DATE DUE

Mar 26 '65			
May 14 '69			
Oct 19 '71			
GAYLORD			PRINTED IN U.S.A.

JOHN THE BAPTIST

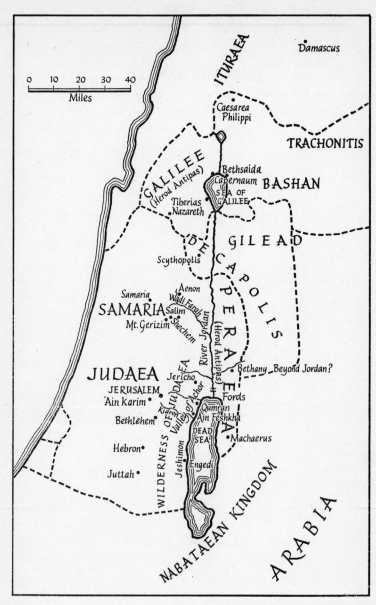

Palestine in the Time of John the Baptist

John the Baptist

Charles H. H. Scobie

FORTRESS PRESS

PHILADELPHIA

TO MY FATHER AND MOTHER

225.92
Sco 1 j

48638

Jan., 1965

CONTENTS

Foreword   7

Abbreviations   9

I THE QUEST OF THE HISTORICAL   11
   JOHN

II THE SOURCES   13
    1 The New Testament   13
    2 Josephus   17
    3 Early Christian Writers   22
    4 The Mandaean Literature   23

III JOHN'S BACKGROUND   32
     1 The Sectarian Background   33
     2 The Geographical Background   41

IV BIRTH AND INFANCY   49

V JOHN THE PREACHER   60
   1 The Proclamation   60
   2 He That Cometh   62
   3 John's Message and Jewish Expectations   73
   4 Man's Response   79
   5 John's Message and Political Questions   86

VI JOHN THE BAPTIST   90
    1 Lustrations in Judaism   94
    2 Proselyte Baptism   95
    3 The Baptist Movement   102
    4 The Meaning of John's Baptism   110

VII JOHN THE PROPHET   117

VIII THE DISCIPLES OF JOHN   131

IX JOHN AND JESUS   142

X THE SAMARITAN MINISTRY   163
   1 The Samaritans   165
   2 Samaritan Sectarianism   168
   3 John the Baptist and the Samaritans   173

XI ARREST AND MARTYRDOM   178

XII THE BAPTIST SECT   187

XIII WHAT MANNER OF MAN?   203

Index of Subjects   215

Index of Authors   218

Index of References   220

FOREWORD

No detailed, critical study of John the Baptist has been published in this country for many years, and it is hoped that this book may in some way contribute towards filling that gap. It is based on a Ph.D. thesis the research for which was conducted at the University of Glasgow under the supervision of the late Prof. G. H. C. Macgregor whose untimely death was such a loss to all who admired him as a scholar and who knew him as a friend.

In preparing the manuscript for publication, the original thesis has been completely rewritten and considerably altered. The aim has been, so far as possible, to present the material in a way which is both scholarly, and 'popular' in the best sense. For those who wish a more detailed study, the notes provide further evidence on some points, and full references to the original sources and to the modern literature. Inevitably much of the material is compressed, and it may well appear that certain writers and certain theories are rather arbitrarily dismissed. The notes, however, in most cases give references to other works in which the arguments for and against each position are more fully stated.

In addition to the debt I owe to the late Prof. Macgregor, I would also like to thank Prof. William Barclay for his advice and assistance. In connection with the preparation of the book for publication I wish to thank my sister-in-law, Mrs Margaret Miller, who typed the manuscript; SCM Press for their kind co-operation and guidance; and my wife and family for their help and for their patience.

The New Testament references are taken from the New English Bible except where otherwise stated, while the Old Testament references are taken from the Revised Standard Version.

This book has been written in the midst of a busy ministry;

the author is conscious of its imperfections and can only trust that these are not too obvious or too numerous.

CHARLES H. H. SCOBIE

Clark Memorial Manse, Largs
February, 1964

ABBREVIATIONS

BASOR	Bulletin of the American Schools of Oriental Research
ERE	Encyclopaedia of Religion and Ethics
HUCA	Hebrew Union College Annual
HDAC	Hastings' Dictionary of the Apostolic Church
HDB	Hastings' Dictionary of the Bible
HDCG	Hastings' Dictionary of Christ and the Gospels
HJ	Hibbert Journal
HTR	Harvard Theological Review
ICC	International Critical Commentary
JBL	Journal of Biblical Literature
JE	Jewish Encyclopedia
JJS	Journal of Jewish Studies
JTS	Journal of Theological Studies
JQR	Jewish Quarterly Review
NT	Novum Testamentum
NTS	New Testament Studies
RB	Revue Biblique
SJT	Scottish Journal of Theology
TWNT	Theologisches Wörterbuch zum neuen Testament (Kittel)
VT	Vetus Testamentum
CD	The Damascus Document
1 QS	The Manual of Discipline
1 Qp. Hab.	The Habakkuk Commentary
1 QH	The Thanksgiving Hymns

I

The Quest of the Historical John

No life has been so closely studied as that of Jesus of Nazareth. Innumerable 'Lives of Jesus' have been produced; innumerable attempts have been made to penetrate behind the Gospel records in order to discover 'the historical Jesus'. Modern critical methods, especially form-criticism, have raised the question of the validity of this quest, and recently attempts have been made to approach the problem in a new light.

This book sets itself a humbler task, the investigation of the life of one of Jesus' contemporaries, John the Baptist. John's name must be almost as well known as that of Jesus, so firmly embedded is it in Christian tradition and literature and art. Yet to most people, John is a somewhat shadowy figure. He is glimpsed only in the background, and then forgotten as interest concentrates on Jesus.

That this should be so is inevitable when we consider the nature of our sources. The Gospels have no interest in John (or in anyone else for that matter) for his own sake; they are concerned with him only in so far as he is connected with Jesus. No 'biography' of John exists in the modern sense; we do not even possess a document which would present John as the Gospels present Jesus. We have only a meagre quota of information culled from sources whose chief interests lie elsewhere.

What this book attempts to do is precisely what the Gospels do not do: to investigate the life of John for its own sake. Here we are concerned to ask what John was and did and said, not in relation to someone else, but simply in himself.

Such a task must, if it has any hope of success at all, make full use of modern, critical, historical methods. To collect and harmonize what the Gospels and other sources have to say about John would give us a picture based on later traditions and interpretations, but would not be true to our self-imposed quest of the historical John. Our first concern is therefore a careful investigation of the sources for the life of John, and a critical assessment of their historical value. Only when this has been done can we attempt a detailed study of the ministry and message of John.

If our sources are meagre they can be supplemented by, and set against our knowledge of the background of John's life. Modern discoveries and studies have contributed a great deal to our understanding of this background, enabling us to see it in a new light and thus, in turn, casting new light on our understanding of John.

Many modern scholars have joined in, or at least contributed to, the study of John the Baptist. The leading views and theories are summarized in the following pages even when they do not seem entirely to fit the facts. It is only by constant study and discussion, by advancing theories, testing them, and if need be rejecting them, that we can advance towards the truth.

In this process it should never be forgotten that we are dealing not with an object, but with a person. How near we can approach to the personality of John remains to be seen. But this we can say: one who was so greatly admired and highly praised by Jesus himself deserves our most careful and sympathetic study.

II

The Sources

THE picture which we gain of John the Baptist will depend to a very large extent on the sources of information from which our picture is built up, and therefore any treatment of the life and work of John must be preceded by a careful and a critical investigation of the source material.

1. The New Testament

Our most important source is the New Testament. From the very start, John had a place in the Christian message, and the early Church preserved quite an amount of information concerning John in written form.

John figures prominently in 'Q', the source common to Matthew and Luke[1]; this was probably a sayings collection, and it may have been compiled around AD 50. Q had little or no narrative material, but it did have an account of John's preaching of repentance (Matt. 3.7b-10; Luke 3.7b-9), and of the Coming One (Matt. 3.11, 12; Luke 3.16, 17). It recounts John's question from prison (Matt. 11.2-6; Luke 7.18-23), and gives quite a large section of sayings of Jesus concerning John (Matt. 11.7-11; Luke 7.24-28; Matt. 7.12; Luke 16.16; Matt. 11.16-19; Luke 7.31-35).

The earliest of the Gospels is *Mark*, written most probably

[1] On 'Q' see B. H. Streeter, *The Four Gospels*, Macmillan, 1924, pp. 271-92; V. Taylor, *The Gospels: A Short Introduction*, Epworth Press, 1938, pp. 36-43; T. W. Manson, *The Sayings of Jesus*, SCM, 1949, pp. 15-21.

about AD 65-70. Like Q, it begins with an account of John the Baptist, but unlike Q, it contains much narrative material. Both Matthew and Luke draw upon Mark's account at many points. Mark tells of John's appearance in the wilderness (Mark 1.1-8), and of his baptism of Jesus (Mark 1.9-11). John's death is narrated in Mark 6.17-29, but apart from this, Mark's chief concern is with Jesus, and John is only mentioned in passing (Mark 2.18; 8.27, 28; 9.11-13; 11.30-33).

It is evident that *Luke*'s Gospel, like Q and Mark, originally began with the ministry of John the Baptist, for Luke 3.1f at one time served as the opening of the book. The narratives of the infancy of John and of Jesus have been added later, and appear to have come from a quite separate source. From Chapter 3 onwards, Luke draws almost all his account of John from either Mark or Q. Apart from a few editorial verses, the only material which is found in Luke and nowhere else is Luke 3.10-14, which gives some of John's preaching to special groups.

Matthew, written perhaps around AD 85 to 90, appears to have had no independent source concerning John the Baptist; with the exception of one verse (Matt. 21.32), all his material comes from Mark or Q.

The *Fourth Gospel* stands apart from the first three in many respects, and appears to have quite independent information concerning John. The Prologue to the Gospel is twice interrupted (John 1.6-8; 1.15) by references to John. These verses, which stress John's inferiority, seem awkward and interrupt the rhythmical scheme of the Prologue, which reads naturally without them; probably they were added by a later editor. John is the chief character in the events of John 1.19-42, which are narrated as having taken place on three successive days. These verses tell of the deputation to John, of his testimony to Jesus, and of how some of John's disciples transferred their allegiance to Jesus. John 3.22-30 deals with a subsequent period when the ministries of John and Jesus overlapped. John is mentioned again only in the passing (John 4.1; 5.33-36; 10.40, 41).

The only other references to John in the New Testament are

in *Acts*, but they are few and meagre, and add nothing to what is to be gleaned from the Gospels.

The question has to be raised of the trustworthiness of the New Testament evidence. The accounts of John the Baptist have come under fire, especially by the form-critical school. In many cases, these scholars have undoubtedly gone too far as when, for example, the words 'in the wilderness' in Mark 1.4 are regarded as a secondary addition, inserted by the early Church, in order to make John fulfil the prophecy of Isa. 40.3.[1] Generally speaking, however, form-criticism has been of great value in reminding us of how the Gospel tradition was passed on by the Christian community, and how therefore the selection, adaptation and preservation of the stories and sayings depended on the life and activities of the community. While on the whole there is no reason to disbelieve the historical accuracy of much of the material which has been preserved, yet in the case of John the Baptist especially, there are grounds for holding that the early Christian community was far from unbiassed in its attitude.

This can be seen, partly from the fact that the New Testament material is inconsistent, and bears traces of development. In the Synoptic Gospels (Matthew, Mark and Luke), for example, John is regarded as the returning Elijah, whereas the Fourth Gospel makes John deny this[2]; in the Synoptics, John and Jesus come into contact only at the time of Jesus' baptism, whereas the Fourth Gospel knows of a period of contact[3]; the Synoptics state that Jesus began his ministry after John's arrest, while this is specifically denied in the Fourth Gospel.[4] Then again, the excessive stress on the subordination of John gives rise to suspicion. We are constantly being reminded of his inferiority to Jesus, but the fact that he continued his ministry after the baptism of Jesus, and the fact that when in prison he appears not yet to have decided whether Jesus was the Coming One

[1] This is the view of K. L. Schmidt, cf. R. Bultmann, *Geschichte der synoptischen Tradition*, Vandenhoeck and Ruprecht, 1957, p. 261.
[2] John 1.21. [3] Cf. John 3.22-30.
[4] Cf. Mark 1.14; Matt. 4.12; John 3.24. John 1.43-2.22 represents Jesus as ministering in Galilee prior to John's imprisonment.

or not[1] suggest that he was in fact more of an independent religious figure than the New Testament allows. There is further a suspicion that John's message has been 'Christianized'. For example, Luke concludes his account of John's message by saying that 'he made his appeal to the people and announced the good news' (*eueggelizeto*) (Luke 3.18). Here John seems to be regarded simply as the first Christian preacher.

These tendencies can be more easily understood when we realize that there is much evidence for the existence of a continuing baptist sect, made up of some of the followers of John who had not gone over to the Christian Church. It was the need to combat the claims of this group which, in all probability, led the Christian community to adapt some of its material concerning John.

Along with these tendencies to alter or adapt the traditional material, we must also note that there are reasons for holding that much of the New Testament evidence is authentic. Many eyewitnesses would still be available when the first documents were produced, and it is significant that one of the qualifications of an apostle was that he should be 'one of those who bore us company all the while we had the Lord Jesus with us, coming and going, from John's ministry of baptism' (Acts 1.21, 22). The very tendency to minimize the figure of John in the early Church lends weight to those passages which give a high estimate of John; even a radical critic like Bultmann accepts as preserving early and authentic tradition such passages as Matt. 3.11, 12; 11.7-11a, 16-18 (and parallels); Mark 11.28-30 (and parallels). Even where the evidence is contradictory, it is usually possible to see where and why the change has been made, and so to determine which version is the more historical. Then, there are many factual details recorded in the New Testament, which can be accepted as true, since they obviously do not serve any dogmatic or apologetic interest. Finally, there is some evidence of underlying Semitic sources in much of the material with which we are concerned.[2]

[1] Matt. 11.1f; Luke 7.18f.
[2] The theory of Semitic sources has been worked out by Dalman, Torrey

From all these considerations, it would appear that the Q source is the most reliable: it is the earliest, it contains the greatest proportion of material concerning John, it has the highest estimate of John, and it contains the clearest evidence of Semitisms. Mark has slightly less to tell, but preserves a number of factual details of great value, and on the whole is a fairly unbiassed work as far as John is concerned. Matthew and Luke have very little independent information, and in their editorial verses, they tend to display the interests of the early Church. The Fourth Gospel is a paradox, to some extent much the most biassed of the Gospels, yet at the same time clearly drawing on an early and accurate source, unknown to the Synoptics.

2. Josephus

In addition to what the New Testament tells us, we have the evidence of Flavius Josephus, the Jewish historian, born in AD 37 and the author of many works including *The Antiquities of the Jews* and *The Jewish War*. It is in the *Antiquities* (XVIII, 5, 2) that we find Josephus' reference to John. After relating how the army of Herod Antipas was defeated by that of Aretas, Josephus says:

Some of the Jews believed that Herod's army was destroyed by God, God punishing him very justly for John called the Baptist, whom Herod had put to death. For John was a pious man, and he was bidding the Jews who practised virtue and exercised right-eousness toward each other and piety toward God, to come together for baptism. For thus, it seemed to him, would baptismal ablution be acceptable, if it were used not to beg off from sins committed, but for the purification of the body when the soul had previously been cleansed by righteous conduct. And when everybody turned to John—for they were profoundly stirred by what he said—Herod feared that John's so extensive influence over the people might lead to an uprising (for the people seemed likely to do everything he might counsel). He thought it much better, under the circumstances, to get John out of the way in

and Burney. The most recent contribution to this question is M. Black's scholarly and objective work, *An Aramaic Approach to the Gospels and Acts*, Oxford, 1954.

advance, before any insurrection might develop, than for himself
to get into trouble and be sorry not to have acted, once an insurrection had begun. So because of Herod's suspicion, John was
sent as a prisoner to Machaerus, the fortress already mentioned,
and there put to death. But the Jews believed that the destruction
which overtook the army came as a punishment for Herod, God
wishing to do him harm.[1]

In modern times the authenticity of this passage has been
questioned by many scholars. But the style and vocabulary are
those of Josephus, and the passage is referred to in Origen's
Contra Celsum (c. AD 250) and is quoted in full by Eusebius (c.
AD 330). It has been asserted that, while Josephus did write
something about John, the text as we now have it bears the
marks of Christian interpolations. But this is most unlikely; if
any part of this passage came from Christian hands, we would
expect at least some reference to John's preaching of the
Messiah and to his testimony to Jesus. But as it stands, the
passage makes no mention of these, nor is it even directly in
line with the Gospels, ascribing a quite different motive for
Herod's execution of John. We can therefore be confident in
accepting this passage as an independent account, from the pen
of Josephus.

The reliability of Josephus' account is another matter. As a
historian Josephus is suspect for many reasons, and he was on
occasion capable of great exaggeration.[2] Above all, he was
clearly guilty both of distorting and omitting much material
in order to serve the two main purposes of his writings, namely,
to defend his own life and conduct (which at times left much
to be desired), and to defend the Jewish people, raising them
in the estimation of the Roman world. This latter motive,
especially, led him to throw all the blame for the Jewish revolt
on a few fanatics, to play down Jewish hatred of Rome, to

[1] Translation by H. St John Thackeray, in Loeb Classical Library. A
critical edition of the Greek text will be found in B. Niese, *Flavii Iosephi Opera*,
Vol. IV, Berlin, 1890.
[2] For estimates of the value of Josephus, see C. Guignebert, *The Jewish
World in the Time of Jesus*, Routledge and Kegan Paul, 1939, pp. 15-19; G. F.
Moore, *Judaism in the First Centuries of the Christian Era*, Harvard, 1927, I,
pp. 208-10; B. Niese, 'Josephus', *ERE*, VII, pp. 569-79.

omit all references to the Messianic expectations of the Jews, and to idealize certain aspects of Judaism, representing the Pharisees, Sadducees and Essenes, for example, as if they were Greek philosophical sects.

In this passage dealing with John the Baptist, Josephus has no particular axe to grind. Some have regarded it with suspicion because of the high estimate of John which it gives, but it is quite in line with Josephus' purpose to present John as yet another example of Jewish piety and virtue. The main criticism which must be levelled at Josephus is the complete absence of any reference to John's Messianic preaching and expectations; here certainly his bias is to be detected. There are therefore no grounds for doubting most of what Josephus tells us, but we must regard it as a one-sided account; it is largely the truth, but by no means the whole truth.

Before leaving the evidence of Jospehus, note must be taken of the controversy over the value of the Slavonic version. The discovery of this version of The Jewish War, written in a dialect of Old Russian, and surviving in a number of Russian manuscripts of the fifteenth and sixteenth centuries, was announced by A. N. Popov in 1866. Its contents did not become generally known until the publication of a German translation in the 1920s.[1] From this it became apparent that the Slavonic version contained hitherto unknown passages on John the Baptist and Jesus. The suggestion was made by Alexander Berendts, and later worked out in great detail by Robert Eisler, that this Slavonic version can be traced back to the original Aramaic version of The Jewish War, which we know Josephus made, before it was translated into Greek. The passages on Jesus and John the Baptist, it is argued, were left out when the Greek version was made, and so have been lost until their rediscovery in the Slavonic version. If this theory were correct, these passages would be most important evidence of the life of John the Baptist.

---

[1] A. Berendts and K. Grass, *Flavius Josephus vom Jüdischen Kriege, Buch I-IV nach der slavischen Uebersetzung deutsch herausgegeben und mit dem griechischen Text verglichen*, Dorpat, 1924-27.

There are two passages dealing with John, although in neither of them is he actually mentioned by name. The first simply begins by saying, 'Now at that time there walked among the Jews a man in wondrous garb. He had put the hair of beasts upon his own body, wherever it was not covered by his own hair; and in countenance he was like a wild man. He came to the Jews and enticed them to liberty, saying, "God has sent me to show you the way of the law, whereby you may be free from many masters. And there shall be no mortal ruling over you, save only the Highest who has sent me." And when the people had heard this they were very glad, and there went after him the whole of Judaea which is about Jerusalem. And he did nothing else to them, save that he dipped them in the river Jordan and let them go, admonishing them to cease from evil works. And (he said that) there would be granted to them a king who would set them free and subject all who were not obedient, but himself would be subject to no one.' The passage goes on to relate how he was brought before Archelaus and the teachers of the law for an interview, in the course of which he incurred the wrath of one, Simon the Essene. After he had spoken out boldly in his own defence, we are told that 'he went forth to that region of Jordan, and, since no man durst hinder him, he did what he had done before'.

The second passage from the Slavonic version does not mention John by name either, but refers to 'that man, whom we have before described as walking about in the hair of beasts and cleansing the people in the waters of Jordan'. In this case, he appears to interpret a dream which Philip had seen, after which Philip dies that same day. The account continues, 'And his (i.e. Philip's) kingdom was given to Agrippa, and his wife Herodias was taken by his brother Herod. But for this reason all who were learned in the law abhorred him, but dared not accuse him to his face. That man alone, whom they called a wild man, came to him in wrath and said: "Forasmuch as thou hast taken thy brother's wife, thou evil man, even as thy brother has died a merciless death, so wilt thou too be cut off by the heavenly sickle!" ' Eventually, Herod ordered him to be slain, and the account concludes with these words, 'Now his manner of life was marvellous and his life not human. For as a spirit without flesh so he continued. His mouth knew no bread, nor even at passover did he taste unleavened bread, saying: "In remembrance of God who redeemed the people from bondage is (the unleavened bread) given to eat, and for the flight, since the journey was in haste." But wine and strong drink he would not so much as allow to be brought near him, and every beast he abhorred (for food); and every injustice he rebuked; and wood-shavings served him for his needs.'[1]

Interesting though these passages may be, their value is extremely doubtful. Study of the Slavonic version has shown that it was translated from Greek, probably in the twelfth or thirteenth century AD. If then it is the work of Josephus, it must stand at two removes from the Aramaic original. In spite of this, Eisler claims to find traces of a Semitic original, but his arguments are very far from convincing. Further, there are good reasons for doubting that these passages could ever have come from the hand of Josephus. There are historical errors in them; for example, Herodias' first husband is said to be Philip the Tetrarch (it is significant that the Gospels make the same mistake). In this, and other cases, the information differs from that given in the authentic works of Josephus. Again, the

---

[1] Translation by J. M. Creed, HTR, 25 (1932), pp. 303-14. Eisler's controversial work, based on the Slavonic version, is *ΙΗΣΟΥΣ ΒΑΣΙΛΕΥΣ ΟΥ ΒΑΣΙΛΕΥΣΑΣ. Die messianische Unabhängigkeitsbewegungen vom Auftreten Johannes des Täufers bis zum Untergang Jacob des Gerechten nach der neuerschlossenen Eroberung von Jerusalem des Flavius Josephus und den christlichen Quellen*, 2 Vols., Heidelberg, 1929-30. The English translation from which all quotations are taken is, *The Messiah Jesus and John the Baptist, according to Flavius Josephus' recently rediscovered 'Capture of Jerusalem' and other Jewish and Christian sources*, translated by A. H. Krappe, Methuen, 1931. Eisler's views have been widely criticized, and the best treatment is to be found in J. W. Jack, *The Historic Christ*, James Clarke and Co., 1933. Recently, however, a number of writers have shown a more favourable attitude to Eisler's theories; these include S. G. F. Brandon, *The Fall of Jerusalem and the Christian Church*, SPCK, 1951; R. Dunkerley, 'The Riddles of Josephus', HJ, 53 (1954), pp. 129-34; R. Dunkerley, *Beyond the Gospels*, Pelican, 1957; G. A. Williamson, *The Jewish War*, Penguin Classics, 1959.

Slavonic version is very anti-Roman in tone, in complete contradiction to the attitude of Josephus, who admired the Romans, and sought to ingratiate himself with them.

In addition to these objections, there are definite indications that the Slavonic version is a compilation, made from various sources, in the Byzantine period.[1] It is related to, and probably based on the ordinary Greek version of Josephus, and indeed it can be shown to have close affinities with one particular branch of manuscripts. There are passages in it which obviously imply a knowledge of the New Testament. The compiler may well also have had access to the *Hegesippus* and the *Josippon*, versions of Josephus produced in the fourth and ninth centuries respectively, and in addition appears to have known various Church Fathers and Christian apocrypha.

Thus it becomes clear that there was no Aramaic original underlying the Slavonic version, but that it is based on a Greek text compiled from the ordinary Greek Josephus, and a variety of sources, most of them Christian. The author of the additions concerning Jesus and John the Baptist was clearly a Christian, for when they are placed together they are seen to make up a connected series which testify to all the chief events of the New Testament. The Slavonic version is therefore of no value as an historical source for the study of John the Baptist.

3. Early Christian Writers

John the Baptist is mentioned by various early Christian writers including Justin Martyr, Tertullian, Hippolytus and Origen, but while these writers are interesting in so far as they reflect the views of the Church about John, they obviously have no independent historical traditions about his life.

John figures in several apocryphal works. *The Gospel according to the Hebrews* (possibly *c.* AD 110) enlarges on the story of

---

[1] See J. W. Jack, *The Historic Christ*; S. Zeitlin, 'The Slavonic Josephus and its Relation to Josippon and Hegesippus', *JQR*, 20 (1929), pp. 1-50; R. Eisler, 'Flavius Josephus on Jesus Called the Christ', *JQR*, 21 (1930), pp. 1-60; S. Zeitlin, 'Josephus on Jesus', 21 (1930), pp. 377-417; J. M. Creed, 'The Slavonic Version of Josephus's History of the Jewish War', *HTR*, 25 (1934), pp. 277-319.

Jesus going to be baptized by John. According to Epiphanius, *The Gospel of the Ebionites* also expanded the account of Jesus' baptism. It contained this passage, 'John was baptizing, and there went out unto him Pharisees and were baptized, and all Jerusalem. And John had raiment of camel's hair and a leathern girdle about his loins; and his meat was wild honey, whereof the taste is the taste of manna, as a cake dipped in oil.' Epiphanius adds his own comment, 'That, forsooth, they may pervert the word of truth into a lie, and for locusts put a cake dipped in honey.' The Ebionites were vegetarians and substituted 'cake' (*egkris*) for 'locust' (*akris*). *The Gospel of Nicodemus* (*Acts of Pilate*), which may date from about the fourth century, recounts John's preaching in Hades, to prepare the way for Christ there.[1]

John figures also in several apocryphal infancy gospels. *The Book of James* (*Protevangelium*), which probably dates from the second century, enlarges considerably on the story of John's infancy. Other infancy gospels depend on *The Book of James*.

Finally, there are a series of references, mainly to the disciples of John, in the *Clementine Homilies* and *Recognitions*.

4. The Mandaean Literature

In view of the claims that have been made for it, the literature of the Mandaeans must also be examined as a possible source for our study of John the Baptist. The Mandaeans still exist in Iraq at the present day,[2] and they were first discovered by missionaries in the seventeenth century who termed them 'Christians of St John' because of the high regard in which they appeared to hold John the Baptist. This is a most misleading designation, however, as they are in fact strongly anti-Jewish and anti-Christian. We are not concerned to give here a survey of Mandaeism, nor of the literature as a whole which has been described as 'an extraordinary farrago of theology, myth, fairy-

[1] For the texts of the apocryphal Gospels (in English), see M. R. James, *The Apocryphal New Testament*, Oxford, 1924.

[2] An excellent description of the present day Mandaeans is given in E. S. Drower, *The Mandaeans of Iraq and Iran*, Oxford, 1937.

tale, ethical instruction, ritual ordinances, and what purports to be history'.[1]

On the face of it, a literature of this type, compiled about the eighth century AD would not seem to be of importance in the study of John the Baptist. The theory has been elaborated by several scholars, however, that the Mandaean literature can take us back to a pre-Christian complex of religious ideas which entered Christianity via John the Baptist. John was a 'pre-Mandaean', who took over this redemption mystery, which was itself of Iranian origin. Christianity developed from the Baptist's group, basing itself on the redemption myth, but the baptist sect split away from the Christian Church and continued an independent existence. Within this continuing sect both the redemption mystery and independent traditions concerning John were preserved, and are now to be found embedded in the Mandaean literature. It is not denied that there are post-Christian elements in Mandaeism, but it is held that the pre-Christian elements can be identified and dated.

Proponents of this view suggest that certain beliefs found their way into Christianity via John the Baptist. This theory has been worked out along two main lines.

1. There is the theory of *the redemption myth*, which is said to have entered Christianity via John the Baptist. This has been most fully worked out by R. Reitzenstein who, using a variety of sources, has attempted to reconstruct the original Iranian myth.[2] Central in this is the idea of the Primal Man or Heavenly Man, a pre-existent divine being, who was sent forth from God at the beginning of time, and who came into con-

---

[1] C. H. Dodd, *The Interpretation of the Fourth Gospel*, Cambridge, 1953, p. 115. Copies of the Mandaean sacred books were brought back to Europe, but little progress was made until the publication of a Mandaean grammar by T. Nöldeke in 1895. The main books were translated into German by M. Lidzbarski as follows—*Das Johannesbuch der Mandäer* (1915), *Mandäische Liturgien* (1920), *Ginza, der Schatz, oder das grosse Buch der Mandäer* (1925). For a survey of Mandaeism see W. Brandt, 'Mandaeans', *ERE*, VIII, pp. 380-93.

[2] Especially in *Das iranische Erlösungsmysterium*, Bonn, 1921. A good treatment of Reitzenstein's views will be found in W. Manson, *Jesus the Messiah*, Hodder and Stoughton, 1943, especially Appendix D, 'The Heavenly Man Redemption Myth', pp. 174-90. See also J. M. Creed, 'The Heavenly Man', *JTS*, 26 (1925), pp. 113-36.

tact with the powers of darkness. God raised him again to the kingdom of light, but part of him was left behind in this world, and from this part of his nature the human soul originated. Man is thus linked with the Heavenly Man, and through him can find redemption and access to the kingdom of light. Reitzenstein traces this myth from Persian origins, via Babylonia and Syria, to pre-Christian Judaism, where its influence is to be traced in Daniel, I Enoch and II (4) Esdras. John the Baptist's message was centred in this Heavenly Man Redeemer, and from this the Christian message took shape. Reitzenstein sees the influence of the myth especially in Pauline theology with its ideas of the pre-existent Christ, the man from heaven, the redeemer who has overcome the powers of darkness.

2. This theory has also been worked out with regard to *the Fourth Gospel*.[1] Parallels in thought and wording between the Gospel and certain parts of the Mandaean literature are explained as being due to the Fourth Gospel drawing upon ideas which entered the early Christian Church by means of John the Baptist and his followers. It is undeniable that many such parallels occur, as Bultmann and Bauer have shown. Key words such as 'light', 'life', 'truth' and 'glory', and symbols such as 'water', 'bread' and 'the spring of life' are held in common. Some passages in the Mandaean writings immediately bring Johannine passages to mind. There are similarities between the Christ of the Fourth Gospel and the Mandaean Saviour, who is sent by his father down to earth, to the world of darkness, in order to give life to his own, whom he chooses, and to lead them out of darkness into light. He is hated by the world, but ascends again to the realm of light after praying for his own.

It is further claimed that the Mandaean literature has preserved *independent traditions concerning John the Baptist*. It is true that there are certain references to John in the *Ginza*, and in the *Book of John*. A few examples may be given. In *Ginza* II, 1, 151f, Hibil-Ziwa says,

[1] See V. Taylor, 'The Mandaeans and the Fourth Gospel', *HJ*, 28 (1930), pp. 531-46.

In those days, a child shall be born who will receive the name of Yōhānā; he will be the son of old Zakhriā, who shall receive this child in his old age, even at the age of a hundred. His mother, Enishbai, advanced in years, shall conceive him and bring forth her child. When Yōhānā is a man, faith shall repose in his heart, he shall come to the Jordan and shall baptize for forty-two years, before Nebou shall clothe himself with flesh and come into the world. While Yōhānā lives in Jerusalem, gaining sway over Jordan and baptizing, Jesus Christ shall come to him, shall humble himself, shall receive the baptism of Yōhānā and shall become wise with the wisdom of Yōhānā. But then shall he corrupt the sayings of Yōhānā, pervert the baptism of Jordan, distort the words of truth, and preach fraud and malice throughout all the world.

The Book of John, as the name suggests, contains material concerning John, though much of it is simply Mandaean teaching placed on John's lips. One passage deals with portents at John's birth:

I slept not and rested not, (and I beheld) that a star appeared and stood over Enishbai. Fire burned in Old Father (Abā Sābā) Zakhriā; three heaven-lights appeared. The sun sank and the lights rose. Fire lit up the house of the people (synagogue), smoke rose over the temple. A quaking quaked in the Throne-chariot, so that Earth removed from her seat. A star flew down into Judaea, a star flew down into Jerusalem. The sun appeared by night, and the moon rose by day.[1]

John's birth is described in the *Book of John*, 32:

'My father', says Yahyā, 'was ninety and nine and my mother eighty and eight years old. Out of the basin of Jordan they took me. They bore me up and laid me in the womb of Enishbai. "Nine months", said they, "thou shalt stay in her womb, as do all other childen." ... I was born from Enishbai in the region of Jordan.'
The region of Jerusalem quakes and the wall of the priest rocks. Elizar, the great house, stands there and his body trembles. The Jews gather together, come unto Old Father Zakhriā and they speak to him: 'O Old Father Zakhriā, thou art to have a son. Tell us now, what name shall we give him? Shall we give him for

[1] *Book of John*, 18. The translations from the *Book of John* are taken from G. R. S. Mead, *The Gnostic John the Baptizer*, John M. Watkins, 1924, pp. 35f.

name "Yaqif of Wisdom", that he may teach the Book in Jerusalem? Or shall we give him for name "Zatan the Pillar", so that the Jews may swear by him and commit no deceit?'

When Enishbai heard this, she cried out and she said: 'Of all these names which you name, will I not give him one; but the name Yāhyā-Yōhānā will I give him, (the name) which Life's self has given unto him.'

This same section mentions John's upbringing:

When Anōsh, the treasure, heard this he took the child and brought it to Parwan, the white mountain, to Mount Parwan, on which sucklings and little ones on holy drink are reared up.

(There I remained) until I was two and twenty years old. I learned there the whole of my wisdom and made fully my own the whole of my discourse. They clothed me with vestures of glory and veiled me with cloud-veils.

Other passages speak of John as a preacher, of his invulnerability to fire or sword; a dialogue with Eshu Mshiha (Jesus) is recorded, and an account given of John's marriage. On his death John ascends triumphantly into the realms of light.

Supporters of this point of view require to show that the Mandaeans originated in Palestine in pre-Christian times, and they advance various proofs of this, such as the fact that the Jordan is frequently mentioned in the Mandaean texts, that Jerusalem is regarded as the holy city, and that the Mandaean dialect is very similar to Nabataean.[1]

In considering these variant forms of the 'Mandaean hypothesis' it is obvious that the crux of the problem lies in *the dating and evaluation of the material*. The Gospels date from the first century AD, while the Mandaean literature was compiled around the eighth century AD. The natural explanation would seem to be that some form of Christianity was one factor contributing to the Mandaean synthesis. If the matter is really the other way round, the onus of proof lies very much with those who assert this.

It must be said that the 'Mandaean' scholars are very far from having proved their case. Reitzenstein's mass of evidence

[1] For a discussion of these arguments see J. Thomas, *Le Mouvement Baptiste En Palestine Et Syrie (150 av. J.C.-300 ap. J.C.)*, Gembloux, 1935, pp. 220-40.

is often far more ingenious than convincing, and it has to be remembered that even the Iranian origin of the myth on which he lays such great stress has to be reconstructed from writings ranging, in their present form, from about the third to the seventh century AD.[1] The work of Bultmann is similarly very open to criticism. The Johannine parallels to the Mandaean passages tend to be shorter and simpler in form, and for this reason Bultmann contends that they are therefore later in date. But as C. H. Dodd points out, when Bultmann 'suggests that the simple allusions in the Fourth Gospel to the sending of the Son by the Father presuppose the elaborate mythical apparatus of the Mandaean passages, he is arguing against the natural supposition in such a case'.[2]

The Dead Sea Scrolls might well be expected to shed light on this question, for they have revealed to us almost exactly what Reitzenstein and others have postulated—a pre-Christian, Jewish fringe sect, reflecting Iranian influence, and itself in an excellent position to influence John the Baptist, and through him, early Christianity.[3] On the Mandaean hypothesis, the Scrolls are the very place where we would expect to find the ideas which entered Christianity via a 'pre-Mandaean' John the Baptist. Comparatively little work has as yet been done in this field, but comparison does show that for the greater part the two literatures are quite different, the Scrolls being basically Jewish, the Mandaean writings basically Gnostic. There are certain areas of agreement, but these must be carefully analysed. Three main points should be noted.

1. The main area of agreement lies in the concept of *dualism*, or modified dualism. In both Mandaeism and the Scrolls this is expressed primarily in terms of the Light-Darkness contrast.[4]

---

[1] Cf. W. Manson, *Jesus the Messiah*, pp. 179-83; C. H. Dodd, *The Interpretation of the Fourth Gospel*, pp. 121, 122, 128.

[2] *The Interpretation of the Fourth Gospel*, p. 123.

[3] On the Dead Sea Scrolls sect, see further, pp. 35ff.

[4] The division between the world of darkness and the world of light, ruled by the 'High King of Light' is basic to Mandaeism; a similar feature expressing itself, for example, in 'the war of the sons of light with the sons of darkness' is a striking feature of the Scrolls. 'Sons of light' is also a Mandaean term, designating angels.

Similarly Truth and Error are opposed to each other. The Scrolls speak of the 'Sons of Truth', and of 'knowing the Truth', but the term is generally equivalent to the Torah; whereas although the Mandaeans use the term Truth (*Kushta*) the content of it is to them very different.

It is more than likely that the Scrolls' form of dualism is of Iranian origin, and had infiltrated into Judaism in pre-Christian times. But there is no need of any 'pre-Mandaean hypothesis' to account for this; these ideas were very widespread, and not necessarily tied to any Gnostic system. In any case, the Qumran dualism is really, as Burrows comments, 'a dualism of good and evil, not of spirit and matter'.[1]

2. There are a variety of *terms and ideas* common to Mandaeism and the Scrolls. T. H. Gaster mentions, for example, 'the elect', 'God's plantation', 'enlightened', 'crown of glory' and 'false prophets'.[2] We note also, of course, the rite of baptism, practised in 'living water'. On close examination, however, these parallels are not impressive, and offer no support at all for the Mandaean hypothesis. They can either be traced to an origin in the Old Testament, or else are terms in widespread use in many religions. In some cases, for example 'the elect' and 'the enlightened', they probably reached Mandaeism via Manichaeism, in which they figure prominently. All the indications are that these are common terms, passed from one group to another, with Mandaeism being the last in the line, and not the first.

3. Most striking of all are not the parallels which the Scrolls provide to Mandaeism, but the parallels which they do *not* provide. *There is no trace of the 'heavenly man' redemption myth* in the Scrolls. No idea is found of the soul as a spark of light, imprisoned in the world of darkness. The Teacher of Righteousness was revered by the sect, but he was neither heavenly nor a redeemer. The expected Messiahs of Aaron and Israel are poles apart from the figure reconstructed by Reitzenstein,

[1] M. Burrows, *The Dead Sea Scrolls*, Secker and Warburg, 1956, p. 258.
[2] T. H. Gaster, *The Scriptures of the Dead Sea Sect*, Secker and Warburg, 1957, pp. 30, 31 and elsewhere in notes.

while the Qumran sect's eschatology has nothing whatever in common with the perilous upward journey of the soul past the demon-guarded 'wards'.

The Dead Sea Scrolls, therefore, fail completely to support the Mandaean hypothesis, especially as advanced by Reitzenstein.

Examination of *the traditions concerning John* which are preserved in the Mandaean literature does not encourage us to believe that they are either early or genuine. The references, for example, to 'Old Zakhriā' (Zechariah) as John's father, and to 'Enishbai' (Elizabeth) as his mother, along with such incidents as the star appearing in Judaea at John's birth and the debate as to what John should be called, suggest very strongly borrowing from the New Testament. The various passages are obviously padded out with descriptions of how John administered Mandaean baptism, and taught Mandaean doctrine. The keynotes of John's preaching according to the New Testament are, on the other hand, completely lacking; there is no mention of the imminent judgement or of the need for repentance. Nor is there any knowledge of the martyrdom of John. Furthermore, analysis reveals that John does not appear in any of the Mandaean liturgical texts, which is where we would expect to find him, especially in the baptismal liturgy; on the contrary the John passages belong to the latest strata of the literature and for the most part bear the marks of the Arab period. John is, moreover, presented neither as the Messiah nor as the founder of the sect, which is what we would expect if the literature was preserved by a sect of the followers of John.[1]

The conclusion is inescapable that the Mandaean literature cannot provide us with any pre-Christian material which could have entered the early Church via John the Baptist, or with any genuine traditions concerning the life and ministry of John. These conclusions are confirmed by the more sober estimate of Mandaean origins which is now accepted by many scholars. Mandaeism is a synthesis of many diverse sources some of which, especially the Babylonian elements, are undoubtedly

[1] On a continuing baptist sect, see further Chapter XII.

old. The arguments in favour of an early Palestinian origin of the Mandaeans, however, cannot hold water. It is clear that the Jewish and Christian elements entered Mandaeism by way of Marcionism and Manichaeism, probably through certain apocryphal traditions, and certainly in part by way of Syriac Christianity.[1]

The Mandaean interest in and exaltation of John took place only at a comparatively late date. There was a good reason for this; toleration was granted to religious sects by the Arabs only on condition that they had a prophet and a sacred book. It was the Arab invasion which compelled the Mandaeans to present John as their prophet. From Syriac Christian and possibly other late sources, they had some knowledge of John. These traditions were now expanded as the situation required.

It is clear therefore that Mandaeism is of no value in providing source material for the life and teaching of John the Baptist.

[1] See F. C. Burkitt, 'The Mandaeans', *JTS*, 29 (1928), pp. 225-37.

III

John's Background

No person can be properly understood except against the background of the place and the period in which he lived and worked. John the Baptist lived in Palestine and was roughly a contemporary of Jesus, and this means that his general background has been very widely studied since it virtually coincides with that of Jesus. No period in Jewish history has been more intensively investigated than that which forms the background and preparation for the New Testament.[1]

To which branch of the Judaism of this period did John belong? The social, political and religious outlook of the Jewish people varied considerably; in which category can John be placed? He was, as we shall see, a highly individual figure, yet that does not prevent us from assigning him some sort of classification.

Clearly, he would have little or no sympathy with the *Sadducees*, in spite of his priestly descent. He preached a coming judgement, while they denied a future life and retribution. His Messianic proclamation would probably be viewed as politically dangerous by the collaborationist Sadducees. With their wealth and privilege, they would have little in common with the ascetic prophet of the wilderness. The representatives of the

[1] On this see, e.g. C. Guignebert, *The Jewish World in the Time of Jesus*; G. F. Moore, *Judaism*; G. H. C. Macgregor and A. C. Purdy, *Jew and Greek: Tutors Unto Christ*, New Edition, St Andrew Press, 1959.

Jerusalem authorities who asked Jesus the question about authority (Mark 11.27-33 and parallels), and who 'did not believe' John, were very probably of the Sadducean party.

John may have felt more sympathy towards the *Pharisees*, with whose general outlook and whose eschatology he had much in common. Yet their legalistic temper and concern with the tradition which was built up around the Law is foreign to John's radical prophetic outlook. The Fourth Gospel records that a delegation from the Pharisees were sent to question John (John 1.24); they appear in order to seek information, and pass no judgement on him. Thus it would seem that John stood apart from the Pharisees, though not being entirely antagonistic to them. With the *Zealot* party, John certainly had no connections. His message, as we shall see, was not a political one, and he was opposed to violence.

There remains one further major division of Judaism with which John does appear to have had closer connections. This is what we may term the sectarian, or the non-conformist, or the baptist movement. Recent discoveries and recent scholarship have emphasized the importance of this movement which has tended in the past to get less attention than it deserves.

1. *The Sectarian Background*

John appears as a preacher and the leader of a group of disciples, in the Jordan valley, in the early first century AD. His movement is on the fringe of Judaism, in opposition to the accepted ideas of most orthodox Jews; it is chiefly noted for the rite of baptism. All these features remind us that it is in fact only one of a number of groups with similar characteristics which flourished in the same place and around the same time. In Palestine and Syria, especially in the region of the Jordan valley, for a century or more BC, and for several centuries AD, there existed a variety of groups which, though differing from each other in details, are in general remarkably alike. As baptism was one of the most important practices which they had in common, they have been classified together as 'the baptist movement'. In the study of this branch of Judaism, we are indebted to the work of W. Brandt,[1] and in particular to the French scholar Joseph Thomas, whose book, *Le Mouvement Baptiste en Palestine et Syrie* (1935) is the classic work on the subject. In more recent years the discovery and study of the Dead Sea Scrolls have brought startling new evidence of Jewish sectarianism and confirmation of many of the views of J. Thomas.

The picture we now get is of a widespread and vigorous sectarian movement. To it belonged, for example, *the Essenes*, mentioned by Pliny the Elder, and described at some length by Josephus and Philo.[2] Philo speaks of a widespread Jewish sect, noted for their piety, goodness and purity of life. They live in communities, have all possessions in common, reject the practice of slavery, and join together in common meals. Josephus speaks of them, both in his *Antiquities* and in *The Jewish War*, as a sect, settling in large numbers in every town. They live a simple and pious life, and members are only admitted after a probationary period. They have a regular baptism of purification when the members, clothed in white linen, 'bathe their bodies in cold water',[3] and we also hear of their common meals. The Essenes, according to Josephus, reject marriage, but adopt other men's children. There is, however, one order which allows marriage. They believe that the body is corruptible but the soul is immortal, and in their view of the future life they 'share the belief of the sons of Greece'.[4] Pliny, in his *Natural History*, mentions 'the solitary tribe of the Essenes', who live on the west side of the Dead Sea, allowing no women, yet making up their numbers by a stream of new recruits. Josephus indicates that Essenism originated during the reign of Jonathan (161–148 BC), and certainly the movement was in existence well before the start of the first century BC.

[1] *Die jüdischen Baptismen*, Giessen, 1910.
[2] On the Essenes, see J. B. Lightfoot, *St Paul's Epistles to the Colossians and to Philemon*, Macmillan, 1876, especially the 'Dissertations on the Essenes', pp. 349–419; F. C. Conybeare, 'Essenes', *HDB*, I, pp. 767–72; W. D. Niven, 'Essenes', *HDAC*, I, pp. 367–9; M. Black, *The Scrolls and Christian Origins*, Nelson, 1961.
[3] *The Jewish War*, II, 8, 5.
[4] *The Jewish War*, II, 8, 11.

The Dead Sea Scrolls sect formed an important part of the baptist movement.[1] Doubtless it will be many years yet before the dust of controversy settles, yet the consensus of sound scholarship now agrees that the Scrolls came from a Jewish sect, which retreated to their wilderness monastery during the reign of John Hyrcanus (135-104 BC) and remained there with the exception of a break of about thirty years following the earthquake of 31 BC, until the monastery was destroyed by Roman troops in AD 68. The disputed identifications of the Teacher of Righteousness, the Wicked Priest, and other terms used in the Scrolls do not concern us directly here. A feature of the sect was their sacred meals at which bread and wine, blessed by a priest, were distributed; and also their rites of baptism. A strict set of rules governed the conduct of members, and this is preserved for us in the *Manual of Discipline*.

Epiphanius mentions a sect of Nasarenes (*Nasaraioi*), whom he carefully distinguishes from a Christian sect of Nazorenes (*Nazōraioi*) whom he also describes.[2] The Nasarenes, we are told, existed prior to the time of Christ. They were Jewish, in origin at any rate, but lived east of the Jordan, in the region of Gilead and Bashan. They observed circumcision, the Sabbath and the Jewish feasts and honoured the patriarchs, but they rejected the Law. In particular they objected to the laws of sacrifice; they themselves had no sacrifices, and were strict vegetarians. The evidence of Epiphanius has been questioned and much debated,[3] yet he does seem to be describing a pre-Christian sect which had much in common with other groups in the baptist movement.

A Jewish sect known as Hemerobaptists is mentioned by Hegesippus and Epiphanius, in the *Apostolic Constitutions* and in the Pseudo-Clementine literature. According to Epiphanius, it

---

[1] A sound and scholarly treatment of the Scrolls will be found in M. Burrows, *The Dead Sea Scrolls*, and *More Light on the Dead Sea Scrolls*, Secker and Warburg, 1958, and both books contain good bibliographies for further reference. English translations of the Scrolls are given by Burrows, or may be found in T. H. Gaster, *The Scriptures of the Dead Sea Sect*.

[2] See J. Thomas, *Le Mouvement Baptiste*, pp. 37-40; C. Guignebert, *The Jewish World in the Time of Jesus*, pp. 200, 201.

[3] See the discussion in M. Black, *The Scrolls and Christian Origins*, pp. 66-73.

flourished prior to AD 70.[1] As the name suggests, the sect's main characteristic was the rites of washing which were practised every day, before their meal.[2]

The Masbotheans are mentioned by Hegesippus, Ephraem and in the *Apostolic Constitutions*. Apart from the fact that they were a Jewish sect, we know almost nothing about them. The name is probably derived, however, from the Aramaic word meaning 'to baptize', in which case they were also a sect of 'Baptists'.

In the *Tosefta* and in the *Talmud*, reference is made to the 'Morning Bathers', who bathe themselves every morning.[3]

We know of other groups which are of less direct interest to us here since they date from after the time of John, and yet which illustrate the influence and indeed the continuation of earlier tendencies. These include Josephus' ascetic teacher, Banos, who lived in the wilderness, 'using frequent ablutions of cold water, by day and night for purity's sake'[4]; the group which produced the *Sibylline Oracles*, *Book IV*, and which rejected Temple worship and sacrifice, and practised rites of baptism[5]; the Ebionites, Jewish-Christians, one branch of whom laid special stress on asceticism, rejection of sacrifices, and frequent baptisms[6]; the Elkesaites who originated around AD 100 and prescribed ablutions in running water for the forgiveness of sins[7]; and the group which produced the *Vita Adae et Evae*, probably a baptist sect.[8] Though the dating of these groups

[1] *Panarion*, XIX, 5, 6-7.
[2] On the Hemerobaptists see J. Thomas, *Le Mouvement Baptiste*, pp. 34-37.
[3] Tos. Jadaim, II, 20; Berak. 22a. See J. Thomas, *Le Mouvement Baptiste*, p. 44.
[4] *Vita*, II, 10-12.
[5] *The Sibylline Oracles, Books III-V*, H. N. Bates, SPCK, 1918; J. Thomas, *Le Mouvement Baptiste*, pp. 46-60; R. H. Pfeiffer, 'The Literature and Religion of the Pseudepigrapha', *Interpreter's Bible*, Abingdon Press, 1, pp. 432, 433; J. B. Lightfoot, *Colossians and Philemon*, pp. 96, 97.
[6] W. Beveridge, 'Ebionites', *ERE*, V, pp. 139-45; J. Thomas, *Le Mouvement Baptiste*, pp. 156-83; J. A. Fitzmyer, 'The Qumran Scrolls, the Ebionites and their Literature', in K. Stendahl, *The Scrolls and the New Testament*, Harper, 1957; SCM Press, 1958, pp. 208-31.
[7] W. Brandt, 'Elkesaites', *ERE*, V, pp. 262-9; L. Ginzberg, 'Elcesaites', *JE*, V, pp. 89, 90; J. Thomas, *Le Mouvement Baptiste*, pp. 140-56; J. B. Lightfoot, *Colossians and Philemon*, pp. 374, 375.
[8] See commentary by Wells in R. H. Charles, *Apocrypha and Pseudepigrapha*

means that Christian influence cannot be ruled out, in the main they continue the Jewish, sectarian baptist movement.

Our interest lies in the movement in the pre-Christian period. Some of the groups mentioned in the different sources may well of course have been identical with each other. Whether or not the Dead Sea Scrolls sect were Essenes has been much disputed; certainly, they had a great many features in common.[1] Pliny, speaking of the Essene settlement on the west shore of the Dead Sea, is almost certainly referring to the Qumran monastery. But Josephus and Philo seem to have something more widespread in mind—the third philosophy or sect of the Jews, large in numbers, with members in all the chief towns and cities. Josephus, moreover, seems to know of divisions within this Essene movement, for he says that as a rule Essenes are celibate, 'yet there is another order (*tagma*) of Essenes, which, while at one with the rest in its mode of life, customs and regulations, differs from them in its views on marriage'.[2] This branch admits women under certain conditions. The Essenism known to Josephus and Philo seems therefore to have been a wide movement embracing different sects. The Qumran sectarians would therefore be Essenes in this broad sense, but they were not the only Essenes. 'Essenes' may well have been a general term covering much if not all of the sectarian baptist movement.

As regards location, the movement seems to have begun in Palestine, but its real centre was the Jordan valley, partly, no doubt, because of the plentiful supply of water for baptismal rites. After AD 70, the centre of gravity shifted to Transjordan, though there is plenty of evidence that the movement also spread very much further afield. As regards time, we have seen that the movement was well established before the start of the first

of the Old Testament, Oxford, 1913, II; R. H. Pfeiffer, 'The Literature and Religion of the Pseudepigrapha', *Interpreter's Bible*, I, pp. 425, 426.

[1] See W. H. Brownlee, 'A Comparison of the Covenanters of the Dead Sea Scrolls with Pre-Christian Jewish Sects', *Biblical Archaeologist*, 13 (1950), pp. 50-72; M. Burrows, *The Dead Sea Scrolls*, pp. 279-94, and *More Light on the Dead Sea Scrolls*, pp. 263-9.

[2] *The Jewish War*, II, 8, 13.

century BC, and it seems to have been at its most flourishing during the first century AD. Some type of baptism is the most important factor which the different sects have in common, though in most cases we lack much definite information; the Dead Sea Scrolls are particularly valuable here with the new light they cast on sectarian baptism. Opposition to the Temple and its sacrifices is another characteristic of the baptist movement. Most if not all of the sects refrained from participation in the Temple worship, but how far this was due to opposition to sacrifice as such is not clear; in some cases it seems to have been the result of opposition to the Jerusalem priesthood.[1] Another strong tendency running right through the movement is asceticism, in some but not all cases manifesting itself as vegetarianism. Philo remarks on the frugality and simple living of the Essenes, and Josephus tells how they despise riches. The Dead Sea Scrolls sect lived a strict monastic life, and their food was rationed, though archaeological evidence suggests that they were not vegetarians.[2] The Nasarenes, on the other hand, were convinced vegetarians, we are told, and held that the Law forbade all sacrifices and eating of meat. The strength of the movement may be judged by the considerable literature which it produced. Some, perhaps many, of the works classed as Pseudepigrapha may well have come from the movement in its earlier stages.[3] The Dead Sea finds especially have revealed the type of literature which one of the sects produced, and other groups are known to have had their own books.

In origin the movement was basically Jewish; the sects adhered to Jewish ethical monotheism, and with the notable exception of the laws of sacrifice most of them observed the

[1] On this see J. B. Lightfoot, Colossians and Philemon, pp. 371-80; J. Thomas, Le Mouvement Baptiste, pp. 12, 13. On the relation of the Qumran sect to the Temple, see J. M. Baumgarten, 'Sacrifice and Worship among the Jewish Sectarians of the Dead Sea (Qumran) Scrolls', HTR, 46 (1953), pp. 141-59; M. Burrows, The Dead Sea Scrolls, pp. 237, 238, and More Light on the Dead Sea Scrolls, pp. 363-6; M. Black, The Scrolls and Christian Origins, pp. 39f.

[2] J. M. Allegro, The Dead Sea Scrolls, Penguin, 1956, p. 116.

[3] Dupont-Sommer suggests that the Testaments of the Twelve Patriarchs, Enoch, Jubilees and the Psalms of Solomon are Essene works; see A. Dupont-Sommer, The Jewish Sect of Qumran and the Essenes, Vallentine, Mitchell and Co., 1954, p. 38.

Law. Beyond doubt we are to trace the ancestors of the sectarians in the *Hasidim*, the ultra pious and devout Jews who came to the fore at the period of Seleucid persecution, and who at first supported the Maccabees in their fight for independence. As the Maccabaean rulers became more worldly, however, the Hasidim developed into more of an opposition party. From them sprang the Pharisees, as well as the sectarians whom we have been describing; the two movements have some features in common, though they also clearly diverged from one another. Some aspects of the baptist movement, especially asceticism, can be traced much further back than the Hasidim, to a very ancient origin in Israel's religious past.[1] As well as elements which suggest a strong religious conservatism, there are also other features in the movement which are quite strange and which suggest new, outside influences. The question of Neo-Pythagorean influence on the Essenes has been debated, but Iranian influence cannot be disputed. This may be seen in such things as the Essene angelology and their worship of the sun,[2] and the Dead Sea Scrolls, particularly in their doctrine of 'modified dualism', clearly betray Iranian influence.

It is this baptist movement which forms the background of John's life and work. John appears in the middle of the movement both geographically and chronologically. In his wilderness ministry he preached within a few miles of Qumran, and it seems impossible to believe that he was not acquainted with the beliefs and practices of the Qumran and other sects. He lived at a time when the sects flourished and were at the height of their popularity and influence. John's ministry was marked especially by the rite of baptism, which figures so prominently also in the sectarian movement. John's asceticism places him in line with these baptist groups, but out of line with orthodox Judaism. John's attitude to orthodox Judaism and to the Jerusalem authorities marks him out as a sectarian and a nonconformist.

[1] Cf. M. Black, *The Scrolls and Christian Origins*, p. 15.
[2] Josephus, *The Jewish War*, II, 8, 7 and II, 8, 5. For archaeological evidence of the penetration of Iranian religion into Syria, see J. Thomas, *Le Mouvement Baptiste*, pp. 419, 420.

An important indication of John's link with this branch of Judaism is to be found in the description of John by Josephus, as one who 'was bidding the Jews who practised virtue and exercised righteousness toward each other and piety toward God, to come together for baptism'. As Abrahams points out,[1] this is very similar to Josephus' description of the oath to be taken by the Essenes, each of whom must promise that 'in the first place he will exercise piety towards God, and next that he will observe justice towards men'. Here piety (*eusebeia*) and righteousness (*dikaiosunē*) are the chief characteristics of both John and the Essenes, and the other terms used of John by Jospehus (*aretē*, *hagneia*) are also used by him of the Essenes. We may note also that there is a passage in the Pseudo-Clementine Homilies in which John is called a Hemerobaptist,[2] though it is doubtful how much reliability can be attached to this testimony.

As we study John's message and ministry we shall discover many more close points of contact. From the survey we have made, however, we are fully justified in saying that in so far as John was connected with any branch of Judaism, and in so far as he was the product of the background from which he emerged, that background appears to have been the sectarian, baptist movement. This is not in the least to deny that there were original features in his life and work. Every religious leader or reformer, however, has to begin somewhere, to use terms and concepts and practices with which his hearers are familiar before going on to show how he differs from these usually held ideas. Having established the branch of Judaism with which John appears to have had most in common, we must now, in the pages that follow, seek to discover in detail how far he was merely a product of his environment, and how far he broke away from it to become an independent and original thinker and preacher. It is only when we have done this, that we will be able to make a final summary and assessment of John.

[1] I. Abrahams, *Studies in Pharisaism and the Gospel*, I, Cambridge, 1917, p. 34.
[2] *Homilies*, II, 23.

2. The Geographical Background

The New Testament mentions several geographical locations in connection with John, and of these the most important is 'the wilderness'. It was here that John spent his youth (Luke 1.80), that he heard the prophetic call (Luke 3.2), and that he first appeared proclaiming his message (Mark 1.4; Matt. 3.1). From Jesus' remarks about John (Matt. 11.7f; Luke 7.24f) we know that the crowds, in order to hear John, had to 'go out into the wilderness'.

For the Jew of the first century the word 'wilderness' would not only have a geographical reference, but it would also be rich with historical connotations. The New Testament term is *erēmos*,[1] and the principal equivalent term in the Old Testament is *midhbār*. *Midhbār* denotes a region in which, because of the scarcity of pasture and water, flocks have to be driven from place to place; that is to say, it can support only a nomadic, Bedouin type of existence.[2] It is not entirely devoid of vegetation (Joel 2.22) though it can become dried up in the heat (Jer. 23.10). Because there is no settled population, the wilderness can be described as uninhabited by man (Job 38.26), though Josh. 15.61, 62 does mention a wilderness which has a few towns in it. *Midhbār* is used of various parts of Palestine, and of desert regions generally. It is used of the land through which the Israelites passed on their wanderings following the exodus, but where a particular region is meant, a definite name is attached, such as wilderness of Shur, wilderness of Paran, and so on. Another, less common, Old Testament term is *'arābhā*; this is most frequently used to indicate the great depression which includes the Jordan valley and extends to the Gulf of Aquabah, especially the part of this region south of the Dead Sea. It can also, however, have a more general reference as in Isa. 40.3—'A voice cries, In the wilderness (*midhbār*) prepare

---

[1] This is an adjective, with *chōra* understood; the form *erēmia* is found in the New Testament only four times. On the wilderness see R. W. Funk, 'The Wilderness', *JBL*, 78 (1959), pp. 205-14; U. W. Mauser, *Christ in the Wilderness*, SCM, 1963.

[2] Deriving the word from *dābhar*, in the sense of 'to guide or lead (flocks)'.

the way of the Lord, make straight in the desert (*'ªrābhā*) a highway for our God.' Here the two terms are used to refer to the desert regions lying between Babylon and Palestine through which the triumphant returning exiles will pass. A third Old Testament term is *yᵉshīmōn*, usually transliterated as 'Jeshimon' instead of translated; generally it seems to refer to part of the region known as the wilderness of Judah.

As these Hebrew words have only one Greek equivalent it might not be possible to say, out of context, exactly what region was being referred to in the New Testament as the *erēmos*. Matthew, however, is more specific and tells us that John began his ministry in 'the wilderness of Judaea' (Matt. 3.1, RSV). This is the region known in the Old Testament as 'the wilderness of Judah' (*midhbār yᵉhūdhā*). It was bounded on the west by the Judaean plateau, and on the east by the Dead Sea and by the last stretch of the river Jordan. To the north and south its exact boundaries are less easy to define; Jeshimon was probably the most desolate part of this wilderness, lying immediately to the west of the Dead Sea.

Clearly, it was principally in the part of the wilderness at the north end of the Dead Sea that John was to be found during his ministry. The fact that 'they flocked to him from the whole Judaean country-side and the city of Jerusalem' (Mark 1.5) supports this, and, of course, John baptized in the River Jordan, which flows into the north end of the Dead Sea. As G. A. Smith points out,[1] the routes from Judaea to the east were governed by the presence of fresh water. Apart from Engedi and 'Ain Feshkha (which of course have the Dead Sea to the east of them) the only fresh water is at Jericho. Therefore the routes from Bethlehem, from Jerusalem and from Bethel converge at Jericho, for the Jordan was forded at a point to the south-east of that city. There are actually two fords here which can be crossed at most times of year[2]; these are known in the Old Testament as 'the fords of the Jordan' (Judg. 3.28), or 'the

---

[1] G. A. Smith, *The Historical Geography of the Holy Land*, Hodder and Stoughton, 1931, p. 263.

[2] G. A. Smith, op. cit., p. 266.

fords of the wilderness' (II Sam. 15.28). John's hearers from Judaea and Jerusalem would thus come by one or other of these routes, and would reach the Jordan at these fords. This accords well with the traditional site of Christ's baptism by John, which has been pointed out since the early fourth century.[1]

It must not be supposed, however, that John remained anchored to one spot. In Luke 1.80, 'He was in the deserts' (AV) the use of the plural seems to imply free movement. Likewise Luke 3.3 which says that John 'went all over the Jordan valley', also implies some moving around.

The area is a striking one; for all who have visited it in person it has remained indelibly stamped on their memory, and from early times travellers have vied in their descriptions of this awesome region.[2] The Jordan valley is a great cleft in the earth's surface, sloping downwards until at the point where the Jordan enters the Dead Sea, it is 1292 feet below sea level, the lowest point on the earth's surface. South of the Sea of Galilee, the Jordan valley is only about four miles wide, but at its southern end it broadens to a plain fourteen miles wide. The waters of the Jordan make possible an area of lush vegetation extending for a short way on either side of the river, and in New Testament times Jericho and the area immediately surrounding it was a thriving and prosperous region noted especially for its dates and balsam.[3] To the west of Jericho and of the Dead Sea, however, the wilderness rises sharply to meet the Judaean hills. In a few miles as the crow flies, the land rises from 1300 feet below sea level to between 1500 and 2000 feet above sea level. G. A. Smith gives a vivid description of a journey he made through the wilderness, travelling from Judaea down towards the Dead Sea.

[1] G. A. Smith, op. cit., p. 496. For a description of the place, see H. V. Morton, In The Steps of the Master, Rich and Cowan, 1934, pp. 104f.

[2] Fine photographs can be found in L. H. Grollenberg, Atlas of the Bible, Nelson, 1956, pp. 347-52, and especially the collection on p. 124, under the title, 'Where John the Baptist Lived and Died'. See also the finely illustrated volume, J. Steinmann, Saint John the Baptist and the Desert Tradition, Longmans, 1958.

[3] G. A. Smith, op. cit., p. 266.

For an hour or two more we rode up and down steep ridges, each barer than the preceding, and then descended rocky slopes to a wide plain, where we left behind the last brown grass and thistle; the last flock of goats we had passed two hours before. Short bushes, thorns, and succulent creepers were all that relieved the brown and yellow bareness of the sand, the crumbling limestone, and scattered shingle. The strata were contorted; ridges ran in all directions; distant hills to north and south looked like gigantic dust-heaps; those near we could see to be torn as if by water-spouts. When we were not stepping on detritus, the limestone was blistered and peeling. Often the ground sounded hollow; sometimes rock and sand slipped in large quantity from the tread of the horses; sometimes the living rock was bare and jagged, especially in the frequent gullies, that therefore glowed and beat with heat like furnaces.[1]

H. V. Morton writes of the wilderness area:

Some writers have described this hot gash in the earth's crust as the most horrible place in the world, while others have found it strangely beautiful. It is, I suppose, a matter of temperament or, perhaps, liver. If you are not feeling too well, I can imagine that the Jordan valley with its overwhelming heat and its airlessness, and Jericho with its flamboyant vegetation, its reptiles and its insects, could be a terrible nightmare. . . . All around are piled dead rocks twisted in the agony of some prehistoric convulsion, unlike the good clean rocks from which men can build their homes; obscene rocks stained with yellow slime and covered with a ghastly shroud of salt.[2]

The term 'wilderness' seems to have had in New Testament times a certain vagueness. We have seen how the one Greek word has to do duty for three Hebrew ones. It would appear that historical events connected with any particular wilderness came to be identified in a loose way with 'the wilderness' in general. This explains why the word is unusually rich in religious and historical associations.

It was, for example, in the wilderness that God revealed himself to Moses (Ex. 3). It was in the wilderness that Israel was delivered, received the Law and entered into the Covenant.

[1] G. A. Smith, op. cit., p. 313.
[2] H. V. Morton, *In The Steps of the Master*, p. 95.

Elijah fled to the wilderness, to Horeb, where he heard the still small voice (I Kings 19); and David also took refuge in the wilderness (I Sam. 23-26; Ps. 63.1). The river Jordan, flowing through the wilderness, also had important associations. The crossing of the Jordan by the Israelites (Josh. 3) marked the end of the wilderness wanderings and the entry into the promised land. Naaman the Syrian was cured of his leprosy by washing in the Jordan (II Kings 5). At the southern end of the Dead Sea is the site of Sodom and Gomorrah, the scene of the drama of Genesis 19. 'In this awful hollow, this bit of the infernal regions come up to the surface, this hell with the sun shining into it, primitive man laid the scene of God's most terrible judgement on human sin.'[1] We are reminded that although John lived in the wilderness, he was never far from the wickedness of cities; the apostasy of Jerusalem, and the luxury and immorality of Jericho would be the targets of his preaching.

It is because of these historical associations that various eschatological associations became attached to the area also. Just as the wilderness had been the scene of God's deliverance of Israel, so it would be the scene of his future deliverance. Thus in Hos. 2.14, 15 God says of Israel,

> Therefore, behold, I will allure her,
> and bring her into the wilderness,
> and speak tenderly to her.
> And there I will give her her vineyards,
> and make the valley of Achor a door of hope.
> And there she shall answer as in the days of her youth,
> as at the time when she came out of the land of Egypt.

In Ezekiel's vision of the river flowing from the Temple, the water flows eastwards, through the wilderness, into the Dead Sea (Ezek. 47.1-12).

It may have been partly its eschatological associations which led many to take refuge in the wilderness during the Maccabaean revolt (I Macc. 2.29; II Macc. 5.27, 6.11, 10.6; Ps. of Sol. 17.19). Certainly this was in the mind of the 'Egyptian false prophet', mentioned by Josephus, who gathered a band of men

[1] G. A. Smith, op. cit., p. 504.

and led them 'by a circuitous route from the desert to the
Mount of Olives'; and it must also have been at the back of the
rebellion led by Theudas, who led his followers to the Jordan,
expecting that the waters would divide as on the first entry
into Canaan.[1] Similar eschatological expectations would doubtless be at least partly responsible for the wilderness and the
Jordan valley becoming the focus of the baptist sectarian movement. The Qumran monastery is located in the wilderness of
Judaea, and the sect believed that they were thus fulfilling the
prophecy of Isa. 40.3, as the Manual of Discipline shows:

> When these things shall come to pass for the community in Israel,
> by these regulations they shall be separated from the midst of the
> session of the men of error to go to the wilderness to prepare
> there the way of the Lord; as it is written, 'in the wilderness
> prepare the way of the Lord; make straight in the desert a high-
> way for our God.' This is the study of the law, as he commanded
> through Moses, to do according to all that has been revealed from
> time to time, and as the prophets revealed by his holy spirit.[2]

It is probable that in the positioning of their monastery the sect
had in mind the prophecies both of Hosea and of Ezekiel. The
valley of Achor (the modern Buqei'a) lies a few miles west of
Qumran,[3] and if the sect took Ezekiel 47 literally, they would
expect the river to emerge either at Qumran itself, or else a
little further south, where the Kidron enters the Dead Sea.
Thus we can see that for the sectarian movement especially, the
wilderness was a place with important eschatological significance.

John's choice of the wilderness as the scene of his ministry is
bound to have been affected by these considerations, and we
can see how he shared the 'wilderness eschatology' of the sectarian movement. It has been pointed out that Isa. 40.3, quoted
by the Dead Sea Scrolls sect, is also used in the New Testament
of John, though only the Fourth Gospel places the words on

---

[1] On these passages see also p. 124 where they are quoted in full.
[2] 1 QS 8.12-16. Cf. 1 QS 9.16f. See U. W. Mauser, *Christ in the Wilderness*,
pp. 58-61.
[3] See J. Allegro, *The Dead Sea Scrolls*, p. 149; M. Burrows, *More Light on
the Dead Sea Scrolls*, p. 21.

John's lips. It has also been noted that the expression 'The Way' is used in Acts to denote the Christian movement.[1] This comes very close to the usage of the Qumran sect, who referred to the faithful as 'those who choose the Way' (1 QS 9.16-21), 'the Way' being a contracted form of 'the Way of the Lord' of Isa. 40.3. It seems certain that the usage of the early Church has been derived in some way from that of Qumran, and there is also clearly some link between the homily on the 'two ways' of light and darkness, truth and error in the Manual of Discipline, and similar homilies in such early Christian works as the *Didache*, the *De Doctrina Apostolorum* and the *Epistle of Barnabas*.

It is possible that it was John the Baptist himself who provided the link between the Christian and the sectarian usages of the expression 'the Way'. John had close links with the sectarian movement as we have already suggested. Whether he actually spoke the words or not, it is very likely that he was influenced by Isa. 40.3. And it is significant that Jesus should say of John that he 'came to you in the Way of righteousness' (Matt. 21.32, RSV). It may well have been through John that the term entered the Christian movement.

Finally, we note that the wilderness was looked upon as the home of evil spirits by some people. In Lev. 16, Azazel, the spirit to whom the scapegoat is sent bearing the sins of the people, dwells in the wilderness; in the inter-testamental period, he becomes the leader of the evil angels.[2] In IV Macc. 18.8 Satan is called 'the seducer of the desert', and in Matt. 12.43, the ejected unclean spirit wanders through the desert places. The charge levelled against John, 'He has a demon' (Matt. 11.18; Luke 7.33, RSV), may have therefore been suggested by his residence in the wilderness, the home of evil spirits.

In all these ways the wilderness must have influenced the life of John. We recognize also, of course, that another reason for going to that area would be that it suited the life of asceti-

[1] Acts 9.2; 19.9, 23; 22.4; 24.14, 22. On this subject see S. V. McCasland, 'The Way', *JBL*, 77 (1958), pp. 222-30.
[2] See S. R. Driver, 'Azazel', *HDB*, I, pp. 207, 208; C. Guignebert, *The Jewish World in the Time of Jesus*, p. 100.

cism to which John committed himself, while the river Jordan would also serve as a most convenient place for baptism.

The wilderness must also have left its mark on John in other ways less easy to define, but of deep significance. Steinmann speaks of the 'simplifying, unifying and cleansing influence' of the desert.[1] The wilderness imposed a life of self-discipline. The wild grandeur of the scenery would speak to John of the majesty and the awfulness of the deity. Long periods of solitude would give time for prayer and meditation, and pave the way for piercing insights into the divine nature and purpose. In the stark simplicity of John's message, in the severity of his condemnation of sin, and in his own burning and passionate conviction, we can see the influence of the wilderness in which he lived.

[1] J. Steinmann, *Saint John the Baptist and the Desert Tradition*, p. 171.

IV

Birth and Infancy

FOR our information concerning the birth of John the Baptist we are dependent on the first chapter of Luke's Gospel where a detailed account is given not only of the birth of John but of the circumstances which preceded it and of those which immediately followed it. Along with the narrative of the infancy of Jesus, the story of John's infancy constitutes a distinct and separate section, Luke 1.5-2.52. The preface to the Gospel (Luke 1.1-4) is composed in elegantly worded Greek, on the model of the prefaces to ancient histories such as those of Herodotus, Thucydides and Polybius; the contrast with the section beginning at Luke 1.5 could hardly be more marked, for here the style, grammar, vocabulary and thought forms are unmistakably Semitic. This is true of the narrative up to the end of Chapter 2, where there is another distinct break, the opening verses of Luke 3.1f, with their elaborate sixfold dating, reading exactly like the beginning of a new book. Clearly, the infancy narratives of Luke 1 and 2 were added to the Gospel after the main body of it had been written, perhaps at a time when a second edition of the Gospel was issued.[1]

Within the section Luke 1.5-2.52 there are two more or less parallel sets of stories concerning the infancies of John and Jesus. The two stories are integrated by the placing of the

---

[1] The addition may well have been made when Proto-Luke was expanded into the full Gospel (B. H. Streeter, *The Four Gospels*, pp. 208f), but acceptance of the Proto-Luke Hypothesis is not necessary in order to recognize that the infancy narratives are a secondary addition.

annunciation to Mary (1.26-38) after the annunciation to
Zechariah (1.11f), and by the insertion of the story of Mary's
visit to Elizabeth (1.39f). The narrative concerning John can
easily stand apart, for it is complete in itself, and some scholars
hold the view that the infancy narrative of Jesus was composed
later with the stories of John serving as a model.[1] It is clear that
the story of Jesus, whatever its exact origins, has been integrated into that of John, and not *vice versa*. Thus, for example,
the phrase 'in the sixth month' in Luke 1.26, relates the annunciation to Mary to the narrative concerning John, for the sixth
month of Elizabeth's pregnancy is meant. There is thus a strong
probability that, as well as Luke 1.5-2.52 being a separate unit,
at a still earlier stage the narrative of John's infancy stood by
itself.

When we come to examine the story of the birth of John
in detail, we cannot but be struck by the distinctive character
of the narrative, for almost every sentence contains words,
phrases or ideas which echo Old Testament passages. Moreover,
the stories as a whole are obviously legendary and based on
Old Testament models. This is not to deny that there is some
historical fact around which pious imagination has woven the
legendary material. But obviously the source of many of the
ideas is to be found in the birth stories of Isaac (Gen. 17.15-21),
of Samson (Judg. 13.2-24), and of Samuel (I Sam. 1.1-23). A
knowledge of Jewish customs is also evident, such as the divisions of the priesthood (1.5), the duties of the priests (1.8f), the
layout of the Temple (1.9-11), and circumcision (1.59). Further,
the very grammatical constructions and sentence formations
are in many cases Semitic in character, and there are some
phrases which no Greek author in his senses could have written.[2]

One possible explanation is the view put forward by Dalman,
Moulton, Harnack and other scholars who hold that the infancy
narrative was composed by Luke himself and that Luke deliberately wrote in the style of the Septuagint, the Greek version

[1] Cf. R. Bultmann, *Die Geschichte der synoptischen Tradition*, pp. 320f;
C. H. Kraeling, *John the Baptist*, Charles Scribner's Sons, 1951, p. 16; J. M.
Creed, *St Luke*, Macmillan, 1930, p. 7.
[2] Streeter, for example, cites Luke 1.51 and 1.69, *The Four Gospels*, p. 266.

of the Old Testament. Modern English writers can produce a style modelled on the Authorized Version of the Bible, and as Luke was a skilful author it would have been possible for him to have done something similar.[1]

The skilful and detailed arguments of those who support this point of view cannot lightly be set aside, and yet there is another and much more likely explanation, and this is that the infancy narrative is based on an earlier source which was originally written either in Hebrew or Aramaic and later translated into Greek. It is not surprising to find that the narrative can be translated into Hebrew with ease. But the important point is that when it is turned into Hebrew, the poetic character, not only of the Magnificat and the Benedictus which are obviously hymns, but of several other parts as well, immediately becomes apparent. It has been shown that there are perhaps six poetical sections in Luke i—vv. 14-17, 30-33, 35-37, 42-45, 46-55 and 68-79. It is important to notice that when these sections are seen to be translations of Hebrew poems the most natural conclusion is that the rest of the narrative too was in Hebrew, as some of the poetical sections are so closely bound up with the narrative.[2]

It has often been held that the source lying behind the infancy narrative was Aramaic rather than Hebrew. Against a Hebrew source it has been argued that by the beginning of our era the writing of Hebrew poetry was a lost art, this belief being based in part on the fact that Josephus at one point seems to betray an ignorance regarding Hebrew metre. Both the *Psalms of Solomon*, however, and the Qumran *Thanksgiving Psalms* were composed within a century or so, if not even closer to the time

---

[1] A detailed exposition of this view is to be found in A. Harnack, *Luke the Physician*, Williams and Norgate, 1907, pp. 96-102, 199-218. For two recent discussions of the subject from this point of view, with references to the earlier literature, see N. Turner, 'The Relation of Luke I and II to Hebraic Sources and to the Rest of Luke-Acts', *NTS*, 2 (1955), pp. 100-109; and P. Benoit, 'L'Enfance de Jean-Baptiste selon Luc I', *NTS*, 3 (1956), pp. 169-94. For a survey of the earlier literature see J. Moffatt, *An Introduction to the Literature of the New Testament*, T. and T. Clark, 1911, pp. 266-73.

[2] See further, R. A. Aytoun, 'The Ten Lucan Hymns of the Nativity in their Original Language', *JTS*, 18 (1917), pp. 274-88.

of the composition of the infancy narrative. The Qumran Psalms in fact offer a very close analogy, though there is no indication of literary dependence.[1] A second and even more basic objection has been the claim that by the first century AD, as far as new composition was concerned, Hebrew was a dead language. But recent discoveries in the Judaean desert have shown, as Allegro points out, that 'Hebrew was still being used in the first half of the second century of our era among Jews of Palestine, in a live and forceful manner which gives no sign either of being at its last gasp or of artificial resurrection for political or nationalistic ends.'[2]

These two objections to a Hebrew source thus fall to the ground. The most recent study of the Aramaic approach to the problem is that by Matthew Black, and it is significant that he is much more cautious than his predecessors in this field. He does show how some features of Luke 1 could have come from Aramaic sources, but the majority of constructions and features of style which he cites can equally well be explained as coming from a Hebrew original.[3] On top of this there are points, such as the form of John's name in the narrative, which strongly favour a Hebrew original, and there are also places where Old Testament references seem to be based on the Hebrew original rather than on the Greek Septuagint version. All things considered, the likeliest view is that the story of John's infancy is based on a Hebrew original.

The theory that Luke used an earlier source is borne out when we examine the thought and theology of Luke 1, considering it as a separate unit. H. L. MacNeill goes so far as to say that 'there is nothing whatever that is distinctively, neces-

---

[1] See A. Dupont-Sommer, The Dead Sea Scrolls: A Preliminary Survey, Blackwell, 1952, p. 69; J. Daniélou, Les Manuscrits De La Mer Morte Et Les Origines Du Christianisme, Editions de l'Orante, 1957, pp. 17, 18. Daniélou points out parallels to the Scrolls especially in the Benedictus, but these are confined to ideas and thought forms which were in widespread use, and do not in any way suggest literary dependence.

[2] The Dead Sea Scrolls, p. 175. Cf. also J. M. Grintz, 'Hebrew as the Spoken and Written Language in the Last Days of the Second Temple', JBL, 79 (1960), pp. 32–47.

[3] See M. Black, An Aramaic Approach to the Gospels and Acts, pp. 111, 112.

sarily, Christian. Everything in these two chapters, on the contrary, is definitely, positively, patriotically, and enthusiastically Jewish.'[1] Whatever may be true of Luke 2, this is certainly true of Luke 1, for on examination this chapter reveals a quite distinctive outlook.

One feature of Luke 1 concerns the use of the word *kurios*, 'Lord', which clearly refers to God and translates the Old Testament *Yahweh*. Thus in Luke 1.46:

> Tell out, my soul, the greatness of the Lord,
> rejoice, rejoice, my spirit, in God my Saviour,

'Lord' is paralleled by 'God, my Saviour'. This is in striking contrast to the rest of the Gospel where *kurios* is a favourite title of Jesus.[2]

Then again, in Luke 1 there is a very high estimate of John. Up to a point the infancy narrative agrees with the Christian view of John as a prophet (1.76), the new Elijah (1.17), who will preach repentance (1.17, 77). But it goes further than this and further than any other part of the New Testament, for, since 'the Lord' means God himself, John is presented as the forerunner of God, and not of the Messiah.

> 'And he will bring back many Israelites to the Lord their God,
> And he will go before him (i.e. God) as forerunner, possessed by
>   the spirit and power of Elijah'

(Luke 1.16, 17). He will 'be the Lord's forerunner to prepare his way' (1.76). There is no room here for a Messiah, indeed John himself is virtually cast in that role; his birth is due to an act of divine intervention, he is filled with the Holy Spirit from his mother's womb (1.15), and with his birth God has already 'turned to his people, saved them and set them free' and 'raised up a deliverer of victorious power' (1.68, 69). John's position in Luke 1 could hardly be more exalted.

---

[1] H. L. MacNeill, 'The Sitz im Leben of Lk 1.5-2.20', *JBL*, 65 (1946), pp. 126, 127.

[2] The one exception is Luke 1.43 where Mary is referred to as 'the mother of my Lord'; this marks it out clearly as an editorial alteration, probably by Luke himself. See P. Winter, 'Some Observations on the Language in the Birth and Infancy Stories of the Third Gospel', *NTS*, I (1954), p. 113.

Still further, the infancy narrative of John is unique in the New Testament in the place it gives to the *priest*. John is born of priestly parents; Zechariah is a priest, and his wife was 'of the daughters of Aaron' (Luke 1.5, RSV). Elizabeth was, significantly, the name of Aaron's wife (Ex. 6.23). As Kraeling remarks, 'It is a priest, officiating in God's presence, to whom it is revealed that God's plan of national deliverance is about to be put into execution.'[1]

These features of Luke 1 all support the view that it is based on a separate source, with its own distinctive language, style and point of view. There is nothing surprising in this for Luke himself states that he knew 'many' sources (Luke 1.1), and his use of Mark and of Q are cases in point. Since Luke was a Gentile it may well be that the source had already been translated into Greek before he got it. In any case, it would be in accordance with what we know of Luke's methods if he polished up the Greek a little and made a few minor modifications as he incorporated the narrative into his Gospel.

Two of the poetic passages in Luke 1 call for special mention. *The Magnificat* (Luke 1.46-55), as it stands, is a psalm attributed to Mary, in which case it belongs to the narrative of the infancy of Jesus. But in the oldest Old Latin manuscripts and in some quotations in the Church Fathers, the reading in Luke 1.46 is 'And Elizabeth said'. This had led scholars to the belief that the Magnificat should properly be attributed to Elizabeth, and that it thus belongs to the story of John's infancy. It is difficult to see why anyone should change 'Mary' into 'Elizabeth' but easy to see why the reverse change should be made by a Christian writer. Moreover, in v. 56, immediately after the Magnificat, we read, 'Mary stayed with her'; but if it was Mary who had just been speaking, we should have expected, 'She stayed with Elizabeth'. It should further be noted that the Magnificat is clearly based on the song of Hannah in I Sam. 2.1-10, in which Hannah praises God for the birth of her son, after a long period of childlessness. It is Elizabeth, not Mary, whose situation corresponds to that of Hannah. The likelihood

[1] *John the Baptist*, p. 21.

is that in the original, Elizabeth was the speaker, but that someone, in all probability Luke in the course of his editing, changed it to Mary in order to lay more stress on the birth of Jesus and less on the birth of John.[1]

The Benedictus (Luke 1.68-79) also poses a problem. It is a psalm of praise to God who has visited and redeemed his people. The context shows beyond all doubt that it is the birth of John which is being celebrated in the Psalm. The phrase, 'from the house of his servant David' in v. 69 is, however, meaningless, for John was of priestly descent; it was Jesus who was of the house of David. How did this reference to Davidic descent come to be in a psalm which is applied to John? When the original Hebrew of the psalm is reconstructed the phrase in question spoils the metre, and is therefore almost certainly to be excluded as a later gloss. Very probably it was inserted by Luke when he revised his source, with the object once again of toning down the high estimate of John. The result has been (from Luke's point of view) very successful, for the usual interpretation is that the first part of the psalm, vv. 68-75, refer to Jesus, and that it is only the last part, vv. 76-79, which refers to John. Clearly, however, in the original source, the whole psalm celebrated the birth of John.

What historical value can we attach to the narrative of Luke 1? Two considerations prevent us from placing too much reliance on the details of the story. The first is that, as already pointed out, the origin of much of the narrative obviously comes from Old Testament models. The second is that there is a strong suspicion that the point of view of a later day has been read back into the narrative. After John's death he was acknowledged to have been a great figure, hence at his birth it

---

[1] Harnack, Loisy and others have suggested that in the original text no name was indicated and that this led to the double reading, but this is not very likely; see J. M. Creed, *St Luke*, p. 22; M. Goguel, *Au Seuil De L'Évangile: Jean-Baptiste*, Payot, 1928, p. 72 n. Although it was noted how several of the poetic passages in Luke 1 are closely linked with the prose narrative, this is not so true of the *Magnificat*, and a case can be made out for regarding it as having originally been a separate composition; cf. R. Bultmann, *Die Geschichte der synoptischen Tradition*, pp. 322, 323. The same may be said for the *Benedictus*; see M. Goguel, *Jean-Baptiste*, p. 74.

was foretold, 'He will be great' (Luke 1.15); he turned out to have a considerable part in the purposes of God, hence there must have been unusual circumstances attending his birth; during his life he was an ascetic (Luke 7.33; Matt. 11.18), hence it was foretold at his birth, 'he shall never touch wine or strong drink' (Luke 1.15).

Beyond the fact that John was of priestly descent, and that the names of his parents were Zechariah and Elizabeth, it is uncertain how much historical basis there is for the narrative. The general impression may be gained, however, of the type of people John's parents were. Zechariah belonged to the rural priesthood; he would officiate at the Temple for only two weeks of the year. Kraeling has pointed to the evidence of a deep cleavage between the rural priesthood, and the more aristocratic and worldly Jerusalem priests.[1] John's parents were humble and deeply pious folk; 'both of them were upright and devout' (Luke 1.6), and prayer and reading of the Scriptures would play a prominent part in their lives.

Much has been made of the statement in Luke 1.36 that Elizabeth was the 'cousin' of Mary, and later tradition and art have linked the two families closely together, and pictured John and Jesus as children playing with one another. The Greek word *suggenis*, however, means only 'kinswoman', and could easily mean that they merely belonged to the same tribe. It has been suggested that the word *suggenis* is introduced merely as a device to link the two narratives together, or in order to suggest that Jesus, through his relation to a priestly family, was himself of priestly as well as Davidic descent, thus strengthening his Messiahship in the eyes of those Jews who looked for a priestly as well as kingly Messiah. Certainly, it would be unwise to suggest any close family connection; the rest of the New Testament does not support the idea and indeed casts doubt on the idea of any previous link between John and Jesus (cf. John 1.31—'I myself did not know who he was').

We do not know exactly where John was born, Luke 1.39 merely stating that his parents lived in 'a town in the uplands

[1] *John the Baptist*, pp. 24f.

of Judah', by which is meant the mountainous, central part of Judaea in which Jerusalem is situated. There were certainly priestly towns, of which Hebron was the chief, but there is no evidence that priests were confined to these towns only, in New Testament times. The suggestion that *Iouda* is the name of the town and should be taken as representing Juttah, which lay just south of Hebron, has little likelihood either. The modern traveller to Palestine is shown 'Ain Karim, a beautiful village a few miles west of Jerusalem, as John's birthplace, but this tradition cannot claim to be earlier than the sixth century AD. Although we know the general region from which John came, his exact birthplace remains unknown.

Accounts of the birth and infancy of John are found in some non-canonical books, but of these only one can be considered at all early, probably dating from the second century AD. *The Book of James* (also referred to as the *Protevangelium*) is an infancy Gospel dealing largely with the childhood of Jesus, and expanding considerably the canonical narratives on which it obviously depends. Some details are added to the story of John, and it is told how Herod's massacre of the infants puts John's life in danger also. Elizabeth escapes with her child, and a mountain swallows them up to keep them in safety. Herod's officers question Zechariah, but when he claims to know nothing of his son's whereabouts, he is slain in the Temple.

There is nothing here of historical value. The author, though he draws heavily on the Old Testament, is clearly ignorant of first century Judaism; apart from the New Testament narratives, his main source was his own imagination. In any case, it is probable that the main section, which deals with John and with Zechariah's martyrdom, is a later addition, since Origen, who knew the *Book of James*, relates a quite different version of the death of Zechariah, according to which he was put to death because he allowed Mary, after the nativity, to take her place among the virgins of the Temple (an obviously pagan idea!). The fact that more than one version of the story existed may indicate a fairly early tradition that Zechariah was martyred, but no great reliance can be placed on stories of this type.[1]

For our knowledge of the infancy and youth of John we are dependent on one verse, Luke 1.80, 'And the child grew and became strong in spirit, and he was in the wilderness till the day of his manifestation to Israel' (RSV).

During much of his ministry John lived the life of an ascetic preacher in the wilderness area, but what was he doing there as a boy? Why was he not in the care of his pious and priestly parents in his home town in the Judaean hills? The answer to these questions is largely a matter of conjecture, but we can recall how the wilderness area was the heart of the baptist movement. We have already noted that this movement formed the background of John's ministry, although he went on to become an original and independent preacher. It is therefore possible that John, as a boy, was adopted by one of the baptist sects.

Brownlee was among the first to ask, 'What was John the son of a priest doing in the wilderness in his tender years?' He called attention to what Josephus says of the Essenes:

> Marriage they disdain, but they adopt other men's children, while yet pliable and docile, and regard them as their own kin and mould them in accordance with their own principles. (*The Jewish War*, II, 8, 2.)

The *Rule of the Congregation*, discovered by the Dead Sea, gives instructions for the training of boys, apparently from the age of ten upwards, within the Qumran sect.[2]

Brownlee's original suggestion was taken up by many scholars, among them A. S. Geyser, who notes the similarities between the beliefs and practices of John and those of the sect of the Scrolls and concludes that John's 'outward appearance, words and acts betray the fact that he has been formed by one

---

[1] For a translation of the *Book of James*, see M. R. James, *The Apocryphal New Testament*, pp. 38-49.

[2] See W. H. Brownlee, 'A Comparison of the Covenanters of the Dead Sea Scrolls with Pre-Christian Jewish Sects', *Biblical Archaeologist*, 13 (1950), pp. 50-72.

or other of the Essene sects inhabiting that very region between Khirbet-Qumran and Massada'.[1]

Geyser argues that in Luke 1 and 2 we have two exactly parallel infancy accounts, one of John and the other of Jesus. For example, the angel appearing to Zechariah (1.11) parallels the angel appearing to Mary (1.28); 'You shall call his name John' (1.13, RSV) parallels 'You shall call his name Jesus' (1.31, RSV); the hymn of Zechariah (1.67ff) parallels the hymn of Mary (1.46ff), and so on. The one place where the strict parallelism breaks down is at Luke 1.80, the single verse being the only thing which corresponds to Luke 2.41-51, the story of Jesus at the Temple at the age of twelve. Geyser suggests that a full parallel did exist in the original source, but that this part of the story was suppressed by Luke, and he goes so far as to sketch what must have been in the missing section. 'It would have told us', he says, 'an episode from the life of John as *bar-mizwa*, it would have supplied an illustration of his exceptional knowledge of the law as revealed in an examination by the Essene teachers. It would further have told us something in relation to his parents, perhaps the fact that, owing to their advanced age, John was already orphaned by this time, that he was nevertheless conscious of the fact that he belonged to his heavenly Father. He went with his adoptive parents to the Judaean desert and obeyed them.'

While this reconstruction of Geyser's is rather far-fetched, the general idea of adoption by some baptist sect is an attractive one. The break with home life could be explained by the fact that John's parents died, or by the fact that they entrusted him to the care of some monastic community. To suggest that John was probably brought up in this way does not, of course, in the least prejudice the belief that as an adult he broke away from his immediate background to become an independent figure.

[1] Geyser's views are to be found in 'The Youth of John the Baptist', *NT*, I (1956), pp. 70-75, from which these quotations are taken.

V

John the Preacher

APART from the infancy narrative in Luke's Gospel, our sources know of John only as a grown man. He is revealed to us above all else as a preacher, as a man with a message. What was the message that John proclaimed?

1. *The Proclamation*

There can be little doubt that the keynote of John's teaching and preaching was the proclamation of the imminent approach of the end of days and of the judgement. This is evident from John's sayings preserved in Q, with their vivid pictures of the vipers fleeing the wrath to come, the tree about to be cut down, and the separating of the wheat from the chaff.

Behind the saying about the vipers (Matt. 3.7; Luke 3.7) probably lay the picture of a wilderness fire, in which dry grass and scrub can blaze for miles, sending animals such as scorpions and vipers scuttling for safety. Here is a warning of the destruction which will take place unless people repent.

The figure of the tree being cut down (Matt. 3.10; Luke 3.9) may also have been based on John's personal experience; the tree would not have been seen in the wilderness, but it might have been close by, near the Jordan, which in Old Testament days was a place where trees were felled (as II Kings 6.1-4 shows). The figure, however, has a literary background as well, for in the Old Testament the cutting down of a tree is a symbol of judgement, as for example in Isa. 10.33, 34 which speaks of the judgement which will fall on the Assyrians, and says:

> Behold, the Lord, the Lord of hosts,
>   will lop the boughs with terrifying power;
> the great in height will be hewn down,
>   and the lofty will be brought low.
> He will cut down the thickets of the forest with an axe
>   and Lebanon with its majestic trees will fall.

Kraeling points out that in the Old Testament this figure is used only of judgement which will fall upon the Gentiles; but in the inter-testamental literature it is applied to Jews (Ecclus. 6.2, 3; 23.25; Wisd. 4.3-5).

The metaphor of winnowing is an even more familiar one. Sheaves were taken to a circular threshing floor and there threshed by means of an ox-drawn threshing sledge. The grain was then separated from the chaff and broken straw by winnowing. In this process, the mixture was tossed up into the air with a winnowing fork, the heavy grain falling directly back to the ground again, while the lighter straw and chaff were blown further away by the wind. Both threshing and winnowing are referred to in Isa. 41.15, 16, where God says to Israel:

> Behold I will make of you a threshing sledge,
> new, sharp, and having teeth;
> you shall thresh the mountains and crush them,
> and you shall make the hills like chaff;
> you shall winnow them and the wind shall carry them away,
> and the tempest shall scatter them.

In the Old Testament the wicked are frequently referred to as chaff, as, for example, in Ps. 1.4—'The wicked are not so, but are like the chaff which the wind drives away'. Cf. also Job 21.18; Ps. 35.5; Isa. 17.13; 29.5; Hos. 13.3.

John thus spoke in words which had their roots in the preaching of the prophets, words which were simple, clear and direct and which would be readily understood by his audience. What then was the outline of this message which he proclaimed?

John proclaimed a coming judgement, in which the righteous would be separated from the wicked, as the chaff is from the good grain, and the bad tree is from that which bears fruit. This judgement, moreover, was to take place in the immediate future; the great crisis was almost upon men. 'Already the axe is laid to the roots of the trees', and the judge already has the winnowing fork in his hand. As a result of this judgement, the wicked will be punished. The chaff is removed and burned, while the bad tree is cut down and thrown into the fire.

How far John's proclamation also included the reward of the righteous and the coming Kingdom has been the subject of debate. In the saying about separating the wheat from the chaff (Luke 3.17; Matt. 3.12) the wheat is to be gathered into the granary, and this certainly implies that just as the wicked will be punished so the righteous will be rewarded. The only place where it is stated that John proclaimed the coming Kingdom is Matt. 3.2, where he is represented as preaching, 'Repent; for the kingdom of Heaven is upon you'. This verse has been cited, however, as an example of the 'Christianizing' of John's message. On the other hand, the high esteem in which John was held by Jesus suggests an area of agreement between the two, and as Jesus differs strikingly from John on quite a number of points surely we must find in the idea of the coming Kingdom one of the points on which they *did* agree.

We can accept, then, that John did proclaim the coming of God's Kingdom, but with two provisos. Firstly, we know very little of the nature of the rewards of the righteous and of the coming reign of God as they were pictured by John. We shall see that he did speak of a future outpouring of God's holy spirit, but beyond this we cannot go. Secondly, while this element was present in John's message the very paucity of the evidence for it suggests that John concentrated by far the greater part of his attention on stern warnings of future punishment, and on practical counsels as to how the punishment may be avoided.

2. He That Cometh

Not only did John proclaim the imminent judgement, with the punishment of the wicked and the reward of the righteous, he also foretold the advent of a person, who would come at the fast-approaching end of days to execute this judgement. The saying about the mightier one who is coming after John, whose sandals he is not worthy to untie, and the contrast between John's baptism and the future Messianic baptism appears to have stood in both Mark and Q; but the Q saying was longer and went on to develop the role of the coming one as the judge, with the winnowing fork in his hand separating the wheat from the chaff (Matt. 3.12; Luke 3.17).

The saying about the one who is to come after John actually appears in the New Testament seven times, never in exactly the same form (Mark 1.7; Matt. 3.11; Luke 3.16; John 1.15, 27, 30; Acts 13.25). Apart from differences in detail which are unimportant, the saying seems to have come down to us in two forms:

1. 'After me comes one who is mightier than I.'
2. 'The one who comes after me is mightier than I.'

The later New Testament references assume that in this saying John was referring to Jesus. Indeed, in John 1.15 and 1.30, we find a still later development of the saying, 'He who comes after me (or, after me comes a man who) ranks before me, for he was before me' (RSV). Here the saying has been altered so as to make John testify to Christ's pre-existence, and thus emphasize his own inferiority.[1]

When we turn to the earliest sources, however, in Q and Mark, it is quite clear that originally John was not referring to Jesus. He was speaking of a coming Messianic figure, one who was not here yet but who would come in the future, albeit the very near future.

It has been argued that the saying about the coming one does refer to Jesus, on the grounds that the words 'he who comes after me' reflect a New Testament expression for a disciple 'following after' his master, e.g. Mark 1.17 (Matt. 4.19) 'Jesus said to them, Follow after me . . .'; Mark 8.34 (and parallels,

---

[1] John 1.15 is almost certainly an editorial addition, and John 1.30 may also be. See G. H. C. Macgregor, *The Gospel of John*, Hodder and Stoughton, 1928, pp. 19, 20, 29.

RSV) 'If any man would come after me, let him deny himself...' The expression, it is true, is a well-known Rabbinic
one with the double meaning of 'walk after' and 'be a pupil
of'. On this interpretation, therefore, the saying means, 'One
who follows after me, i.e. one of my disciples, i.e. Jesus, is
mightier than I.' This is an ingenious explanation, though rather
far-fetched.[1] It contradicts the clear evidence that John pictured
this figure as being still in the future. John had no thought of
identifying the coming Judge with Jesus.

How then did John regard the coming Messiah? Which form
of the saying is the original one? Did John speak of a Mightier
One who was to come, or of a Coming One who would be
mightier than he?

Walter Grundmann would explain the saying in terms of
the coming of a Mightier One.[2] He turns to the only other
place in the New Testament where the form 'mightier'
(ischuroteros) occurs, which is in Luke 11.20-22, where Jesus says,

> But if it is by the finger of God that I cast out demons, then the
> Kingdom of God has come upon you. When a strong man (ho
> ischuros), fully armed, guards his own palace, his goods are in
> peace; but when one stronger (ischuroteros) than he assails him and
> overcomes him, he takes away his armour in which he trusted,
> and divides his spoil.

Grundmann interprets the strong man (ho ischuros) guarding
his palace and his goods, as Satan who has dominion over the
kingdoms of this world (Luke 4.6) and has men bound (Luke
13.16). The mightier one (ischuroteros) is then the Messiah, with
whom Jesus here identifies himself, who is already overcoming
the power of Satan. Grundmann further suggests that the
phrase 'and divides his spoil' (Luke 11.22) is based on Isa. 53.12
—'and he shall divide the spoil with the strong', so that Jesus
here claims to be both the conquering Messiah and the Suffering Servant.

Whatever we may think of this theory of Jesus' view of

---

[1] For this view see K. Grobel, 'He That Cometh After Me', *JBL*, 60 (1941),
pp. 397-401.

[2] W. Grundmann, 'ἰσχύω etc.', *TWNT*, III, pp. 402-5.

himself (and it may well be reading too much into a simple parable) it is difficult to see its relevance for the earlier saying of John. There is no evidence that the term 'mightier one' was in use as a Messianic title. The use of *ischuroteros* in Luke 11.22 is probably only a coincidence, and it is noteworthy that the term does not appear in the shorter forms of the saying found in Matt. 12.29 and Mark 3.27. Moreover, in John's saying the contrast is between John and the Messiah, who is mightier than John; whereas in the saying of Jesus, the comparison is between Satan and the Messiah, who is mightier than Satan.

It has also been pointed out that the word 'mighty' can be used to describe a person given special powers by God. In Isa. 9.6 one of the titles of the Messiah is 'Mighty God'. In Ps. of Sol. 17.43, 44, it is said of 'the anointed of the Lord' that 'he will be strong and stumble not ... he will be mighty in his works.' But on the whole it is unlikely that John used the phrase 'Mightier One' as a Messianic title. The meaning is rather that the Messiah, when he comes, will be mightier than John because, whereas John only spoke and prophesied about the judgement, the Messiah will actually execute the judgement.

We are on much more fruitful ground when we turn to the other form of John's saying in which he speaks of the figure he expects as the Coming One, for there is ample evidence that this phrase was current as a Messianic title. The Greek is *ho erchomenos*. The crowds hailed Jesus as he entered Jerusalem, 'Blessings on him who comes (*ho erchomenos*) in the name of the Lord!' (Mark 11.9, and parallels). While it is possible to interpret these words as being addressed to a precursor, it is more likely that they were intended to hail the Messiah. Certainly Matthew interprets them in that way; for him *ho erchomenos* is paralleled by 'the Son of David' (Matt. 21.9). Luke inserts the term 'king' after *ho erchomenos* (Luke 19.38). Cf. also John 12.13. A similar use of the term is seen in John 11.27, where Martha confesses to Jesus, 'I now believe that you are the Messiah, the Son of God, who was to come (*ho erchomenos*) into the world.' Hebrews 10.37 applies the expression to Christ, 'For ... he who is to come (*ho erchomenos*) will come;

he will not delay.' The origin of the title is probably to be found in the expression, 'Blessed is he that comes in the name of the Lord', a quotation from Ps. 118.26 originally addressed to pilgrims coming up to the Temple, but later interpreted as referring to the Messiah. It may be that through Daniel 7 the Coming One was linked with the Son of Man since the form *erchomenos* is used in the Septuagint version of Dan. 7.13, 'Behold, with the clouds of heaven there came one like a son of man.'[1] John, it is clear, was using a phrase with strong Messianic overtones when he proclaimed the advent of the Coming One.

John is reported as saying three things of this figure: that he holds the winnowing fork in his hand; that he is mightier than John; and that in contrast to John's baptism, he will baptize with holy spirit and with fire. Each of these sayings contributes to our picture of John's Coming One.

The saying about the winnowing fork (Matt. 3.12; Luke 3.17) tells us that the Coming One is to be the agent of the judgement. He is the one who will separate the wheat from the chaff, and administer the punishments and rewards. It is worth noting that in Rev. 14.14, a passage which very probably reproduces an earlier Jewish apocalypse, the Son of Man is pictured as holding a sickle and reaping the earth.[2]

The saying about the Coming One being mightier than John can also tell us something. In this saying John compares himself to the Coming One, to his own disadvantage; he is not worthy even to untie the thong of his sandals. This comparison 'shows that the person in question is not God, for to compare oneself with God, even in the most abject humility would have been presumptuous for any Jew in John's day'.[3] That is to say, John is definitely speaking of a Messiah, and not of God himself. Further, even allowing for figurative language, the fact that John could speak of the Coming One as wearing sandals

[1] In Theodotion only. Rabbinic sources speak frequently of 'the Coming Age' (see G. F. Moore, *Judaism*, I, p. 271) but do not use the expression 'the Coming One'.

[2] Cf. M. Goguel, *Jean-Baptiste*, p. 41.

[3] C. H. Kraeling, *John the Baptist*, p. 54.

suggests that he thought of him, to some extent at least, as a man. A Rabbinic saying provides a parallel, 'Every work which a slave performs for his lord, a disciple must do for his teacher, except loosing his shoe.'[1]

This leaves us with the saying about the baptism of the Coming One which is contrasted with John's baptism, 'I baptize you with water; he will baptize you with the holy spirit and with fire.' (Matt. 3.11; Luke 3.16; and Mark 1.8, Mark omitting 'with fire'; in Acts 1.5; and 11.16, in both cases without 'fire', the saying is attributed to the risen Christ; cf. also John 1.33.) The original form and the exact meaning of the saying have been the subject of much study and discussion.

The future baptism with fire is almost certainly to be understood in connection with the other references to fire in John's preaching, where fire is to be the instrument of punishment following the judgement. 'Every tree that fails to produce good fruit is cut down and thrown on the fire'; 'he will burn the chaff on a fire that can never go out'; and the vipers, we suggested, were fleeing from a wilderness fire.

In foretelling punishment by fire John stood firmly within the Old Testament and apocalyptic tradition. Amos 7.4, for example, pictures the Lord God 'calling for a judgement by fire', while in Ezek. 38.22, the Lord rains down on Gog and his hordes, 'torrential rains and hailstones, fire and brimstone'. According to Mal. 4.1, 'the day comes, burning like an oven, when all the arrogant and all the evildoers will be stubble; the day that comes shall burn them up . . .' (cf. also Isa. 31.9; Mal. 3.2).

In the post Old Testament period, especially in the apocalyptic literature, the idea of the punishment of the wicked by fire was greatly developed and elaborated. In Enoch 90.24-27 the judgement is described with the guilty being 'cast into an abyss, full of fire and flaming, and full of pillars of fire'. In the Ps. of Sol. we hear of 'flaming fire and wrath against the ungodly' (15.6). In the Dead Sea Scrolls, the wicked are condemned to 'the gloom of the fire eternal' (1 QS 2.8); they will

[1] Ketubot 96a. R. Joshua ben Levi (c. AD 250).

be punished 'with fire and brimstone' (1 Qp. Hab. 2.11); in the end they will 'come into judgements of fire' (1 Qp. Hab. 2.12, 13). The New Testament has numerous references to future punishment by fire (see, e.g. Matt. 5.22; 13.40, 42, 50; 25.41; Luke 17.29; I Cor. 3.13-15; II Thess. 1.8), and the Lake of Fire in Revelation (19.20 etc.) is also derived from this tradition.

But how can this punishment by fire be thought of in terms of a baptism? Even more relevant than the examples just cited are others which contain the idea of a river of fire. In Dan. 7.9, 10 it is said of the 'one that was ancient of days' that

> His throne was fiery flames,
> its wheels were burning fire.
> A stream of fire issued
> and came forth from before him.

We meet this fiery stream again in II (4) Esd. 13.10.[1] Almost certainly we are to see in this idea an example of Iranian influence on Judaism. Kraeling sums up the position concisely— 'In Persian eschatology, the mountains which are made of metal melt at the end of the world, and the molten metal pours over the earth like a river. All men pass into this river of molten metal and in doing so are either purified or destroyed.'[2] In one of the hymns of the Dead Sea Scrolls sect we now have the most striking description of the river of fire hitherto known. T. H. Gaster translates as follows:

> When the hour of judgement strikes,
> when the lot of God's anger is cast
> upon the abandoned,
> when His fury is poured forth upon dissemblers,
> when the final doom of His rage
> falls upon all the works of Belial;
> when the torrents of death do swirl,
> and there is none escape;
> when the rivers of Belial
> burst their high banks
> —rivers that are like fire

---

[1] II (4) Esdras, however, dates from the period following the destruction of Jerusalem in AD 70.

[2] C. H. Kraeling, *John the Baptist*, p. 117. Cf. also M. Goguel, *Jean-Baptiste*, p. 40.

devouring all that draw their waters,
rivers whose runnels destroy
green tree and dry tree alike,
rivers that are like fire
which sweeps like flaming sparks
devouring all that drink their waters
—a fire which consumes
all foundations of clay,
every solid bedrock;
when the foundations of the mountains
become a raging blaze,
when granite roots are turned
to streams of pitch,
when the flame devours
down to the great abyss,
when the floods of Belial burst forth
unto hell itself . . .[1]

It is now easy to see how John could speak of future punishment as a 'baptism' of fire. John himself baptized people in a river, but the Coming One would immerse the wicked in a river of fire. In the Old Testament it is usually God who punishes with fire, but the idea of the Messiah as the agent of punishment is found in the post-Old Testament literature; for example, in II (4) Esdras it is from the mouth of the Son of Man that the fiery stream comes:

He sent out of his lips as it were a fiery stream, and out of his lips a flaming breath, and out of his tongue he shot forth a storm of sparks. . . . And these were all mingled together . . . and fell upon the assault of the multitude which was prepared to fight, and burned them all up. (13.10, 11)

In a number of the references to judgement by fire which we have noted the idea is present of fire as a purifying or refining force. The messenger of Mal. 3.2 is 'like a refiner's fire' and 'he will purify the sons of Levi and refine them like gold and silver'. This appears to have been part of the original Iranian conception, according to which all men must pass through the river of fire in which they will either be purified or destroyed.

---

[1] 1 QH 3.27-32. *The Scriptures of the Dead Sea Sect*, pp. 142, 143.

This is the idea present in I Cor. 3.13-15. More common than this, however, is the simple idea of the punishment of the wicked, and it is this idea of punishment, not of purification which John preached. For John, it is only after a separation has been made between the good and bad trees, that the bad trees are thrown into the fire (Matt. 3.10; Luke 3.9); it is only after the wheat and chaff have been separated that the chaff is burned with unquenchable fire (Matt. 3.12; Luke 3.17).

The baptism with holy spirit has proved a more difficult problem to solve, and many have even denied that John ever spoke the phrase, since baptism with the Holy Spirit looks very like a Christianizing of John's message. The phrase, 'He will baptize you with the Holy Spirit and with fire' appears, however, to have stood in Q, which is the earliest and most reliable source for the reconstruction of John's message.[1]

It should be noted that what appears in the phrase is 'holy spirit' (en pneumati hagiō), which should be written without capitals and without the definite article. The later Christian writers obviously interpreted it in the sense of 'the Holy Spirit', but to suggest that John may nevertheless have used the words does not imply that he was anticipating the doctrine of the Trinity.

Further, the term 'spirit of God' is found in the Old Testament and in the literature of Judaism. The actual phrase 'holy spirit' is found in the Old Testament (Isa. 63.10, 11; Ps. 51.11), is mentioned in the Ps. of Sol. 17.42, and occurs in the Rabbinic

---

[1] It has been held that the Q form of the saying was, 'I have baptized you with water, but he will baptize you with fire'; Mark re-interpreted this in a Christian sense and reproduced it as, 'I have baptized you with water, but he will baptize you with the Holy Spirit'; and finally both Matthew and Luke conflated Mark and Q to produce their version, 'He will baptize you with the Holy Spirit and with fire'. For this view see, e.g. F. C. Grant, *Interpreter's Bible*, 7, p. 651; T. W. Manson, *The Sayings of Jesus*, p. 41. A serious weakness of this view is that it involves the coincidence of both Matthew and Luke making an identical conflation, whereas normally, since Matthew and Luke use exactly identical Greek, it would be assumed that both were drawing on Q. Further, the saying in both Matthew and Luke is intimately linked with the saying which follows, 'whose winnowing fork is in his hand' etc., which certainly comes from Q. Therefore the normal principles of criticism suggest that Q did have 'He will baptize you with holy spirit and with fire', and this has the strongest claim to be considered as the original version.

literature. It is also found in the Dead Sea Scrolls (1 QS 4.20, 8.16; CD 2.12). There is thus nothing improbable in supposing that John did in fact speak of God's 'holy spirit'.

Obviously the baptism with holy spirit closely paralleled the baptism with fire in John's preaching: just as the baptism with fire stands for the future punishment of the wicked, so the baptism with holy spirit would stand for an outpouring of God's spirit at the end of days. The reference is clearly not to the future institution of another rite of baptism; to suppose that John foresaw the development of Christian baptism would be most improbable. But there is nothing at all improbable in the view that John was proclaiming a future outpouring of God's spirit. Such an event is indeed foretold in the Old Testament itself, the classic passage being Joel 2.28, 29 (quoted in Acts 2.17f)—'And it shall come to pass afterward, that I will pour out my spirit on all flesh. . . .' In Ezek. 39.29, God says of Israel, 'I will not hide my face any more from them, when I pour out my spirit upon the house of Israel', and Isa. 32.15 looks to the time when 'the spirit is poured upon us from on high, and the wilderness becomes a fruitful field'.

How could this future outpouring of God's spirit be thought of as a baptism? Here again it is unlikely that John was being original; he was rather using ideas which would be familiar to many of his hearers. Already in Ezek. 36.25-27, the future gift of the spirit is linked with the idea of sprinkling with water:

I will sprinkle clean water upon you, and you shall be
clean from all your uncleannesses, and from all your idols
I will cleanse you. A new heart will I give you,
and a new spirit I will put within you . . .

Similarly, in Isa. 44.3 we read:

For I will pour water on the thirsty land,
and streams on the dry ground;
I will pour my spirit upon your descendants,
and my blessing on your offspring.

Abrahams has pointed out that in two of the passages cited

above (Joel 2.28, 29; Ezek. 39.29) the word used for the 'pouring out' of God's spirit is properly applicable only to liquids.[1]
Once again, however, the most striking parallel comes from
the Dead Sea Scrolls, for the Manual of Discipline speaks of a
time when 'God will refine in his truth all the deeds of man,
and will purify for himself the frame of man, consuming every
spirit of error hidden in his flesh, and cleansing him with holy
spirit from all wicked deeds. And he will sprinkle on him a
spirit of truth like water for impurity' (1 QS 4.20, 21).[2] Here
the eschatological sprinkling of the spirit is thought of in terms
of a rite of baptism, thus providing a close parallel to John's
thought. Usually it was God who was thought of as pouring
out the spirit; whether the Messiah was ever so pictured is a
matter of debate.

What exactly is the meaning of the outpouring of the spirit
at the end of days? Kraeling links it closely with the baptism
of fire, pointing to the tradition of the 'fiery breath' of the
Messiah by which the unrighteous will be destroyed (cf.
II (4) Esd. 13; Isa. 11.4; Rev. 11.5). On this basis Kraeling
wants to regard the spirit foretold by John as 'a purgative and
destructive force working through the Messiah'.[3] Similarly,
Goguel wants to equate fire and spirit. Eisler takes spirit
(*pneuma*) in the sense of 'wind', by which God punishes sinners
as, for example, in Ps. 1.4 where the wicked are 'like chaff
which the wind drives away'.[4] The evidence for this view is
slight, however, and most of the passages cited above as examples of the idea of the outpouring of God's spirit do not
regard it as a destructive force. It is not on the wicked, but on
God's people that the spirit will be poured. The spirit is gener-

[1] *Studies in Pharisaism and the Gospels*, I, p. 43.
[2] The translation of this passage has been a matter for dispute. See W. H.
Brownlee, 'The Servant of the Lord in the Qumran Scrolls, II', *BASOR*, 135
(1954), pp. 36, 37; M. Burrows, *More Light on the Dead Sea Scrolls*, p. 316;
Y. Yadin, 'A Note on DSD IV 20', *JBL*, 74 (1955), pp. 40-43.
[3] *John the Baptist*, p. 62.
[4] See M. Goguel, *Jean-Baptiste*, p. 40; R. Eisler, *The Messiah Jesus and John
the Baptist*, pp. 275f. Eisler believes John had in mind a threefold trial of water,
wind and fire which will annihilate the wicked, but through which the just
will pass unscathed. Cf. also G. R. Beasley-Murray, *Baptism in the New Testament*, Macmillan, 1962, pp. 37-39.

ally regarded as a blessing, as for example the parallelism in Isa. 44.3 clearly shows:

> I will pour out my spirit upon your descendants,
> and my blessing on your offspring.

In view of all this there is little reason to doubt that John did speak of a Messiah who would baptize, not with water as John himself did, but with both fire and holy spirit. Upon the wicked, the Coming One will pour out a river of fire to punish and destroy them; but on God's people the Coming One will pour out God's spirit and all the blessings which that entails.[1]

3. John's Message and Jewish Expectations

Having surveyed John's proclamation, it remains to ask with which branch of Jewish expectation John allied himself.

In his preaching of the coming judgement, John stood in the true prophetic tradition. To a certain extent, John was also in line with the apocalyptic branch of Jewish thought, which developed the ideas of the prophets especially in the inter-testamental period. Whereas the prophets often thought of

---

[1] That Mark omits the baptism of fire is not surprising; most likely this is a Christianizing of John's message since for the Christian baptism and the gift of the Holy Spirit were closely linked. Could it also be that Mark, compiling his Gospel in Rome after the Neronic persecution, is anxious to avoid references to fire, since the Christians were blamed by Nero for causing the fire of Rome? Cf. Tacitus, *Annales*, XV, 44.

Objection has been raised to John's prophecy of the holy spirit on the basis of Acts 19.1-7, where Paul finds at Ephesus a group of disciples who know only John's baptism. When Paul asks them, 'Did you receive the Holy Spirit when you believed?' they reply, 'No, we have never even heard that there is a Holy Spirit.' How, it is argued, could John have spoken of a Holy Spirit if these disciples have never heard of it? Cf. T. W. Manson, *The Sayings of Jesus*, p. 41. But this interpretation completely fails to understand the text. The reply of the disciples does *not* mean that they had never heard of the idea of the outpouring of the spirit; to be ignorant of this, they would have to be ignorant of Ezekiel, Isaiah, Joel and so on. What they did not know, however, was that 'there *is* a holy spirit', i.e. that the Holy Spirit was a present reality. Paul's question was, '*Did* you receive the Holy Spirit?' These disciples still thought the spirit was in the future, so their reply naturally means: we are quite unaware of the fact that the new age has already dawned and that the spirit has already been given. It was this that Paul explained to them, and it was this defect that Paul remedied by the laying on of hands, so that 'the Holy Spirit came upon them' (Acts 19.6).

judgement as being administered on earth, by some nation whom God used for his purposes, the apocalyptists expected the judgement to take place at the end of days, following the resurrection, and preceding the ushering in of a new age when God and/or his Messiah would reign supreme. The apocalyptists usually expected the end to take place soon, and sometimes ventured to predict exactly when and how it would occur. In so far as John looked for a judgement by fire, by the Coming One, at the fast-approaching end of days his message has a very apocalyptic ring.

Further, John can be seen to have many affinities with the baptist sectarian movement. The ideas both of the river of fire and of the future outpouring of the holy spirit find their closest and most striking parallels in the Dead Sea Scrolls. This supports our contention that it was the sectarian movement which formed John's background.

In one important respect, however, John's picture of the future constrasts strongly with that of the apocalyptic-sectarian strain in Judaism. John seems to have concentrated on essentials, and to have gone back to the vigorous simplicity of the prophetic message. We saw that although he probably spoke of the coming Kingdom, he declined to go into details. There is no hint in John's message of an elaborate blueprint of the future. Not for him the apocalyptic arithmetic of Daniel, or the conducted tours of Enoch, or the military strategy for the war against Gog and Magog; his was a simple message of punishment for evil and reward for righteousness.

Turning now to the Coming One foretold by John, can we identify this figure, as we have tried to sketch him, with any particular Jewish expectation?

Various identifications have been proposed, including the view that he was none other than Elijah. This was the claim of Albert Schweitzer,[1] who thus challenged the normal Christian view that John was Elijah, and therefore the forerunner of the Messiah. According to Schweitzer, John never thought of him-

[1] A. Schweitzer, *The Quest of the Historical Jesus*, A. & C. Black, 1910, pp. 371-4.

self as Elijah; 'Jesus was the first and only person who attributed this office to him', the identification being part of the 'secret' of Jesus' Messiahship. G. S. Duncan revived this view,[1] pointing to John's denial that he is Elijah in John 1.19ff, behind which passage Duncan says 'we may trace an undeniably genuine tradition'. Elijah fits the description of John's Coming One for he called down fire from heaven. Duncan suggests that John may have thought of himself in terms of Elijah's servant who is briefly mentioned in I Kings 18.43; 19.3.[2] More recently, J. A. T. Robinson has supported this idea that John's Coming One was to be Elijah. He follows previous writers in pointing to Elijah as 'the man of fire *par excellence*', and he quotes the gloss on Luke 9.54 where James and John say to Jesus, 'Lord, may we call down fire from heaven to burn them up, as Elijah did?'

One defect of the view of Schweitzer and Duncan is that John emerges as the forerunner of Elijah, who is the forerunner of the Messiah. Being the forerunner of the forerunner seems rather far fetched. Robinson, however, gets round this difficulty by arguing that John expected that Elijah would come as the Messiah. But this contradicts the view which was held that Elijah would not carry out the judgement, but would rather come before the judgement, and call the people to repentance. Altogether, the view that John's Coming One was Elijah is full of difficulties, and the arguments in favour of it do not carry conviction. John's Coming One, as we have sketched him, was no forerunner; he was to be the judge, the instrument of the punishment of the wicked and of the outpouring of God's spirit. This can only be a Messiah of some description.

Is there then any branch of Messianic expectation with which we can connect John's Coming One?

Was he a national, Davidic Messiah? T. W. Manson suggests that the figure expected by John was akin to the Messiah of Psalms of Solomon 17, a king who is to 'purge Jerusalem' and

---

[1] See G. S. Duncan, *Jesus, Son of Man*, Nisbet, 1947, pp. 82–87.
[2] See G. S. Duncan, op. cit., p. 85.

'destroy the Godless nations', and 'gather together a holy people'.[1]

'For God will make him mighty by means of His holy spirit . . .
And the blessing of the Lord will be with him; he will be strong
    and stumble not,
His hope will be in the Lord: who then can prevail against him?'
                                                (Ps. of Sol. 17.42-44)

In spite of the statement that this figure 'shall not put his trust in horse and rider and bow', he is nonetheless very much an earthly Messiah; the judgement he brings will be directed against the Romans who have defiled the Holy City.

There is no evidence that John looked for such a warrior king who would lead his armies against the Romans. In our sources, no mention is made by John of judgement upon the Gentiles; it is the unrighteous Israelites whom he calls to repentance. There is no mention in Psalms of Solomon 17 of a fiery judgement; and it is to the Messiah, not to the righteous that God's holy spirit will be given.

It has also been suggested that John's Coming One may have been a priestly Messiah. For a certain time, and in certain circles, a priestly rather than a Davidic Messiah was expected; though probably the two beliefs existed side by side in the Qumran community.[2] John was of priestly descent, and his followers showed an interest in the priesthood. It has therefore been suggested, for example by Stauffer, that 'it is possible that . . . the Baptist expected a levitical Messiah, and meant to prepare for his coming'.[3] The main objection to this view is simply the lack of direct evidence for it; nowhere in our sources does John ever speak of a priest or of the priesthood, and it may therefore be doubted whether this idea can have been important

[1] See T. W. Manson, *The Sayings of Jesus*, p. 41. On the Psalms of Solomon, see R. H. Charles, *Apocrypha and Pseudepigrapha*, II, pp. 625-52, from which also the translation has been taken.

[2] On the priestly Messiah, see S. Mowinckel, *He That Cometh*, Blackwell, 1956, pp. 286f. On the Messianic expectations of the Qumran sect see K. G. Kuhn, 'The Two Messiahs of Aaron and Israel', in K. Stendahl, *The Scrolls and the New Testament*, pp. 54-64; and M. Burrows, *More Light on the Dead Sea Scrolls*, pp. 297-311.

[3] E. Stauffer, *New Testament Theology*, SCM, 1955, p. 24.

to him. Nevertheless it is quite possible that priestly ideas did play some part in John's expectation.

Can we then identify John's Coming One with the heavenly Son of Man of apocalyptic expectation? We have already seen how John was influenced by apocalyptic ideas. The judgement of all men, and the punishment of the wicked by a river of fire strongly suggest a supernatural Messiah. We noted how II (4) Esdras 13 portrays the Son of Man as destroying the wicked with a fiery stream, how the term 'Coming One' may reflect the Son of Man of Dan. 7.13, and how the picture of the winnowing fork is akin to the picture of the Son of Man in Rev. 14.14.

While these points all favour an apocalyptic, supernatural Messiah of the Son of Man type, there is another and apparently quite contradictory line of evidence which points to an earthly rather than a supernatural Messiah. This is suggested by the fact that John dares to compare himself to the Coming One, albeit to his own disadvantage, when he says, 'The Coming One is mightier than I'. Similarly, John's saying about untying, or carrying the Coming One's sandals points to an earthly human figure. Furthermore, if John sent his disciples to ask Jesus, 'Are you the Coming One, or are we to expect some other?' (Luke 7.19; Matt. 11.3), he can hardly have regarded the Coming One as a supernatural figure.

The evidence appears to point to two quite contradictory conclusions. Escape from the dilemma can be sought by denying either one or other term of the equation. Some have denied or ignored the apocalyptic or supernatural element, and T. W. Manson, for example, holds that 'there is no indication that John thinks of the Messiah as a supernatural being', he is merely 'a human Messiah endowed with supernatural power and authority'.[1] Such a conclusion can only be arrived at, however, by setting aside a considerable part of the evidence. Others, for example Goguel and Kraeling, seek to deny the earthly attributes of John's Coming One. But this does not do justice to all the evidence either, and it involves the

[1] *The Sayings of Jesus*, p. 41.

denial of historical value to the question of John from prison.

One explanation which might account for the contradictory evidence would be to suggest that John looked for an earthly figure who would subsequently be exalted to become the heavenly judge. There is, according to some scholars, evidence that such an expectation did exist in John's day, and it has been claimed that it formed the closest approach to the thought of Jesus which we can find in the literature of Judaism at this period. In the Book of Enoch, Chapters 70 and 71, the secret is revealed of the identity of the Son of Man, who has been described in previous parts of the Book. Enoch himself is translated to heaven, where the Head of Days 'came to me and greeted me with His voice, and said to me; Thou art the Son of Man'.[1] Here we have the idea of an ordinary man, a preacher of right-eousness, being exalted to heaven and appointed Son of Man by God. This view has been worked out with reference to our understanding of Jesus by Rudolph Otto.[2] Otto's conclusions have, however, been widely disputed on the grounds that the dating and interpretation of Enoch 70 and 71 are very un-certain. Nevertheless we can see how all the evidence concern-ing John's Coming One could be fitted into such an expecta-tion. John looked for a historical figure, walking this earth, as yet unrecognized, who would be exalted to heaven as Son of Man at the fast-approaching end of days. Jesus could then have taken over this conception from John, his own original contri-bution being the idea that the exaltation of the Son of Man could only come about through suffering and death.

Such a view must, however, fall far short of proof. We can only say that in so far as John's Coming One can be identified

[1] Enoch 71.14. R. H. Charles in *The Book of Enoch, Translation and Com-mentary*, Clarendon Press, 1912, makes a series of emendations for which there is no textual evidence, on the grounds that Christian scribes must have altered the text. This is most improbable since (a) if Christians had altered the book the alterations would be more numerous and more obvious, and (b) it is inconceivable that Christians, who believed Jesus to be the Son of Man would deliberately alter a document to make it state that Enoch was the Son of Man.

[2] See R. Otto, *The Kingdom of God and the Son of Man*, Lutterworth 1938, especially pp. 176-243. For the other point of view see O. Cullmann, *The Christology of the New Testament*, SCM, 1959, pp. 137-52; W. Manson, *Jesus the Messiah*, especially pp. 113-20; S. Mowinckel, *He That Cometh*, pp. 437-44.

in current Jewish expectation he appears to be linked in some way with the Son of Man. It should be noted, however, that to a certain extent John appears to have been deliberately vague as to the exact type of Messiah he expected. We have noted already his reluctance to go into details regarding the coming Kingdom. It is significant that he is not reported as using the term Son of Man, nor for that matter, Son of David, Son of God, The Branch, The Elect One, or any other Messianic title. He speaks only of the Coming One, which is the vaguest possible title.[1] The fact that the Messiah will come is an obvious one, and beyond this the user is not committed. Instead of speculating when and in what manner the Messiah will come, people would be better employed in preparing themselves by repentance for his coming.

4. Man's Response

John's proclamation of the Coming One and of the coming judgement was followed by a demand upon his hearers that they should respond in a certain way.[2] John's demand was a threefold one; his hearers must repent, they must be baptized, and they must live righteous lives. The demand for baptism will be dealt with in the next chapter; here we shall examine the other two demands.

First and foremost, John called for repentance. 'Prove your repentance by the fruit it bears', he warns his hearers (Matt. 3.8; Luke 3.8); 'I baptize you with water, for repentance', he states (Matt. 3.11). Mark and Luke characterize John's message as 'a baptism of repentance' (Mark 1.4; Luke 3.3, RSV), and Matthew summarizes it, 'Repent; for the kingdom of Heaven is upon you' (Matt. 3.2).

Repentance is never defined in the New Testament. It is

---

[1] It is noteworthy that Mowinckel uses the phrase, 'He That Cometh' as a title for his book which describes the whole range of Messianic beliefs.

[2] Josephus (*Antiquities*, XVIII, 5, 2) and the New Testament (Mark 1.5; Matt. 3.5) agree that John's preaching attracted large crowds. The Q passage (Matt. 3.7-12; Luke 3.7-9) probably had no introduction, and the evangelists thus added their own, Matthew addressing John's message to 'many of the Pharisees and Sadducees', and Luke, to the 'crowds of people' who 'came out to be baptized by him'.

assumed that its meaning is known, and this is not to be won-
dered at as repentance lay at the very heart of the prophetic
message, and is 'a cardinal doctrine of Judaism'.[1] Numerous
passages in the Old Testament speak of the need for repentance,
and of the forgiveness which it brings, not only in the Prophets
but also in the Law. The penitential Psalms are expressions of
repentance. Originally it was the nation that was addressed,
but from Ezekiel onwards the idea of repentance was indivi-
dualized; it is the wicked man who must turn from his sin as,
for example, in Ezek. 18.21—'But if the wicked man turns
away from all his sins which he has committed and keeps all
my statutes and does what is lawful and right, he shall surely
live; he shall not die.' In the teaching of the Rabbis repentance
was given an exalted place; according to them, it was created
before the world.[2]

The Hebrew verb for 'repent' (shūbh) means literally to turn,
to go back, or to return. Wickedness is viewed as a departure
from or a falling away from God and from the will of God.
Repentance therefore involves both a turning away from evil
and a returning towards God.

Repentance presumes a state of sin, and it is in the light of
this that John's addressing his hearers as a 'brood of vipers' is
to be understood. It was the serpent who tempted Eve to sin
and by the time of Rev. 12.9, if not earlier,[3] the serpent was
identified with Satan himself.[4] Obviously John did not pull his
punches in denouncing the wickedness of his hearers and their
need, therefore, of repentance.

Repentance involves the recognition of and the confession

[1] G. F. Moore, *Judaism*, p. 500; on repentance, see pp. 500-2, 507-34; and
also W. Morgan, 'Repent, Repentance', *HDB*, IV, p. 225.

[2] For references see G. F. Moore, *Judaism*, I, p. 526.

[3] See G. F. Moore, *Judaism*, I, pp. 478, 479.

[4] Kraeling wants to distinguish between snake (*ophis*) and viper (*echidna*).
A viper, he claims, was looked upon as 'basically noxious in character, a
creature of venomous malignity', and to call anyone a viper was 'not merely
to accuse him of improper motives, but to castigate him as evil in his inner-
most being'. See C. H. Kraeling, *John the Baptist*, p. 48. Another suggestion
is that of G. R. S. Mead (*The Gnostic John the Baptizer*, p. 13) that the phrase
reflects Micah 7.17 where it is said of the Gentiles that 'they shall lick the dust
like a serpent'.

of sins: 'He who conceals his transgressions will not prosper, but he who confesses and forsakes them will obtain mercy' (Prov. 28.13). But repentance must involve a real change of mind and heart and will. Ezekiel says, 'Repent and turn from all your transgressions, lest iniquity be your ruin. Cast away from you all the transgressions which you have committed against me, and get yourselves a new heart and a new spirit' (Ezek. 18.30, 31). It was recognized that this inner change had to be genuine; according to the Mishnah (Yoma 8, 9) if anyone repents, but with the intention of sinning again, and again seeking forgiveness, then his repentance is not true repentance at all. Moreover, it is fully recognized in Jewish thought that repentance must be manifested in deeds. 'Prove your repentance by the fruit it bears' (Matt. 3.8; Luke 3.8) represents the Jewish view exactly. The New Testament word for repentance (*metanoia*) is not therefore adequately defined as a 'change of mind'; we must attach to it also the wider meaning it held in Judaism, including especially the good works which prove its genuineness.

John, in his call for repentance, was thus very much in line with one of the central beliefs of the Old Testament and of the Judaism of his day. His proclamation of the imminence of the end would, however, give his teaching on repentance a special urgency.

It has often been pointed out, in connection with John's message, that repentance and the coming of the Messianic age were frequently connected in one strand of Jewish thought. The continual non-appearance of the Messianic age posed a serious problem for Jewish thought, especially as one foreign yoke succeeded another. An explanation was devised to account for the delay which had its origin in the Old Testament teaching that if only Israel would repent and return to God, they would be pardoned and God would restore the national fortunes. During the Roman period, the idea gained ground that what was holding up the day of deliverance was the wickedness of the Jewish people. According to this point of view, there is no one fixed time for the coming of the Messiah; he will appear only when the proper conditions are fulfilled, whenever that may be. The Rabbinic references to this belief mostly date from the third century AD, but this does not mean that the doctrine did not exist much earlier. Writing of the belief that the coming deliverance is conditional on repentance, G. F. Moore reminds us that 'This is the burden of the prophets from first to last; it is written in some of the most pertinent and impressive chapters of the Law.'[1] There are records of a debate between two Rabbis of the late first century AD who discussed the question.[2] Rabbi Eliezer ben Hyrcanus held that 'If the people of Israel do not repent, then they will never be redeemed' i.e. he held that the Messianic deliverance is conditional on repentance. He was opposed by Rabbi Joshua ben Hananiah, who could not accept the logical conclusion of this, that if Israel never repented they would never be redeemed. He believed that the deliverance did not depend on man at all, but would come in God's own time. It was the view of Rabbi Eliezer ben Hyrcanus which became dominant in the orthodox eschatology of Rabbinic Judaism. The view is stated concisely by Rabbi Jose the Galilean (c. AD 110) who said, 'Great is repentance, for it brings near the (Messianic) redemption'.[3] In the majority of cases the condition is repentance, but there are a number of Rabbinic sayings which mention other conditions such as almsgiving, the study of the Law, and the correct keeping of two or even one Sabbath. Rabbi Simeon ben Yochai (c. AD 150) said, 'If Israel kept only two Sabbaths according to the rule they would be immediately delivered' (Shabbat, 118b).

If John's message were to be interpreted in the light of this line of thought, then his idea would have been to call the nation to repentance and to the performance of good works in order to make possible and indeed to hasten the advent of the Coming One.

It must be noted, however, that 'Great is repentance, for it brings near the redemption' expresses only one approach to

[1] G. F. Moore, *Judaism*, II, p. 350.
[2] See H. L. Strack-P. Billerbeck, *Kommentar zum Neuen Testament aus Talmud und Midrasch*, Munich, 1922-28, I, pp. 162f.
[3] For further references see Strack-Billerbeck, I, pp. 162f, 598f.

the question, that which became dominant in Pharisaic, ortho-dox Judaism. John's sympathies, on the other hand, lay more with the apocalyptic outlook which tended to expect the new age at a fixed time. When we study John's message we find there is nothing conditional about his proclamation of the approaching crisis; it is in the face of the inevitable end that men are called to repent in order that they might escape the wrath of God. The Rabbinic view, while it is interesting, does not thus coincide with that of John at all. Abrahams expresses the difference between the two points of view as follows, 'The formula of John (or Jesus) was: Repent *for* the Kingdom is at hand. The Pharisaic formula was: Repent *and* the Kingdom is at hand.'[1]

Closely linked with John's call to bring forth fruits that befit repentance is his warning, 'Do not presume to say to yourselves, "We have Abraham for our father". I tell you that God can make children for Abraham out of these stones here' (Matt. 3.9; Luke 3.8). This saying has sometimes been interpreted as meaning that in the sight of God all racial distinctions are abolished and that only repentance and righteousness count, but this is to go beyond John's meaning. His hearers were Jews (cf. Mark 1.5; Matt. 3.5); the fact that he warned them against relying on descent from Abraham shows that those being addressed *were* in fact descended from Abraham. John's warn-ing to the Jews was that mere physical descent from Abraham was not enough, but that repentance and a righteous life were also necessary. Nothing is said of John's attitude to the Gentiles, and there was presumably nothing distinctive or startling in his attitude to that question.

Once again, John is but repeating and emphasizing the teach-ing of the prophets. The conception of a chosen people had always been open to abuse: the danger was that the privilege of choice was stressed, but the responsibility forgotten. 'Even if we sin we are thine, knowing thy power', says Wisdom of Solomon 15.2; in the popular mind this could easily be misinterpreted, and the next phrase forgotten—'but we

[1] *Studies in Pharisaism and the Gospels*, I, p. 34.

will not sin, because we know that we are accounted thine'.

Behind this saying of John we should probably see not only a general reference to membership of the Chosen People, but also a reference to the common belief that God had been and might still be, especially merciful towards Israel for the sake of his servant Abraham, or for the sake of the patriarchs, Abraham, Isaac and Jacob. (Cf. Gen. 26.3, 5; II Kings 13.22, 23; II Macc. 8.15.) In Exodus 32.11ff, after the incident of the golden calf, Moses pleads with God not to destroy the Israelites, but it is only when Moses says, 'Remember Abraham, Isaac and Israel, thy servants...' that 'the Lord repented of the evil which he had thought to do to his people'. Rabbi Hezekiah ben Hiyya commented on this passage, 'Moses' intercession was not accepted by God until he made mention of the good desert of the forefathers'.[1] It is perhaps misleading to talk of belief in a 'treasury of merit' by means of which Jews could draw upon 'the merit of the fathers'[2]; nevertheless it is not difficult to imagine how, in the popular view, descent from Abraham could lead to moral complacency. It was such a complacency that John sought to shatter by declaring that each Jew would be judged entirely on his own merits.

In John's view, God did not depend on Israel; if they all broke the covenant and defied God's Law, the omnipotent God could easily create a new people. In the passage cited above from Exodus 32 this is what God threatens to do when he says to Moses, 'Now therefore let me alone, that my wrath may burn hot against them and I may consume them; but of you I will make a great nation' (Ex. 32.10). God threatens to destroy all the Israelites except Moses, who would become the father of a new Israel. John looks at the stones strewn over the face of the wilderness, and declares that 'God can make children for Abraham out of these stones here'. Perhaps John had in mind Isa. 51.1, 2 where Abraham is the stone from which Israel is hewn:

---

[1] Tanhuma, Wayyera 9. This Rabbi was of the third century AD, but he is merely illustrating this long-standing belief.
[2] See G. F. Moore, *Judaism*, I, p. 544.

Look to the rock from which you were hewn,
And to the quarry from which you were digged,
Look to Abraham your father,
And to Sarah who bore you.

Mere physical descent from Abraham, John stressed, will by itself count for nothing at the judgement.

Turning now to John's other demand that men should respond by living righteous lives, we find that this demand was expressed in various ways. Josephus, anxious to portray Judaism as a religion of high moral standards concentrated almost entirely on this aspect of John's teaching; John, he tells us, 'commanded the Jews to exercise virtue, both as to righteousness towards one another, and piety towards God...' Jesus said that 'John came to show you the right way to live' (Matt. 21.32), and we have seen how John himself demanded righteous living as the essential fruit of repentance.

What was 'the right way' advocated by John? Undoubtedly it would consist mainly of governing one's life in accordance with the Law, and this is borne out by the four sayings of John which preserve definite moral injunctions.

There is firstly his fearless word to Herod Antipas, 'You have no right to your brother's wife' (Mark 6.18; Matt. 14.4), the grounds for this being found in Lev. 18.16; 20.21.[1] The other three rulings are found in Luke 3.10-14, which is peculiar to Luke. The authenticity of this passage has been questioned, but we may agree with B. S. Easton when he says that 'there is every reason to suppose that details of the Baptist's teaching were preserved in Palestine and, at all events, the present section contains the kind of instruction he must have given'.[2]

The command to share clothing and food with those in need (Luke 3.11) has been compared to the teaching of Jesus in Matt. 5.40—'If a man wants to sue you for your shirt, let him have your coat as well.' The comparison is a false one,

---

[1] This is dealt with more fully in Chapter XI.
[2] B. S. Easton, *The Gospel According to St Luke*, T. and T. Clark, 1926, p. 39. On the significance of the three categories of questioners, cf. G. C. Darton, *St John the Baptist and the Kingdom of Heaven*, Darton, Longman and Todd, 1961, p. 18.

however, because Jesus' saying is part of a much more radical ethical demand; it is given as an example of returning good for evil, for it is to the person who is suing you for your shirt that you are to give your coat. John's saying, on the other hand, is in keeping with the usual Jewish teaching on almsgiving.[1] 'Is not this the fast that I choose ... to share your bread with the hungry, ... when you see the naked, to cover him ...?' (Isa. 58.6, 7). 'He who oppresses a poor man insults his Maker, but he who is kind to the needy honours him' (Prov. 14.31). The Rabbinic writings similarly abound with praise for charity to the poor and needy, and it is significant that the usual word for almsgiving is $c^e dh\bar{a}q\bar{a}h$, 'righteousness'.

The tax collectors ($tel\bar{o}nai$) who were told, 'Exact no more than the assessment', were especially despised as collaborators with the Romans and as traitors to their own people; the system of farming out taxes offered ample scope for oppression and fraud. They are extorted by John to act justly, and to take only exactly what is their due.

The soldiers ($strateuomenoi$) who were told, 'No bullying; no blackmail; make do with your pay!' were most probably Jewish, and may well have been engaged on police duties rather than being on active service.[2] John's answer is enough in itself to suggest how their powers could be misused.

5. John's Message and Political Questions

We have already seen how John's Coming One was in no sense a political figure or a warrior Messiah. In so far as John did preach the coming Kingdom, it was a Kingdom which would be ushered in by God and by the Coming One, and not by man's efforts either by way of repentance or by way of force of arms.

A massive attempt has been made, however, by Robert Eisler to interpret the whole of John's ministry in political terms. Eisler believes John to have been 'Johanan b. Zekharjah,

---

[1] See G. F. Moore, *Judaism*, II, pp. 162-79.
[2] See A. Plummer, *The Gospel according to St Luke*, ICC, T. and T. Clark, 1896, p. 92.

a priestly Rekhabite descended from a famous sept of wonder-workers and rain-charmers'.[1] Building on the statement of the Slavonic Josephus that John enticed the Jews to liberty by declaring to them, 'God has sent me to show you the way of the Law, whereby ye may be freed from many masters', Eisler portrays John as condemning all Jews who had submitted to the Idumaean line and to Rome. He demanded that all who had done so should receive proselyte baptism before being counted as true Jews again, and he preached the coming of a liberator-king.

Eisler connects John and his disciples with the 'fourth sect' of the Jews, the rebel party founded by Judas of Galilee. These were known, Eisler believes, as the 'barjonîm', those who 'stand outside', the 'extremists'[2]; and they are to be identified with the later sect of 'Dosithean Ṣadoqites', who produced the Damascus Document. Since, according to the Slavonic version, John's ministry began in the time of Archelaus, he is connected with the revolt under Judas the Gaulanite, Simon of Peraea and Athrongas. Ten years later he was concerned in the revolt occasioned by the census of Quirinius. Eisler pictures John as the 'army chaplain' of the rebels; Luke 3.10ff he considers to be 'a sort of field sermon delivered before the march into battle' on the occasion of one or other of these two revolts.[3] John's baptism also is seen as being largely political in significance,[4] a *sacramentum* in the sense of a soldier's oath of allegiance, by which he enrolls in the army of the new Israel. 'The new Israel, regenerated through the baptism of John into a "new covenant" with the national God, is primarily a Militia of the coming Messiah, an army of the Christ, the future anointed national king who is their war-lord and army commander, and to whose service their soldiers' lives are devoted.'[5]

After the failure of the two revolts, Eisler pictures John as living in hiding in the bush of the Jordan valley, 'appearing only now and then, like a bodiless spectre, a jinn of the wilder-

[1] *The Messiah Jesus and John the Baptist*, p. 566.
[2] Op. cit., pp. 252, 253.   [3] Op. cit., pp. 262f.
[4] Op. cit., pp. 267f.   [5] Op. cit., p. 270.

ness, a wild man or a satyr, causing consternation with his ever
and anon repeated announcement of the coming terror of the
last days, now and then baptizing newly won fighters for the
last messianic war'.[1] A fresh impetus was given to the revolutionary movement, however, by Pilate bringing the Roman
standards into Jerusalem, fulfilling in the eyes of pious Jews,
Daniel's prophecy of 'the abomination of desolation'. It was
at this time (AD 19) so Eisler believes, that Jesus went to be
baptized by John. Though a follower of John for a period,
Jesus went on to proclaim his own distinctive message and to
form his own band of disciples, some of whom had previously
been adherents of John. Eisler's reconstruction of the life and
ministry of Jesus do not concern us here, and we can merely
note that he holds that John continued his hermit-like existence
until he was arrested and executed by Antipas in AD 35.

Eisler's theory is so manifestly false that one hardly knows
where to begin to criticize it. Basically, it distorts the truth
because Eisler rejects the most reliable sources, and builds on
the least reliable. The keystone of the theory is the two passages
on John in the Slavonic Josephus which Eisler believes to go
back to an original Aramaic version of *The Jewish War*, but
which are in fact, as we have already seen, Byzantine interpolations in a Greek version of Josephus, and which have no claim
to be regarded as reflecting an independent historical source.
Moreover, he does not hesitate to drag in fragments of 'evidence' from the latest and most unreliable sources if they appear
to offer the least support for his conjectures; these references
range from the apocryphal gospels to the Josippon, the Toledoth Jeshu and the Arabian Nights! Eisler's theory can only
stand if the clear evidence of the Gospels is to be dismissed as
utterly false. This Eisler is prepared to do, for he believes the
Gospels have come down to us 'covered with a thick layer of
pious frauds, as is the case with the sacred writings of all
peoples'.[2] But he is not even consistent, for he is ready to accept

[1] Op. cit., p. 567.
[2] See J. W. Jack, *The Historic Christ*, p. 13; this book is a fine treatment of
Eisler's views.

any parts of the Gospel record (e.g. Luke 3.10-14) which fit in with, or can be made to fit in with his pre-conceived notions. Eisler's methods are unscientific, and his treatment of texts is in many cases purely arbitrary. Whatever does not suit his theory he rejects as Christian interpolations; when evidence is lacking this is held to be due to Christian censorship, and so the text is 'emended' and 'reconstructed'.[1]

Eisler's theories rest primarily on the Slavonic Josephus, but it is not at all clear that even the Slavonic version regards John as a political figure.[2] Eisler's theories are open to many other objections, such as the fantastic chronology he is forced to accept. His reconstructions of the rebel movement do have, of course, a historical basis. There was a fanatical Zealot party, always ready to spring into armed rebellion against the Roman oppressors, and eventually it was this party which brought about the disastrous revolt of AD 66-70 which resulted in the destruction of Jerusalem and a fearful loss of life. There is no indication, however, in any of the reliable sources, that John had any close links with the Zealot party, or that he preached armed rebellion against Rome. Eisler's fantastic theories merely show the length one has to go in order to import a political significance into John's message.

[1] See J. W. Jack, The Historic Christ, pp. 99f.
[2] The statements of John in the Slavonic version do not necessarily constitute incitement to armed rebellion, but are in fact quite in line with the New Testament picture of John, who demands obedience to God and to the Law, and who promises the coming of a (non-political) Messiah. That the Slavonic version is not thinking in political terms is also suggested by the fact that John appears before 'the teachers of the Law', and is questioned on theological, not political questions. Further, the fact that he is thereafter released shows that Archelaus is not thought of as suspecting him of having political motives.

VI

John the Baptist

JOHN's ministry was characterized not only by the preaching and teaching which we have just been considering, but also by the rite of baptism. So prominent a feature was this of his ministry that he was generally known as 'John the Baptist', or 'John the Baptizer'.[1]

Our information about John's baptism is very limited. The principal place where the rite was performed was in the river Jordan, though in the Fourth Gospel we hear of him baptizing also at Aenon near Salim (John 3.23) and at Bethany beyond Jordan (John 1.28).[2] Baptism was doubtless preceded by an

---

[1] This is also doubtless as A. Oepke says ('βάπτω, βαπτίζω, etc.' Kittel, *TWNT*, I, p. 544), an example of the Jewish custom of differentiating between people of the same name by adding another name. Cf. the four Simons of Matt. 10.2; Mark 3.18; Mark 14.3; Acts 10.6. Both Josephus and the New Testament have the form *Iōannēs ho baptistēs* (Josephus once, the New Testament 13 times). *Ho baptizōn* appears three times, in Mark 1.4; 6.14, 24, but the fact that the form *baptistēs* also appears in Mark (6.25; 8.28) suggests that they were used interchangeably.

[2] On the location of Aenon near Salim, see pp. 163, 164. Bethany beyond Jordan poses a problem, as no such place is known from any other source. The variant reading 'Bethabara' (*Bēthabara* or *Bētharaba*), textually inferior, can probably be traced to a textual emendation on the part of Origen, who could not find a suitable 'Bethany' when he visited Palestine. Nor can we accept that the well-known Bethany is meant, *peran* being taken to mean 'across from, opposite' the Jordan. (This is argued by P. Parker, 'Bethany Beyond Jordan', *JBL*, 74 (1955), pp. 257-61.) The whole point of the phrase 'beyond Jordan' is to distinguish this place from the well-known Bethany. We must content ourselves by saying that it was a small place on the east side of the Jordan, the name of which in later centuries became forgotten.

exhortation by John, and then the people were baptized, 'confessing their sins' (Mark 1.5; Matt. 3.6). This is the only trace of the service which must have accompanied the rite, but whether this confession was a formal one prescribed by John or an extemporary prayer of confession by those about to be baptized, we are not told. John himself presided in some way at the actual ceremony for he is said to have baptized people, and people could be said to be baptized by him. Although it is not specifically stated, the baptism was almost certainly by total immersion; this is suggested by the fact that when Jesus had been baptized, he 'came up out of the water' (Mark 1.10; Matt. 3.16).

The information in our sources concerning the meaning of John's baptism is meagre, and contradictory. The only statement of John himself which is reported for us is the saying in which he contrasts his baptism, which is 'with water', with the coming Messianic baptism with holy spirit and fire. Mark 1.4 states that 'John the Baptist appeared in the wilderness proclaiming a baptism in token of repentance, for the forgiveness of sins'. This statement is paralleled in Luke 3.3. Josephus, on the other hand, tells us in *Antiquities*, XVIII, 5, 2 that, according to John, 'baptismal ablution would be acceptable, if it were used not to beg off from sins committed, but for the purification of the body when the soul had previously been cleansed by righteous conduct'. Mark seems to suggest baptism had a *moral* significance, conferring forgiveness of sins, following on repentance, whereas Josephus seems to suggest that it had a purely *ritual* or ceremonial significance and definitely states that it was not for the remission of sins.

It is not specifically stated in our sources whether John's baptism was repeated or whether it was performed on each person only once. Usually it is assumed to have been performed only once because of its close connection with Christian baptism. The only individual baptism described is that of Jesus, and he was baptized only once. It might be argued that his was a rather special case, but the fact that John baptized large numbers of people who then returned to their homes and to their daily occupations suggests that John's baptism was in fact only administered once.[1]

What exactly would the word 'baptize' imply in New Testament times? The verb *baptizein*, although common in the New Testament occurs only four times in the Septuagint.[2] It is the intensive form of *baptein*, which is common in Classical Greek and in the Septuagint, meaning usually to 'dip'. Hence it can be used of dyeing cloth (i.e. by dipping it into a dye); of drawing water (i.e. by means of dipping a bucket into a well); and of a ship sinking (i.e. dipping under the sea). *Baptizein* can mean virtually the same, to 'dip', or immerse in a liquid, but from this two further meanings seem to have been derived.

(a) *Baptizein* can mean to 'wash' by dipping or immersing in water. Thus it is used in the Septuagint version of the story of Naaman the leper, who was told to go and wash in the Jordan that he might become clean (II Kings 5.14).[3] Similarly, in Ecclus. 34.25, it is used of ritual washing after pollution— 'If a man washes (*baptizomenos*) after touching a dead body, and touches it again, what has he gained by his washing?' The law requiring this washing after contact with the dead is found in Num. 19.11-13. Again, in Judith 12.7, *baptizein* is used of Judith washing herself at a fountain every night, this probably being some type of ritual lustration.[4] This meaning of to 'wash' with special reference to Jewish ritual lustrations is found in

[1] In *Clementine Homilies*, II, 23, John is described as a Hemerobaptist, but no reliability can be attached to this statement. There is some evidence of baptismal rites being repeated in the early Christian Church. Cf. Heb. 6.1, 2 ('baptisms' in the plural); Tertullian, *De Corona*, 3; Hippolytus, *Apostolic Tradition*, 20; See further, M. Black, *The Scrolls and Christian Origins*, pp. 99-101.

[2] See A. Oepke, Kittel, *TWNT*, I, pp. 527-44; Liddell and Scott, *A Greek-English Lexicon*, Clarendon, 1940, pp. 305, 306; Arndt and Gingrich, *A Greek-English Lexicon of the New Testament* (based on Bauer), University of Chicago Press, 1957, pp. 131, 132; Moulton and Milligan, *The Vocabulary of the Greek Testament, Illustrated from the Papyri and other Non-Literary Sources*, Hodder and Stoughton, 1930, p. 102.

[3] Here it translates the Hebrew *tābhal*, to 'dip'. In the post-Old Testament period it, and the Aramaic *t^ebhal*, came to be used rather of the Levitical lustrations. From this root comes *t^ebhīlah*, the word used for the ritual bath, especially that of proselytes.

[4] For these last two examples see, A. Oepke, Kittel, *TWNT*, I, p. 533.

the New Testament in Luke 11.38 and Mark 7.4, both of these referring to the ritual washing of hands before meals.

(b) A second meaning of *baptizein* also appears in the sense of to 'overwhelm'. In Isa. 21.4, the Septuagint uses *baptizein* in the phrase 'horror has appalled me'. The idea here is the metaphorical one of being overwhelmed or swamped with horror, just as a person might be if water swept over him. Josephus uses the word in this sense of refugees flooding into Jerusalem —*ebaptisan tēn polin*, 'they swamped the city' (*The Jewish War*, IV, 3, 3).[1] This metaphorical meaning of being overwhelmed is found in the New Testament in Mark 10.38, 39 and Luke 12.50.

Baptizein does not necessarily imply total immersion, but John's baptism was almost certainly by this method. There is no definite evidence as to whether the ritual washings of the Old Testament were by total immersion but it is very likely that they were (except, of course, where sprinkling is laid down as the method). Certainly the later proselyte baptism, which evolved from the earlier washings, was by total immersion.[2]

It cannot be claimed that a study of the meaning of *baptizein* sheds a great deal of light on the meaning of John's baptism. That the candidates were dipped into water is fairly obvious, and that the immersion was total is very likely. The metaphorical meaning of overwhelm with disaster does not seem to offer any direct clue. The best approach would appear to be through the meaning of to 'wash', possibly in connection with the Jewish ritual and ceremonial washings.

In considering the question of the origin and meaning of John's baptism, we now seek to discover the closest parallel which can be found to John's rite. We would do well to realize here that religious rites involving the use of water are a most frequent phenomenon in the study of Comparative Religion, and can be traced over many centuries and among many

---

[1] Usually the idea is that of being overwhelmed by evil or ill fortune; this meaning is found in a papyrus of the mid-second century BC. See Moulton and Milligan, op. cit., p. 102.

[2] See I. Abrahams, 'How Did The Jews Baptize?', *JTS*, 12 (1911), pp. 609-12.

peoples.[1] It is not enough therefore merely to produce some rite which has similarities to John's baptism in order to establish a connection between the two. The rite must be attested as having existed at a time and in a place which make a connection both possible and likely. Various alternatives therefore now fall to be considered.

1. Lustrations in Judaism

Various rites involving the use of water existed, though they were never of the first importance, in orthodox Judaism. In the Old Testament we meet with various beliefs which were for the most part held in common with other Semitic religions, and indeed with a great many religions throughout the world.[2] These relate almost entirely to ritual and ceremonial purity.

The regulations governing ritual purity, found principally in Leviticus 11-15, deal with unclean animals, and uncleanness due to childbirth, menstruation, various diseases especially leprosy, and various issues. Uncleanness due to death and contact with the dead is dealt with in Numbers 19. Usually a complete bath is prescribed to remove the uncleanness; in some cases, washing of the clothes, and also washing and rinsing of the hands are laid down. Numbers 19.1-10 lays down the laws for the making of 'water for impurity' by mixing the ashes of the sacrifice of a red heifer with water. This water was sprinkled on whatever was to be purified (Num. 19.13, 18, 19, 21).

No unclean person might take part in the worship of God. Hence washings precede the consecration of a priest or Levite; the high priest washes on the Day of Atonement, and priests wash before entering the sanctuary.[3]

The uncleanness dealt with by these washings was apparently thought of largely in material terms, as something exterior; and it had little or nothing to do with moral ideas, as can be

---

[1] Cf. A. Oepke, Kittel, *TWNT*, I, p. 528; J. Thomas, *Le Mouvement Baptiste*, pp. 288-341.

[2] See A. S. Peake, 'Unclean, Uncleanness', *HDB*, IV, pp. 825-34.

[3] Ex. 29.4; 30.17-21; 40.12; Lev. 8.6; 16.4, 24 (cf. Lev. 16.26, 28); Num. 8.6, 7, 21.

seen from the fact that objects, as well as persons, may become unclean.

When we turn to the post-Old Testament period,[1] we find that the rites of lustration were developed considerably. Not only did the Rabbis expound the Old Testament laws, but new regulations were introduced, for example concerning the washing of hands—before sitting down to a meal, before touching sacred books, at morning prayer, and so on. The largest of the six books of the Mishnah is devoted to the laws of purification, and twelve treatises deal in fine detail with the different types of uncleanness, how they can be contracted and how they are to be removed.

John is portrayed in our sources as a man of exceptional piety and as a good Jew it is certain that he must have observed the laws of ritual purity. John 3.25 mentions a dispute which arose between John's disciples and a Jew 'about purification' (*peri katharismou*). 'Purification' seems to mean rites of ritual purity (cf. John 2.6), and John and his disciples must therefore have been interested in these rites.[2]

The statement of Josephus that John's baptism was 'for the purification of the body' suggests that it was a rite of ritual purity. While it is certain that John must have observed these rites, his own baptism, which he administered, which caused such a great stir, and which earned him the name of 'the Baptist' was clearly something quite different from the usual Jewish rites of purity. If it had been merely a ritual lustration such as those we have just been describing, then there would have been nothing remarkable about it. The evidence of Josephus must definitely be called in question, therefore, and it seems certain that he either did not know or did not want to reveal the true nature of John's baptism.

2. Proselyte Baptism

Having failed to explain John's baptism in terms of ritual

[1] See E. Schürer, *A History of the Jewish People in the Time of Jesus Christ*, T. and T. Clark, 1890, Division II, Vol. II, pp. 106-11; J. Thomas, *Le Mouvement Baptiste*, pp. 350-6.

[2] On John 3.25 see further pp. 154, 155.

lustration, we turn now to another type of lustration within Judaism which has been widely held to have been the origin of John's rite, namely, proselyte baptism.

The Jewish attitude to proselytes or converts to Judaism varied considerably. In the Maccabaean period, we hear of considerable proselyting, mostly by force[1]; indeed, Galilee became largely Jewish in this way. By the turn of the era, it is evident that the admission of proselytes was a widespread practice,[2] especially in the Diaspora. The movement for the conversion of the Gentiles was probably at its peak in the mid-first century AD but after the First Revolt a considerable change took place and most Jews took up a more intolerant attitude to Gentiles.[3]

Nevertheless, the admission of proselytes did continue, and from Rabbinic sources we learn that the rite of initiation was threefold, consisting of circumcision, baptism (t^e bhīlāh) and sacrifice. From the Talmud we learn how baptism is to be administered. It follows a course of instruction summarizing the main requirements of the law, and also circumcision. The candidate is partially immersed in water in the presence of two men, learned in the Law, who recite to him some of the lighter and some of the weightier commandments. Then the candidate is immersed in the water, 'and when he comes up he is in all respects an Israelite'.[4]

A rite of baptism by which a person became a convert to Judaism might well have stood in a close relation to John's baptism, but the all-important question which must first of all be dealt with is when proselyte baptism came into being. If it

[1] Josephus, *Antiquities*, XII, 9, 1 and XIII, 11, 3. On Proselytes in general see G. F. Moore, *Judaism*, I, pp. 325-53; W. G. Brande, *Jewish Proselyting, In The First Five Centuries Of The Common Era*, Brown University, Providence, R.I., 1940; E. G. Hirsch, 'Proselyte', *JE*, X, pp. 220-4.

[2] Cf. Philo, *Vita Mosis*, 2; Matt. 23.15.

[3] See C. Guignebert, *The Jewish World in the Time of Jesus*, p. 231.

[4] The main sources are (a) a passage in the Babylonian Talmud (Yebamot 47), and (b) a small work entitled 'On Proselytes' (Gerim) which is an 'extra-canonical' tractate of the Talmud, dating from c. AD 1300. Although late in date, these sources do embody much earlier material. The texts are printed in full, in English, in parallel columns for comparison, in F. Gavin, *The Jewish Antecedents of the Christian Sacraments*, SPCK, 1928, pp. 33-35.

did not appear until after the time of John, then it can have no relevance for the study of the origin of John's rite. It has frequently been assumed that proselyte baptism did provide the origin of both Johannine and Christian baptism, but the descriptions of proselyte baptism which are quoted are mostly from the Talmud and other sources very much later than the period with which we are concerned.

Schürer holds that in the Mishna all three requirements (circumcision, baptism and sacrifice) 'are presupposed as already being of long standing; nay for Rabbinical Judaism they are so much matters of course that, even apart from any explicit testimony, we should have had to assume that they were already currently practised in the time of Christ'.[1] Schürer (and many other scholars) 'assume' the existence of proselyte baptism in the time of Christ because of the fact that Gentiles were considered unclean and would therefore have to take a bath of Levitical purification.

It is true that converts to Judaism would from the first participate in the various rites of ritual purity, for no one could take part in the worship of the Temple, or in the feasts and ceremonies of Judaism until they had carried out the prescribed lustrations and thus ensured that they were clean. But there is no evidence that these lustrations were considered to be any different from the usual Levitical washings, and especially there is no evidence that they constituted part of the rite of initiation.

There can be no doubt that originally, and for a considerable period of time, admission of a proselyte was by circumcision only, followed in many cases by participation in sacrifice. The question of when baptism was added and became part of the ceremony of initiation has been much disputed.

In the frequent proselytizing of the Maccabaean period, admission to Israel was always by circumcision. Philo (c. 30 BC-

---

[1] *History of the Jewish People*, Division II, Vol. II, p. 320. In this connection, cf. the articles by T. F. Torrance, 'Proselyte Baptism', *NTS*, I (1954), pp. 150-4, and 'The Origins of Baptism', *SJT*, 2 (1958), pp. 158-71, in which much of the material quoted is centuries later than the New Testament period. Torrance seems here to side-step the all-important historical question of the date of proselyte baptism; cf. T. M. Taylor, 'The Beginnings of Jewish Proselyte Baptism', *NTS*, 2 (1955), pp. 193-8.

AD 54) while frequently speaking of proselytes, makes no mention of baptism. Even more significant is Josephus (AD 37-c. 100), who writes at such length about the history and customs of the Jews. He often mentions the admission of proselytes; but where the method of admission is given, it is by circumcision only. The silence of the New Testament itself is an important piece of evidence. The Gospels give a prominent place to the baptism of John, but there is no word of proselyte baptism. It is especially strange that Paul, who employs many references to circumcision in his writings, should make no reference to the baptism of those who entered the Old Israel.[1] It is significant too that early Christian literature contains no references at all, even in the case of writers who discuss the subjects of Judaism or baptism or both: for example, Barnabas, Justin Martyr, and Tertullian.

Even in the Mishna there are only two possible references. One passage records a debate between the schools of Hillel and Shammai as to whether or not a Gentile who was circumcised on the eve of the Passover might wash and partake of the paschal lamb. It was apparently usual for proselytes to be admitted before the Passover so that they could then take part in the feast. But there is nothing in the passage to indicate that the washing was part of a ceremony of initiation, and what is referred to is probably the usual purification before Passover.[2]

Another passage has also been cited as evidence in which Rabbi Eleazar ben Jacob said, 'Soldiers were guards of the Gate in Jerusalem; they were baptized and ate their Paschal lambs in the evening'. Because of the reference to Roman soldiers this has been claimed as an example of proselyte baptism prior to the destruction of the Temple.[3] Here again, however, the washing is connected with the Passover, and there is no clear

---

[1] Cf. J. Thomas, *Le Mouvement Baptiste*, pp. 364, 365; G. R. Beasley-Murray, *Baptism in the New Testament*, pp. 19, 20.

[2] For this point of view see T. M. Taylor, 'The Beginnings of Jewish Proselyte Baptism', *NTS*, 2 (1955), p. 195. Cf. J. Thomas. *Le Mouvement Baptiste*, p. 358. See also H. H. Rowley, 'Jewish Proselyte Baptism and the Baptism of John', *HUCA*, 15 (1940), p. 316.

[3] I. Abrahams, *Studies in Pharisaism and the Gospels*, I, p. 37. See also H. H. Rowley, *HUCA*, 15 (1940), p. 317.

indication that it was the ceremony by which the proselyte was admitted to Judaism.

The first definite reference to proselyte baptism is found in a passage in the Babylonian Talmud which reports the differing opinions of Rabbi Eliezer ben Hyrcanos and Rabbi Joshua ben Hananiah. Their discussion may be dated as late first or early second century AD. If a proselyte had been circumcised, but not baptized, R. Eliezer would admit that he was a proper proselyte; if he had been baptized but not circumcised, R. Joshua would admit that he was a proper proselyte. The passage seems to suggest that about the end of the first century AD baptism and circumcision could be regarded as alternative methods of entering the Jewish faith. There is no evidence from any other source that circumcision could be omitted, so that what this passage may really reflect is a stage when baptism was coming to be regarded as an essential part of initiation but was not necessarily regarded as such by all authorities.[1]

Epictetus, the Stoic philosopher, has also been cited as a witness on account of a passage in his Discourses, in which becoming a Jew and being baptized seem to be equated. But both the date and the accuracy of this evidence are in doubt.[2]

It is generally held that proselyte baptism developed from the lustrations prescribed in the Old Testament and expanded in post-Biblical Judaism.[3] Some time during the first century AD the convert's first bath of ritual purity must have begun to take on an added significance, and to be regarded as part of the initiation proper. In spite of the controversy which has taken place with regard to this subject, there would seem to be no reliable evidence of baptism as an initiation rite until the end of the first century. The conclusion is inescapable that the destruc-

---

[1] On this passage, see H. H. Rowley, HUCA, 15 (1940), pp. 317-19.

[2] Epictetus, Discourses, II, 9. P. E. Matheson comments on the passage, 'It is not certain whether in this sentence ... Epictetus is thinking of Jews or of Christians, who at this time were often confused with them' (Epictetus, The Discourses and Manual, Vol. II, Clarendon Press, 1916, p. 249). Cf. also J. Thomas, Le Mouvement Baptiste, pp. 360, 361; and H. G. Marsh, The Origin and Significance of the New Testament Baptism, Manchester University Press, 1941, p. 10.

[3] Cf. F. Gavin, The Jewish Antecedents of the Christian Sacraments, pp. 29, 30.

tion of the Temple must have been a decisive factor. When sacrifice was no longer possible, women converts to Judaism could only be admitted if some kind of baptism were devised or developed. Even granting that the destruction of the Temple led to baptism being elevated to a leading role in the admission of proselytes, there is no evidence that this was a general practice before the second century AD.

Two different interpretations of proselyte baptism, propounded at a later date by some Rabbis, deserve mention. They have, however, nothing to do with the original and basic meaning of the rite.

1. Proselytes raised a legal question when they cut themselves off from their previous life and became Jews. The Rabbis were concerned with such questions as the status of sons born previous to a proselyte's conversion, and how this affected the laws of inheritance. One passage is much quoted in which Rabbi Jose ben Halafta (mid-second century AD) laid down that 'a newly converted proselyte is like a newborn child'.[1] The implication is that the convert's past life has been completely obliterated. But there is no suggestion that the rite of baptism confers forgiveness of sins, and certainly there is no idea whatsoever of 'rebirth' such as is found either in the Mystery Religions, or in Christianity.

2. Proselyte baptism raised another kind of problem; the only rite of initiation mentioned in the Law is circumcision, so how can baptism be justified? Rabbi Judah the Patriarch solved this by pointing out the analogy between the experience of the proselyte and the experience of Israel in the wilderness. The Israelites were circumcised (inferred from Josh. 5.2f); they were baptized (inferred from Ex. 19.10), and they were sprinkled with the blood of the covenant sacrifice (Ex. 24.3-8). This Rabbinic teaching arose merely to find a justification for baptism in the Law, and has no bearing on the original meaning of

---

[1] Yebamot 48b. For further Talmudic references, see F. Gavin, op. cit., pp. 51, 52; G. F. Moore, *Judaism*, I, pp. 334, 335. It should be noted that in Rabbinic teaching the proselyte's 'new life' was connected with his circumcision and not with his baptism; see G. R. Beasley-Murray, *Baptism in the New Testament*, pp. 28, 29.

the rite. It is frequently cited as a close parallel to Paul's teaching on Christian baptism in I Corinthians 10. Paul there certainly uses the Rabbinic method, but his interpretation is original to himself, as his interpretation of the rock as referring to Christ shows. The Rabbinic passages on the subject are too late to have influenced Paul. They represent a line of interpretation in some ways similar to Paul's, but quite independent of it.

As already indicated, it has frequently been held that John's baptism was developed from the baptism of proselytes. In proselyte baptism, a Gentile, regarded as unclean and a sinner was admitted to Israel. On this view, John's inspired originality lay in his proclamation that not only the Gentiles but all Jews as well were sinners and unclean. All Jews had apostatized, and could not be regarded as true Jews until they had confessed their sin and then re-entered Israel exactly as a proselyte does, by baptism.

This is a logical and an attractive explanation of John's baptism.[1] We have just shown, however, that there is very grave doubt as to whether proselyte baptism could have provided the basis of John's baptism, since it almost certainly arose too late to have influenced John. Even if we were to allow that proselyte baptism did exist in the early first century AD, further examination reveals significant differences between proselyte baptism and John's rite.

Apart from the obvious difference that John's baptism was confined to Jews while proselyte baptism was confined to Gentiles, John's baptism had a moral significance, being closely linked with his demand for repentance, whereas proselyte baptism was essentially a ritual washing only.

Further, John's baptism was very closely linked to his intensely eschatological preaching; it anticipated the Messianic baptism of fire and holy spirit. John appealed to people to be

---

[1] This theory was worked out in detail by J. Leipoldt in his book, *Die urchristliche Taufe im Lichte der Religionsgeschichte*, Leipzig, 1928. It is also the line followed by Eisler, for whom Israel's apostasy consisted in their recognizing the non-Jewish royal house of the Herods and the Roman overlords, thus breaking the 'royalty law' of Deut. 17.14, 15; see, *The Messiah Jesus and John the Baptist*, p. 251.

baptized in view of the imminent approach of the end. Proselyte baptism lacked any such vital and direct eschatological reference, although in a general way the acquiring of status as a Jew would be thought of as an advantage in the world to come. Thus the candidate for baptism is reminded that the keeping of the commandments will be rewarded—'Know thou that the world to come was made only for the righteous.'[1] The reception of proselytes in orthodox Judaism, however, must have been quite different from the eschatological fervour which surrounded John's rite.

Again, John's baptism was administered in running water, and frequently in the Jordan. Proselyte baptism, on the other hand, was usually performed in a bath (mikweh) or baptistry. The Rabbis discuss the minimum size and lay down that it must contain at least forty seahs.[2] And it is highly significant that Rabbinic law specifically states that the waters of the Jordan are unsuitable for baths of purification.[3]

Finally, John administered his baptism, whereas proselyte baptism was self-administered.[4] As Stauffer remarks, this administration of baptism was a new and unique feature; it is the real reason why John was called 'the Baptist'.[5]

Thus, in addition to the fact that proselyte baptism arose too late to influence John, there are other cogent reasons for doubting any connection between the two rites. In view of all the evidence we have surveyed, we must now proceed to ask whether there is not a much more likely explanation to be found at the period of time when John lived, and in the branch of Judaism with which he had the closest connections.

3. The Baptist Movement

We have already indicated that the background of John's ministry appears to have been not within orthodox Judaism,

[1] Yebamot 47a.
[2] See C. F. Rogers, 'How Did The Jews Baptize?', JTS, 12 (1911), pp. 437-45.   [3] Parah 8.10.
[4] Cf. H. H. Rowley, HUCA, 15 (1940), pp. 322, 323.
[5] E. Stauffer, New Testament Theology, p. 22. On the differences between John's baptism and proselyte baptism see further, G. R. Beasley-Murray, Baptism in the New Testament, pp. 40-42.

but rather within the non-conformist, baptist movement which flourished especially in the first century BC and the first century AD on the fringe of Judaism. The sects which comprised this movement, as we also saw, had as their most characteristic feature rites of baptism.

To some extent the lustrations of the sects were the usual Jewish baths of ritual purity, which would be strictly observed. Some of the Essene washings were certainly of this type, and the Damascus Document, for example, lays down:

> Let no man bathe in water that is dirty or less than the quantity that covers up a man. Let him not purify a vessel in it. And as for every rock-pool in a rock in which there is not the quantity that covers up (a man), which an unclean person has touched; he renders its water unclean with the uncleanness of water in a vessel. (CD 10.12, 13)

Here reference is made to the ritual cleansing both of persons and of vessels. There are references to 'water for impurity' in the Dead Sea Scrolls (1 QS 3.4,9; 4.21) which suggest that the sect may have carried out the sacrifice of the red heifer which, the Law lays down, was to be done 'outside the camp', away from the sanctuary (Num. 19.3); the ashes would be mixed with water, and the water then used in rites of purification.

To a certain extent the washings of the baptist movement can be regarded as further extensions of the Jewish ritual and ceremonial washings. The tendency in the inter-testamental period to extend the Old Testament washings was carried even further by the sects. The frequency of the washings was increased, and the causes of uncleanness multiplied. Josephus tells us how the Essenes wash after contact with a member of inferior grade, or with a Gentile,[1] after the discharge of excrement, 'though this . . . is a natural function',[2] and also after contact with oil.[3] Many of the sects practised washings *before meals*. This was done by the Hemerobaptists, and Josephus describes how the Essenes, 'after girding their loins with linen

---

[1] *The Jewish War*, II, 8, 10.   [2] *The Jewish War*, II, 8, 10.
[3] *The Jewish War*, II, 8, 3.

clothes, bathe their bodies in cold water' prior to their meal.[1] It is not certain whether this rite was practised at Qumran or not.[2]

Most interest attaches, however, to evidence of baptism as a rite of initiation. Josephus tells us a certain amount about initiation into the Essene movement and mentions that the candidate, after his first probationary year, 'is brought into closer touch with the rule and is allowed to share the purer kind of holy water'.[3] But of the precise method of initiation, Josephus tells us nothing, and it is in the Dead Sea Scrolls that we find evidence of an actual baptism of initiation. In the Manual of Discipline (1 QS 1.16-2.18), there is a description of how 'all who come into the order of the community shall pass over into the covenant'.[4] This initiation apparently took place at an annual covenant-renewal ceremony.[5] The priests and Levites take part in this ceremony, detailed instructions for which are given. The candidates have to make a confession of sin in the following terms:

> We have committed iniquity, we have transgressed, we have sinned, we have done evil, we and our fathers before us, in walking contrary to the statutes of truth; but righteous is God, and true is His judgement on us and on our fathers; and the mercy of His steadfast love He has bestowed upon us from everlasting to everlasting. (1 QS 1.24-2.1)

The priests recite blessings on all those who walk in God's ways, and the Levites recite a series of curses on 'all the men of

---

[1] The Jewish War, II, 8, 5.
[2] A possible reference is 1 QS 5.13, 14, but we may accept the summing up of K. G. Kuhn, 'No passage in the Qumran texts has yet been found where it says expressly . . . that the meal is always preceded by a bath.' (K. Stendahl, The Scrolls and the New Testament, p. 68.)
[3] The Jewish War, II, 8, 7.
[4] For the view that this refers to initiation cf. O. Cullmann, in K. Stendahl, The Scrolls and the New Testament, p. 21; T. H. Gaster, The Scriptures of the Dead Sea Sect, pp. 49f; A. Dupont-Sommer, The Jewish Sect of Qumran and the Essenes, pp. 92-95; J. Allegro, The Dead Sea Scrolls, pp. 105-7; M. Black, The Scrolls and Christian Origins, pp. 92-97; G. R. Beasley-Murray, Baptism in the New Testament, pp. 15-17. For a contrary view see H. H. Rowley, 'The Baptism of John and the Qumran Sect', New Testament Essays, Studies in Memory of T. W. Manson, Manchester University Press, 1959, pp. 218-29.
[5] Cf. M. Black, The Scrolls and Christian Origins, pp. 91f.

Belial's lot', to which the candidates make the response, 'Amen! Amen!'

The next section of the Manual (1 QS 2.25-3.12) takes up the theme of those who refuse to enter God's covenant. We are told of such a person that

> He will not be purified by atonement offerings,
>   and he will not be made clean with the water for impurity;
> He will not sanctify himself with seas and rivers,
>   or be made clean with any water for washing.
> Unclean, unclean will he be all the days that he rejects the ordinances of God, not being instructed in the community of his counsel.

Here, the person who is not a member of the community is considered to be unclean. The fact that a man who does not become a member is not cleansed 'with any water for washing' shows that the man who does become a member *is* cleansed by some rite of baptism.

The passage continues by saying of the man who enters the sect that

> in a holy spirit he will be united in his truth,
> and he will be cleansed from all his iniquities;
> and in an upright and humble spirit his sin will be atoned,
> and in the submission of his soul to all the statutes of God,
>   his flesh will be cleansed;
> that he may be sprinkled with water for impurity,
> and sanctify himself with water of cleanness.

Here different rites of baptism are clearly referred to, and in the context of initiation into the sect, the passage indicates that admission was by 'water of cleanness'.

A further passage in the Manual of Discipline also deals with the ceremony of initiation (1 QS 5.7-20). It tells of how all those who 'enter into the covenant' must take upon themselves 'a binding oath', and must separate themselves from 'all the men of error'. Such wicked people 'shall not enter the water, in order to touch the sacred food of the holy men, for they will not be cleansed unless they have turned from their evil. For there is something unclean in all who transgress his word.'

Here again the statement that those who are wicked 'shall not enter the water' implies that those who join the sect *do* enter the water, in a baptism of initiation.[1]

Ever since the discovery and excavation of the Qumran monastery it has been suggested that the remarkable system of water cisterns was used for the sect's baptismal rites.[2] This may have been the case, the monastery providing a headquarters and a centre of worship for various groups of sectarians. On the other hand, there is nothing unique about the construction of the cisterns, and the steps may not have been to allow people to descend into the water but simply to allow access to the water as the level receded. Much, if not all of the water would be needed by the community which may have totalled several hundred persons at a time.[3] For at least nine months of the year the monastery would be entirely dependent on the cisterns for ordinary domestic uses. It is difficult to conceive of even a large cistern being used regularly by many people, bearing in mind that the water could not be changed for nine months of the year; ordinary hygiene let alone the strict views of the sect on purity would seem to make this impossible.[4]

If the cisterns were not used, where would the baptisms, including that of initiation, be carried out? In the context of initiation baptism in 'seas and rivers' is mentioned. A sea (*yām*) can mean anything from the Mediterranean to the great basin in the Temple; because of the high salt content it is unlikely that the Dead Sea would be used. Allegro is probably nearest the mark when he suggests that 'the sectarians would have preferred the running water of the Jordan with its ancient associations, or even of 'Ain Feshkha to the south, to the static tanks of the settlement'.[5]

---

[1] Cf. J. A T. Robinson, 'The Baptism of John and the Qumran Community', *HTR*, 50 (1957), p. 182.

[2] See, e.g. W. H. Brownlee, 'John the Baptist in the New Light of Ancient Scrolls', in K. Stendahl, *The Scrolls and the New Testament*, p. 39.

[3] J. Allegro, *The Dead Sea Scrolls*, p. 90.

[4] On this subject see J. A. Fitzmyer, in K. Stendahl, *The Scrolls and the New Testament*, p. 226.

[5] *The Dead Sea Scrolls*, p. 90. Cf. the opinion of F. M. Cross Jnr., quoted in K. Stendahl, *The Scrolls and the New Testament*, p. 298. 'There is no reason

The Qumran baptism of initiation will repay a careful study of its meaning and significance.

Firstly, it is clear that the basic idea is that of cleansing. The person who is outside the community is regarded as unclean, but by entering the covenant he is cleansed. The basic metaphor, as in the case of the Old Testament ritual washings, is that of actual physical dirt being washed away by water. There is no suggestion of the idea of death and rebirth; the metaphor is purely that of cleansing.

Secondly, in common with the other lustrations of the sect, the baptism of initiation may have been regarded, up to a certain point, as taking the place of the Temple sacrifices and mediating forgiveness of sins. One of the most important conclusions reached by J. Thomas in his classic study of the baptist movement was the recognition of the tendency for rites of baptism to take the place of sacrifice, and he links this with a widespread tendency of the time towards a spiritualization of religion.[1] Josephus tells us that the Essenes 'do not offer sacrifices, because they profess to have more pure lustrations', and Philo, although he does not mention baptism, says of the Essenes that 'they have shown themselves especially devout in the service of God, not by offering sacrifices of animals, but by resolving to sanctify their minds'.[2] Striking confirmation of this view has come from the Dead Sea Scrolls, in which the washings of the sect, along with other practices of the community, are thought of as being of more value than, and as taking the place of, animal sacrifice. They came to be regarded as having value in atoning for sin, as the parallelism in 1 QS 3.4, 5, for example, shows:

> He will not be purified by atonement offerings,
>   and he will not be made clean with the water for impurity,
> He will not sanctify himself with seas and rivers,
>   or be made clean with any water for washing.

to connect these cisterns with the well known practice of the sect (i.e. baptism); more probably, "living water" was used. . . .'

[1] *Le Mouvement Baptiste*, pp. 425-30.

[2] Josephus, *Antiquities*, XVIII, 1, 5; Philo, *Quod Omnis Probus Liber Sit*, XII, 75.

K. G. Kuhn, in summarizing the evidence, says that 'the baths had . . . over and above their old meaning (to secure cultic purity), the sacramental function of mediating in the divine forgiveness of sins. In place of the sacrificial cultus of the Temple . . . the baths, and apparently also the communal meal, took on a new meaning, mediating salvation from God.'[1]

It might be questioned how far the sins washed away in sectarian baptism were ritual and ceremonial sins and how far they were moral. The references to *confession* and to *repentance*, however, show clearly that the Qumran baptism of initiation did have, in part at least, *a moral significance*. Baptism was preceded by confession of sins, the terms of which were quoted above. The members of the sect called themselves 'the penitents of Israel' (CD 6.5, 8.16). The stress on repentance is especially significant. 1 QS 5.14 says that the wicked 'will not be cleansed unless they have turned from their evil'. The whole point of the passage, 1 QS 2.25f is that the lustrations are of no value whatever if a person 'rejects the ordinances of God'. Here is no *ex opere operato* rite, but a baptism which confers forgiveness of sins only on condition of repentance.

The baptism of initiation also marked the entry of a person into the new Israel. The Qumran sect believed that they alone had remained true to God, and their separation from unfaithful Israel was dramatized by their withdrawal into the wilderness. They called themselves 'the holy congregation', 'the elect', 'the Sons of Light' and the 'Sons of Truth', thus claiming that they were the only true Israel, chosen by God and in receipt of his truth and guidance. Initiation into the sect, as we have seen, is spoken of as 'entering into the covenant'. But those who were baptized were all Jews, and already partakers of the covenant between God and Israel which is such an important concept in the Old Testament.[2] How then could they be thought of as entering into the covenant? The Damascus Document gives us a clue when it speaks of 'all the men that have entered the new

---

[1] In K. Stendahl, *The Scrolls and the New Testament*, p. 68.
[2] Cf. G. Ernest Wright, 'The Faith of Israel', *Interpreter's Bible*, I, pp. 352-7.

covenant'.[1] The covenant into which the sectarians entered was a *'new* covenant', words which immediately recall the prophecy of a new covenant by Jeremiah:

> Behold, the days are coming, says the Lord, when I will make a new covenant with the house of Israel and the house of Judah, not like the covenant which I made with their fathers. . . . But this is the covenant which I will make with the house of Israel after those days, says the Lord: I will put my law within them, and I will write it upon their hearts; and I will be their God, and they shall be my people. And no longer shall each man teach his neighbour, saying, 'Know the Lord', for they shall all know me, from the least of them to the greatest, says the Lord; for I will forgive their iniquity, and will remember their sin no more.
>
> (Jer. 31.31-34)

In this passage we find the keynotes of the life of the Qumran sect—the study and discussion of the Law, the knowledge of God, and cleansing from sin. Jeremiah's new covenant was obviously one of the formative ideas of the sect, and through this new covenant the candidate for baptism would enter the new Israel.

This idea of a new Israel is very largely an eschatological concept. The present time is 'the period of wickedness' and 'the days of the dominion of Belial', but the sect looked forward to the coming consummation in which they would play a leading role, and, as the Sons of Light, would inflict defeat on the Sons of Darkness and on all the enemies of the true Israel. In the glorious future which lies beyond this, the Sons of Truth will enjoy 'healing and abundance of peace in length of days, and bringing forth seed, with all eternal blessings and everlasting joy in the life of eternity, and a crown of glory with raiment of majesty in everlasting light' (1 QS 4.7, 8).

Finally, the baptism of initiation would naturally be a ceremony of dedication, for the candidates were bound to separate themselves from 'all the men of error', and to devote themselves to the worship and service of God within the community. Similarly, Josephus tells us of the 'tremendous oaths' which the

[1] CD 8.21, 20.12.

candidate swore on entry to the Essenes (*The Jewish War*, II, 8, 7).

Here then we appear to have a very close parallel to the baptism of John—a baptism confined to Jews, with a moral significance, conferring forgiveness on condition of repentance, granting admission to the new covenant and to the new Israel, with an eschatological orientation, and probably performed in a river. In all these respects it seems to offer a much closer analogy than proselyte baptism, and of course it is attested at a time and in a place which makes a connection highly probable in any case. We shall, therefore, now consider John's baptism in the light of this sectarian baptism of initiation.

4. The Meaning of John's Baptism

In seeking to explain the meaning of John's baptism, we must return to the contradictory statements of Josephus and of the New Testament (cf. above, p. 91). The contradiction may not be so great as appears at first sight. Though the New Testament speaks of the rite as being for the forgiveness of sins, this does not mean that it was thought of as automatically conferring forgiveness in a magical way at the time of baptism. John, like every Jew, would believe that only God can forgive sins, and probably he would think of the forgiveness as being conferred at the time of the judgement. Josephus, for his part, does not speak of repentance, but does mention that baptism was administered 'when the soul had previously been cleansed by righteous conduct'. This phrase is not far removed from the concept of repentance which, it will be remembered, in Judaism, signified a positive turning towards righteousness, just as much as a turning from sin.

We cannot, however, explain away the definite statement of Josephus that John's baptism was 'for the purification of the body'. It is conceivable that the New Testament writers have been guilty of 'christianizing' John's message, but on the whole it is Josephus who is suspect, for a variety of reasons.

1. Josephus lived later than the time of John and almost certainly had no first hand evidence. He may well therefore

have thought of John's baptism as being identical with that of the hermit Banos, with whom he lived for a while.

2. It may be that Josephus is guilty of distorting the evidence. We know that he constantly leaves out of his writings mention of the Messianic expectations of the Jews, and of their eschatological beliefs. Thus, in his account of John's baptism, he must leave out a vital clue to its meaning, namely its eschatological reference.

3. Further, Josephus can hardly have been unaware of the growing Christian movement, and his statement that John's baptism was not for the remission of certain sins is highly suspicious. Having accepted John as a fine example of Jewish piety, this looks very like an attempt to dissociate him from the new sect of Christians with their baptism for remission of sins.[1]

4. Finally, as we have already argued, if John's baptism was merely a ritual purification, then there would have been nothing remarkable about it. Josephus portrays John as such a harmless and unoriginal figure that his portrait completely fails to make sense. Why should he have been termed 'the Baptist', and why did he attract such large crowds, if there was nothing special about his baptism?

For these reasons, Josephus' view is to be rejected, and the view of the New Testament is much to be preferred.

Now, we have seen that while the ritual purifications of Judaism had no moral significance, yet within the baptist movement there was a tendency to develop a type of baptism which did mediate forgiveness of sins, conditional on repentance. Although our evidence comes from the Dead Sea Scrolls, other sects may well have had similar rites; we must remember always the extreme paucity of the evidence as far as most of the sects are concerned. Such a baptism developed out of the earlier Jewish lustrations, and indeed it probably retained ritual as well as moral connotations. Certainly, the ordinary ritual washings existed alongside of it. John must have known of this baptism, whether or not he was ever actually a member of the

[1] See I. Abrahams, *Studies in Pharisaism and the Gospels*, I, p. 32.

Qumran sect. His baptism seems to have been an extension of the trend which we have traced within the sectarian movement. For John, the moral significance was all-important, and the greatest stress was laid on repentance. Here we see how John's baptism linked up with his preaching, for the demand for repentance in view of the fast-approaching Messianic judgement was the essence of John's message.

Lohmeyer has argued for a very different view of the place of repentance in John's baptism.[1] He does not consider repentance or conversion to have been the condition of baptism, but rather the result of it. He points especially to Matt. 3.11 where John says, 'I baptize you with water, for repentance' (eis metanoian), and holds that repentance is not a human act at all, but a divine act which is experienced through baptism.

It is true that the meaning of John's 'baptism of repentance' is nowhere exactly defined for us. We have, however, already considered in some detail the meaning of repentance in the Old Testament and in Judaism, as a condition of God's forgiveness (pp. 80, 81). The Dead Sea Scrolls in particular show how repentance is a condition of cleansing; participants in the Qumran baptism 'will not be cleansed unless they have turned from their evil' (above, p. 108). John would no doubt assent to the proposition that in one sense all human thought and action depend upon God, 'without him we can do nothing', and yet no one made the demand of God upon man clearer than did John. He demanded that men repent—turn from evil and turn to God—before coming to baptism, and he demanded that after baptism the sincerity of their repentance should be demonstrated by good works.

To this demand for repentance, John added the further demand that the repentance of man and the forgiveness of God be symbolized by the rite of baptism. As we have already suggested, John would not think of forgiveness being conferred at the moment of baptism, but at the judgement itself. This very close connection between John's preaching and his baptism is

[1] E. Lohmeyer, Das Urchristentum, I, Johannes der Täufer, Göttingen, 1932, pp. 67f.

witnessed to by the rather curious phrase used by Mark and Luke—John appeared 'proclaiming a baptism in token of repentance for the forgiveness of sins'. The baptism could not be understood, and had no significance apart from the preaching of the message. Baptism was a symbolic act by which the essence of the message was dramatized in the experience of those who accepted the message. We may compare the idea of prophetic symbolism; Jeremiah, for example, was told to break an earthenware vessel to symbolize the impending destruction of Jerusalem (Jer. 19.10f), and Elisha, on his deathbed, bade Joash fire an arrow to symbolize that he would defeat the Syrian army (II Kings 13.14ff). So the act of baptism symbolized a person's repentance, and his hope that God would wash away his sins and grant him forgiveness when, through the Coming One, he judged the earth.

In arriving at this conception of baptism, the conclusion is inescapable that John must have been influenced by passages in the prophets which interpret cleansing in moral and spiritual terms. To some extent this was already true of the sectarian movement. We have seen, for example, how use was made by them of Ezek. 36.25, where God says to Israel, 'I will sprinkle clean water upon you, and you shall be clean from all your uncleannesses, and from all your idols I will cleanse you' (see above, p. 72). John, however, was far more of a true prophet than the Qumran sectarians were. His message is essentially a prophetic one, and in his conception of baptism we cannot but feel that here is a new Isaiah crying,

> Wash yourselves; make yourselves clean;
> Remove the evil of your doings from before my eyes;
> Cease to do evil, learn to do good . . .
>
> (Isa. 1.16, 17)

In the Psalms also we meet the desire for an inward and spiritual cleansing, and one cannot but feel that John, steeped as he must have been in the Scriptures, must have been strongly influenced also by passages such as Ps. 51.6-11:

> Behold, thou desirest truth in the inward being;
> therefore teach me wisdom in my secret heart.

> Purge me with hyssop, and I shall be clean;
>> wash me, and I shall be whiter than snow.
> Fill me with joy and gladness;
>> let the bones which thou hast broken rejoice.
> Hide thy face from my sins,
>> and blot out all my iniquities.
> Create in me a clean heart, O God,
>> and put a new and right spirit within me.
> Cast me not away from thy presence,
>> and take not thy holy spirit from me.

Hyssop was used for sprinkling blood which, along with various washings, made up the ritual for the cleansing of lepers. In this passage we have combined the ideas of washing, forgiveness of sins, and the gift of God's holy spirit. As in the passages cited from Ezek. 36.25 and Isa. 1.16, 17, these Old Testament writers use the idea of ritual washings in a metaphorical sense only, when they are referring to a moral and spiritual cleansing. John, however, fused the demand for moral cleansing with an actual rite of baptism.

John's preaching was strongly eschatological, and so was his baptism. In this too it was closely related to sectarian baptism, especially the Qumran baptism of initiation. How far the concept of a new Israel and a new covenant was present in John's mind, our sources do not permit us to say. But we may note that this is essentially a moral concept, entirely in keeping with John's outlook. Both John and the sectarians agree that membership of the old Israel is not enough, and in itself is no guarantee of salvation. For the sectarians, Israel had apostatized, and for John, those Jews who came to hear him preach were a brood of vipers, who must not think that they can place any reliance on their descent from Abraham. Following the analogy of the Qumran baptism, we can say with confidence that John's baptism too must have been thought of as admitting people to the eschatological community.

For John, however, this community must have been something very different from the Qumran community. Although a group of disciples did gather round him, he had no intention of founding a sect. The great majority of those baptized were expected to return to their daily tasks (Luke 3.10-14), and certainly there is no hint that they were required to join a highly organized monastic community. There was no pooling of property, no rigorous interview, no period of probation. Nevertheless all those baptized by John could be thought of as an eschatological community in a wide sense—the community of those who by repentance, symbolized in baptism, and by righteous conduct were prepared to face the judgement of the Coming One, and who would in due time share the rewards of the righteous. We cannot go any further than this in deducing the nature of John's expectations on the basis of sectarian beliefs, for our sources are very meagre, and John in all probability gave no detailed picture of what would take place in the last days.

Kraeling has made the idea of the eschatological river of fire the key to the whole understanding of John's baptism, for he suggests 'that the water of baptism represents and symbolizes the fiery torrent of judgement, and that the individual by voluntarily immersing himself in the water enacts in advance before God his willing submission to the divine judgement which the river of fire will perform'.[1] In a general way no doubt the thought of the coming judgement would be in the minds both of John and of those who came for baptism. Yet the basic idea of the immersion in the river is not that of submission to judgement, but that of cleansing or washing away of sins. This is clear from our whole survey, both of the meaning of the word *baptizein*, and of the understanding of baptism in Judaism, especially in the baptist movement.

We can now understand why John's baptism was not a repeated rite. It was not a ritual washing which required to be repeated every time a person became unclean. It marked the once-for-all decision of a person to break with sin and to enter the community of those who sought to prepare for the imminent advent of the Coming One and his twofold baptism of fire and holy spirit.

We can see also why the rite was performed by John and

[1] C. H. Kraeling, *John the Baptist*, p. 117.

not by the person being baptized, as was the case in all other Jewish lustrations. In the next chapter we shall see how John regarded himself as having a definite role to play in the purposes of God. His preaching was the last minute warning before the judgement. Just as his message was divinely authorized, so was his rite of baptism, and it was therefore fitting that he should administer it. As Stauffer puts it, 'The act of baptism is bound up with a unique historical figure who finds his eschatological mission in the administration of baptism'.[1]

Finally, the question has been raised as to whether John's baptizing in the river Jordan had any special significance. We have already seen how the whole area in which John worked was rich in historical and religious associations, and the story of Adam and Eve doing penance while immersed in the waters of the Jordan (from the *Vita Adae et Evae*),[2] as well as the story of the healing of Naaman have frequently been quoted in this connection. The decisive factor, however, must surely be the fact that John did baptize at places other than the Jordan, such as Aenon near Salim.[3] If John could baptize elsewhere, the waters of the Jordan could hardly have been regarded as an *essential* element in baptism, though of course the part the river had already played in Israel's history would naturally be in the minds of John and his hearers during the time that he ministered on the banks of the river.

[1] *New Testament Theology*, p. 22.

[2] The *Vita Adae et Evae* has been subjected to Christian editing, and there is a likelihood that the river was not originally the Jordan, but rather the Gihon, which is certainly what other Rabbinic sources would lead us to expect. Cf. the commentary in R. H. Charles, *Apocrypha and Pseudepigrapha*, Vol. II.

[3] On the location of Aenon near Salim, see pp. 163, 164.

VII

John the Prophet

H AVING dealt with John's message and ministry, the question now arises as to how John regarded himself. 'The people were on the tiptoe of expectation, all wondering about John, whether perhaps he was the Messiah' (Luke 3.15); what was John's own interpretation of his role?

This is not an easy question to answer. Josephus gives us no direct evidence on this point. The only place in the New Testament where John actually speaks of his own office is in John 1.19-23, where in answer to the deputation of priests and Levites sent from Jerusalem to question him, he denies that he is 'the Messiah', 'Elijah' or 'the prophet'; he answers instead in the words of the prophet Isaiah: 'I am a voice crying aloud in the wilderness, "Make the Lord's highway straight".' But we know that the Fourth Gospel is determined to minimize the importance of John at all costs, and this passage must be treated with great caution, and with some suspicion. Apart from this passage, there is quite a bit of evidence of how John's contemporaries regarded him, especially of how Jesus regarded him, and there is also indirect evidence which will in fact help us to answer the original question as to how John regarded himself.

The key term which appears in almost all of the passages dealing with John's office is that of 'prophet'. Unfortunately, our understanding of what this concept meant in John's day has been extremely distorted. We look back at John in the light of the beliefs of the early Church; we also overstress the contrast between prophet and priest. We must, however, think ourselves back to the period immediately preceding the birth of the Church, and discover what the concept of prophecy would mean for John and his contemporaries.

Our starting point must be the realization that, at the start of the Christian era, the Jews believed that prophecy had long since ceased.[1]

The view that the prophetic spirit had been withdrawn is found even in the Old Testament itself. Zech. 13.3-6 makes it clear that the only prophets left were false ones. Psalm 74.9 says:

> We do not see our signs;
> there is no longer any prophet,
> and there is none among us who knows how long.

The fact that the religious writings produced in the inter-testamental period are almost all pseudonymous was due to the popular belief that God's Spirit, which had inspired the prophets of the Old Testament, was now withdrawn. In I Macc. 9.27, in the account of the death of Judas, it is said: 'Thus there was great distress in Israel, such as had not been since the time that prophets ceased to appear among them.' The Rabbinic literature also upholds this view. Zeitlin states, 'The same opinion, that prophets ceased among the Jews after the Persian period, is corroborated in the Talmudic literature where it is stated that Haggai, Zechariah and Malachi were the last of the prophets'.[2]

Yet if prophecy was thought to be dead, there was an equally strong opinion that at some point in the future prophecy would return. To be more precise, the return of prophecy would mark the dawning of the new age. In all the passages which refer to this belief, the revival of prophecy is an eschatological concept.

In the Old Testament, for example, we find that according

---

[1] On this section see especially, O. Cullmann, *Christology of the New Testament*, pp. 13-50; also F. W. Young, 'Jesus the Prophet: a Re-examination', *JBL*, 68 (1949), pp. 285-99.
[2] Quoted by F. W. Young, op. cit., p. 291.

to Joel 2.28f the new age will be marked by the return of the spirit of prophecy:

> And it shall come to pass afterward,
> that I will pour out my spirit on all flesh;
> your sons and your daughters shall prophesy . . .

Sibylline Oracles, III, 781 declares, 'For naught but peace shall come upon the land of the good; and the prophets of the mighty God shall take away the sword'.

In the inter-testamental period, however, the idea developed that *one* prophet would arise at the dawning of the new age. And so most sources speak of 'a prophet' or 'the prophet', and not of 'prophets'. In some forms of this expectation, no special figure is mentioned as the prophet; in others, he was identified as either Elijah or Moses.[1]

A. *The Prophet.* A few passages refer to the prophet in general terms. In I Macc. 4.45, 46, in the account of the purification and rebuilding of the Temple, it is said, 'They tore down the altar, and stored the stones in a convenient place on the temple hill until there should come a prophet to tell them what to do with them'. Here a difficult problem is solved by being shelved until a future prophet should settle the matter. Again, in I Macc. 14.41, we read, 'And the Jews and their priests decided that Simon should be their leader and high priest for ever, until a trustworthy prophet should arise . . .'. In these two cases the coming prophet is to settle any outstanding problems and reveal God's will.

Another reference is found in Test. Benjamin 9.2 which reads, 'And the twelve tribes shall be gathered together there (at the Temple), and all the Gentiles, until the Most High shall send forth his salvation in the visitation of an only-begotten prophet'. Here the coming prophet is the bringer of salvation.

B. *The returning Elijah.* The identification of the eschatological prophet with Elijah originates in Mal. 4.5, 6, 'Behold,

---

[1] Although the great mass of the evidence is divided between belief in a returning Elijah and a returning Moses, there is some evidence of the expectation of Enoch, Baruch and Jeremiah. See O. Cullmann, *Christology of the New Testament*, pp. 17, 18.

I will send you Elijah the prophet before the great and terrible day of the Lord comes. And he will turn the hearts of fathers to their children and the hearts of children to their fathers, lest I come and smite the land with a curse.' Mal. 3.1-4 speaks of a rather different figure, 'the messenger of the covenant', whose task will be to purify the Temple cult and priesthood, preparatory to the coming of the Lord himself in judgement:

> Behold, I send my messenger to prepare the way before me, and the Lord whom you seek will suddenly come to his temple; the messenger of the covenant in whom you delight, behold, he is coming, says the Lord of hosts. But who can endure the day of his coming, and who can stand when he appears?
>
> For he is like a refiner's fire and like fullers' soap; he will sit as a refiner and purifier of silver, and he will purify the sons of Levi and refine them like gold and silver, till they present right offerings to the Lord. Then the offering of Judah and Jerusalem will be pleasing to the Lord as in the days of old and as in former years.

It is now generally conceded that Mal. 4.5, 6 is a later addition in which the 'messenger of the covenant' has been reinterpreted as the returning Elijah whose task is no longer to prepare the Temple, but 'to restore peace and social well-being to the community so as to avert God's wrath in the day of judgement'.[1]

Ecclus. 48.9, 10 provides another clear reference to the belief that 'the prophet' will be Elijah. A passage dealing with Elijah concludes,

> You who were taken up by a whirlwind of fire,
>   in a chariot with horses of fire;
> You who are ready at the appointed time, it is written,
>   to calm the wrath of God before it breaks out in fury,
> To turn the heart of the father to the son,
>   and to restore the tribes of Jacob.

This passage obviously depends on the one in Malachi, with the addition of 'to restore the tribes of Israel'.[2] The close connection with Elijah's translation shows us why Elijah especially

---

[1] R. C. Dentan, *Interpreter's Bible*, 6, p. 1144.
[2] This phrase is probably echoed in Mark 9.12.

was chosen as the future prophet. He did not die as men do, but was taken up by a whirlwind into heaven (II Kings 2.11). In Jewish legend (most of it later than the first century AD), Elijah's activities really only begin with his translation, that unusual occurrence providing ample scope for stories of his frequent returns to earth.[1]

Several New Testament passages bear witness to contemporary Jewish belief in the returning Elijah. When the deeds of Jesus became known, there were some who thought that he was Elijah come again; 'some were saying that Elijah had appeared' (Luke 9.8; Mark 6.15). Again, at Caesarea Philippi, Jesus asked what the popular opinion about him was, and the disciples reported that some thought that he was Elijah (Mark 8.28; Matt. 16.14; Luke 9.19). In Mark 9.11 and Matt. 17.11 it is said that the scribes taught that 'Elijah must be the first to come'. Jesus confirmed this, adding that 'Elijah does come first to set everything right'. In John 1.21, one of the questions John is asked is, 'Are you Elijah?' To these should perhaps be added the incident at the Cross when Jesus cried out in the words of Ps. 22.1, 'Eli, Eli . . .' and the bystanders thought he was calling for Elijah (Mark 15.34-36; Matt. 27.46-49). They misunderstood Jesus' words, but evidently they thought it at least conceivable that Elijah would come to earth and make a dramatic last minute rescue. Alternatively, their words may have been spoken in mockery.

Thus there is quite a body of evidence that there was a widespread belief in John's day that the eschatological prophet would be Elijah come again.

c. *The prophet like unto Moses.* There was another point of view, however, which identified the coming prophet with Moses. The origin of this belief is found in Deut. 18.15f, where Moses says, 'The Lord your God will raise up for you a

[1] See L. Ginzberg, 'Elijah', *JE*, V, pp. 121-8, for a selection of these legends. Possible allusions to the Elijah legend are also found in I Macc. 2.58; Martyrdom of Isaiah 2.14; I Enoch 89.52; II Baruch 77.24; II (4) Esd. 7.109. For Rabbinic references see F. W. Young, op. cit., p. 293. The Jewish belief that Elijah is present as 'angel of the covenant' at the ceremony of circumcision, and the belief about the presence of Elijah at the Passover are worth noting, but they are probably mediaeval in origin.

prophet like me from among you, from your brethren—him you shall heed'. Whatever the original writer meant by these words, they were later interpreted as referring to the eschatological prophet.

The Dead Sea Scrolls have contributed important evidence of this. 1 QS 9.10, 11 reads, '... they shall be ruled with the first laws, until the coming of a prophet and the anointed ones of Aaron and Israel'. Here we have the expectation of three eschatological figures, the prophet and two Messiahs.[1] In the Testimonia text from Qumran,[2] this threefold expectation is expanded and explained by the texts which are quoted—Deut. 5.28, 29 and Deut. 18.18, 19, referring to the prophet like unto Moses; Num. 24.15-17, referring to the 'star out of Jacob', the secular kingly Messiah; and Deut. 33.8-11, the blessing of Moses on the tribe of Levi, referring to the expectation of the priestly Messiah. Here is clear proof of the expectation of the eschatological prophet in the person of the returning Moses.

In the New Testament, we find the deputation to John asking him, when he has denied being either the Christ or Elijah, 'Are you the prophet we await?' (John 1.21). The fact that he has already denied being Elijah makes it clear that the deputation were asking him if he was the prophet like unto Moses. Likewise, in John 7.40, the people say of Jesus, 'This must certainly be the expected prophet'. In John 6.14, following the feeding of the five thousand, the people say, 'Surely this must be the prophet that was to come into the world'; Jesus, having repeated the miracle of the manna, is the prophet like the first Moses. More indirect evidence of the existence of the belief is afforded by the New Testament writers who identify Jesus as the Moses-like prophet.[3]

[1] On the two Messiahs see K. G. Kuhn, 'The Two Messiahs of Aaron and Israel', in K. Stendahl, The Scrolls and the New Testament, pp. 55-64.
[2] See T. H. Gaster, The Scriptures of the Dead Sea Sect, pp. 353-5.
[3] Matthew pictures Jesus as a new Moses giving a new law, and this motif has been traced in Luke also, Luke 9-18 following the outline of Deut. 1-26. Cf. also the quotations of Deut. 18.15 in Acts 3.22, 23 and Acts 7.37. Another reference is almost certainly to be found at John 7.52 where Papyrus Bodmer II (c. AD 200) has the definite article before prophētēs so that this reads, 'The prophet does not arise out of Galilee' (cf. John 7.41, 42). The existing text has

In view of this evidence it may be held that Matthew Black is right when he says that 'there is reason to believe that one of the liveliest of popular Jewish expectations in the New Testament period was that of the coming of a prophet "like unto Moses", foretold at Deut. 18.15 . . .'.[1] It may be added that the Moses-like prophet is a central figure in Samaritan eschatology.

However the coming prophet was pictured, whether without any identification or as either Elijah or Moses come again,[2] he is an eschatological figure. Prophecy was dead; its rebirth would be a sign of the new age. It is quite wrong therefore to speak of someone claiming to be 'merely a prophet' in contrast to someone claiming to be 'a Messianic figure'.[3] Anyone who claimed to be *a* prophet was automatically claiming to be *the* prophet. Anyone claiming to be a prophet was claiming to be a Messianic figure, not in the sense that he was the Messiah himself, but in the sense that he was preparing for the ushering in of the new age.

Thought has been greatly confused by allowing the New Testament to cloud over the picture of pre-Christian Judaism. The New Testament believes that prophecy has returned, notably following the day of Pentecost. There were many prophets in the early Church (cf. I Cor. 12.28; Eph. 2.20; 3.5, etc.). Matthew (10.41) can talk about receiving a prophet as if that was a common occurrence, as indeed it was—in the Christian Church. But 'prophet' has now changed its meaning; there is almost an order of prophets in the Church, and the eschatological prophet is no longer meant. Our survey of the evidence has shown that previous to, and outside of the early

caused much trouble, being in conflict with the Old Testament and Rabbinic evidence; the Papyrus Bodmer II reading looks like the original one.

[1] M. Black, 'Servant of the Lord and Son of Man', *SJT*, 6 (1953), pp. 2, 3.

[2] It would be wrong to set the two views in violent opposition to each other; it is unlikely that most people held dogmatically either to one view or the other. There is a little evidence that sometimes two prophets were expected, and the Transfiguration and also Rev. 11.3f may reflect such a belief, though it is possible that the combining of Moses and Elijah is a Christian idea. See O. Cullmann, *Christology of the New Testament*, p. 18. Both Moses and Elijah had strong links with the wilderness; cf. U. W. Mauser, *Christ in the Wilderness*, pp. 114-16.

[3] Cf. F. W. Young, op. cit., pp. 297, 298.

Church 'prophet' was an eschatological term with a definite limited meaning. This point may be finally driven home by citing two examples of men who claimed to be prophets. The true nature of this claim, and the consequences of it are clear from the quotations.

Josephus (*Antiquities*, XX, 5, 1) relates:

> Now it came to pass, while Fadus was procurator of Judea, that a certain magician, whose name was Theudas, persuaded a great part of the people to take their effects with them, and follow him to the river Jordan, for he told them that he was a prophet, and that he would by his command, divide the river, and afford them an easy passage over it; and many were deluded by his words. However, Fadus did not permit them to take advantage of his wild attempt, but sent a troop of horsemen out against them, and took many of them alive, and cut off his head and carried it to Jerusalem.

This man claimed to be 'a prophet', which could mean nothing else than the eschatological prophet. It is interesting to note that a journey of the people through the desert taking their effects with them recalls Moses leading the Israelites, whereas the dividing of the Jordan recalls Elijah (II Kings 2.8).

Josephus (*The Jewish War*, II, 13, 5) tells another story:

> A still worse blow was dealt at the Jews by the Egyptian false prophet. A charlatan, who gained for himself the reputation of a prophet, this man appeared in the country collecting a following of about 30,000 dupes, and led them by a circuitous route from the desert to the Mount of Olives. From there he proposed to force an entrance into Jerusalem and, after overpowering the Roman garrison, to set himself up as a tyrant.

The man's followers were killed or dispersed, but he himself escaped. This passage, like the previous one, shows that the claim to be a prophet was a momentous one indeed, and one which, in view of a Roman government ever alert for any sign of revolt, could have the most dangerous consequences. Even if a person claiming to be the prophet interpreted the office in a quite peaceful and non-militarist way, he would run a very grave risk of being misunderstood by a certain section of the Jewish people, and by the Roman government.

We should note that the eschatological prophet was some-times regarded as being a priest as well as a prophet. This would be a logical consequence of the fact that both Moses and Elijah were priests.[1] It is clear that the contrast between prophet and priest has been overdrawn in modern times,[2] and that in John's day prophecy and priesthood, so far from being opposed, were expected to be linked in the person of the eschatological prophet.

The relation of the eschatological prophet to the Messiah in Jewish thought is not an easy one to discover. G. F. Moore states that 'it was the universal belief that shortly before the appearance of the Messiah, Elijah should return',[3] and the common view is that Elijah was expected as the precursor of the Messiah. The evidence for this is, however, not as strong as is sometimes supposed. The question of the disciples in Mark 9.11, 'Why do our teachers say that Elijah must be the first to come?' probably indicates such a belief, and Justin Martyr probably passes on an earlier Jewish tradition when he says that it was a common Jewish belief that Elijah would be the precursor of the Messiah.[4] It is, however, the Dead Sea Scrolls which have provided us with the first definite pre-Christian evidence of the prophet as the forerunner, in this case of the two Messiahs.

We noted in Chapter V the arguments of J. A. T. Robinson, who wishes to identify Elijah with the Messiah and who holds that this figure was John's Coming One. The evidence we have surveyed above, however, does not support such a point of view. The eschatological prophet generally has a preparatory role, and certainly does not possess the features of John's Coming One.

The eschatological prophet prepared the way and was a fore-runner, but in many texts he is the forerunner of God himself,

---

[1] See E. Stauffer, *New Testament Theology*, p. 24; T. H. Gaster, *The Scriptures of the Dead Sea Sect*, pp. 38, 315.

[2] See especially Chapter II, 'The Law and the Prophets', in H. H. Rowley, *The Unity of the Bible*, Carey Kingsgate Press, 1953.

[3] *Judaism*, II, p. 357.

[4] *Dialogue With Trypho*, 8.4, 49.1.

and prepares simply for the coming of the new age. While therefore some people believed the prophet to be the forerunner of the Messiah, this was by no means a universal belief.[1]

How then was John linked with this expectation of the coming prophet?

There can be no doubt that Jesus regarded John as the eschatological prophet. Jesus says to the crowds, 'But what did you go out to see? A prophet? Yes indeed, and far more than a prophet. He is the man of whom Scripture says, "Here is my herald, whom I send on ahead of you, And he will prepare your way before you".' (Matt. 11.7-11; Luke 7.24-28.) According to Jesus, John is a prophet in so far as he has the characteristics of the prophets of old; but he is 'far more than a prophet' in so far as he is the eschatological prophet as foretold by Malachi. In Matt. 11.13, 14 Jesus says 'For all the prophets and the law foretold things to come until John appeared, and John is the destined Elijah, if you will but accept it'. Again, in the passage where Jesus confirms the belief that Elijah 'does come first to set everything right', he says that 'Elijah has already come and they have worked their will upon him, as the scriptures say of him' (Mark 9.11-13). Matthew adds the explanatory comment in his version, 'Then the disciples understood that he meant John the Baptist' (Matt. 17.10-13).

Further, the Christian writers themselves obviously regarded John as the eschatological prophet. For example, when Mark (1.2) inserts the quotation from Mal. 3.1 before the quotation from Isa. 40.3, he makes it known that he considered that John was the returning Elijah as prophesied by Malachi. He neither puts the words into the mouth of John nor of Jesus; he merely states that these prophecies were fulfilled in the ministry of John. Whatever may have been the original meaning intended in the source on which Luke draws, in Luke 1 as it now stands, John is certainly pictured as the eschatological prophet, the returning Elijah of Mal. 4.5, 6.[2] Probably we should include

---

[1] Cf. O. Cullmann, *Christology of the New Testament*, p. 23.

[2] The concept of the returning Elijah seems to be somewhat 'spiritualized' in the phrase 'he will go before him as forerunner *by the spirit and power* of Elijah' (Luke 1.17); contrast the rather more literal tone of Matt. 11.14.

here also Luke's statement that 'the word of God came to John son of Zechariah in the wilderness' (Luke 3.2). It is doubtful whether Luke had any authority for saying this, but it clearly shows that he regarded John as a prophet, called to this office through hearing the word of God, exactly as were the prophets of old.

Next, we look for evidence that the people regarded John as the eschatological prophet. Matthew's account of the death of John is found in 14.3-12. Clearly he is abridging the Marcan version of the story, but at v. 5 he slips in almost accidentally the fact that Herod wanted to put John to death, 'But he was afraid of the people, in whose eyes John was a prophet'. Again, in the narrative of the question about authority (Mark 11.27-33; Matt. 21.23-27; Luke 20.1-8), when Jesus turned the tables on the priests and scribes and asked them, 'The baptism of John: was it from God, or from men?', they 'were afraid of the people, for all held that John was in fact a prophet'.

The fact that Jesus, and the early Christian writers, and many of the people all regarded John as the eschatological prophet does not of course by itself establish the fact that John cast himself in this role. We have seen already (in Chapter V) that Schweitzer, for example, held that John did *not* regard himself as the returning Elijah, but that Jesus was the first and only person to make this identification. In the absence of reliable evidence of any saying of John himself on the subject, we seek a solution in what John did rather than in what he said.

The place of his ministry is significant, for the wilderness as we have already seen had strong eschatological associations. We may note further that the wilderness (east of Jordan) was the scene both of Elijah's translation (II Kings 2.1-12) and of the death of Moses (Deut. 34.1-6), and therefore the ideal place for their return. Strangely enough it is the Fourth Gospel which makes John quote Isa. 40.3 as the justification for his wilderness ministry (John 1.23), while all three Synoptics, though quoting the text, do not place it on John's lips.[1] Whether or not John

[1] Mark 1.3; Luke 3.4; Matt. 3.3.

actually quoted this text of himself, it seems certain that he did go into the wilderness because he believed it to be the correct place for an eschatological ministry.

John's dress is also of significance here. He was clothed, Mark tells us 'in a rough coat of camel's hair, with a leather belt round his waist' (1.6). The garment would be of a coarse cloth woven from camel hair,[1] while the girdle or belt would gather in the garment at the waist. Hair and leather would be the cheapest and simplest materials available for the two items of dress, but obviously John's chief consideration in wearing them lay in the fact that they constituted the traditional dress of a prophet. The hairy mantle goes back to Elijah who wore a garment ('adereth) as a sort of badge of office. Elisha's inheriting Elijah's mantle is the equivalent of inheriting his prophetic office (I Kings 19.19; II Kings 2.13, 14). Nothing is said of the exact nature of the garment, but 'adereth is used in Gen. 25.25 of Esau—'all his body was like a hairy mantle'. A leather belt is also mentioned in connection with Elijah (II Kings 1.8), but it was the hairy mantle which became the traditional garb of the prophet. Zech. 13.4 says—'On that day every prophet will be ashamed of his vision when he prophesies; he will not put on a hairy mantle ('adereth) in order to deceive'. Here false prophets are spoken of; they are condemned for being dressed like prophets but not acting or speaking like them. In the *Martyrdom of Isaiah*, Isaiah and the faithful prophets are pictured as being clothed in garments of hair. John's wearing of the hairy mantle proclaimed to all that he was a prophet; of his own free will he deliberately gave this impression.

John's message was essentially a prophetic one, as we have already seen. Here was no Rabbi expounding the intricacies of the Law, but a prophet calling on the people to repent and turn from their wickedness, just as the ancient prophets had foretold the judgement which would fall on the nation which thought that God would protect them though they were morally, socially and politically corrupt. John feared no one, not even

[1] Cf. Matt. 3.4. See E. P. Gould, *The Gospel According to St Mark*, *ICC*, T. and T. Clark, 1901, pp. 7, 8.

the king, for he denounced Antipas, just as Elijah had de-nounced Ahab (I Kings 21.17ff).

Again, the fact that John baptized, in contrast to other types of baptism which were self-administered, suggests that he thought of himself as fulfilling some important office.

The conclusion is inescapable that John deliberately cast him-self in the role of prophet. The place of his ministry, the dress he adopted, his message and his ministry allow of no other description than that of 'prophetic'. But we have already seen that anyone claiming to be *a* prophet, inevitably claimed to be *the* prophet. In the situation in which John appeared his actions must clearly have demonstrated a claim to be the eschatological prophet, ushering in the new age and preparing for the Messiah. John's priestly descent would make him specially fitted for this office, in view of the expectation that the coming prophet would also be a priest.

Did John regard himself as the prophet in the sense of Elijah come again or in the sense of Moses come again? The hairy mantle worn by John went back to Elijah, but on the other hand it became the accepted dress of any prophet. The wilder-ness ministry, as we have seen, could recall either Moses or Elijah. The likeliest explanation is that John was content to picture himself as the prophet in general terms, as in the branch of the expectation where no special person was indicated. In this case it would be Jesus who connected John specifically with Elijah, possibly reserving the role of the second Moses for himself. The Synoptics followed Jesus in casting John as Elijah, but the Fourth Gospel, in clear contradiction to the Synoptics, makes John deny even the office of eschatological prophet, so intent is it in minimizing his importance.

We would therefore hold that John was aware of the ex-pectation of the eschatological prophet who would immediately precede the new age. He believed that God had called him to this office, and so he set out to warn the people of the imminent judgement and to prepare the people by calling them to re-pentance. As with the ancient prophets, this was a dangerous calling and John would realize the dangers full well. Nevertheless, in the true prophetic tradition he spared neither the king nor the religious leaders in his attacks on wickedness. He believed that he had a decisive place in God's plan, that he stood on the threshold of the new age and indeed that he was ushering in the new age. He was the beginning of the end. His task was indeed to prepare the way for the great events about to take place.

VIII

The Disciples of John

JOHN the Baptist had no intention of founding a new sect, far less of starting a new religion. The imminence of the end of days dominated his thought, and ruled out any idea of setting up a permanent organization. Yet there is evidence that a small group of disciples formed around John during his ministry, and continued to exist after his death.

Both Josephus and the New Testament testify to the large numbers of people who flocked to hear John preach and to be baptized by him. John's baptism, however, as we have seen, was not a baptism of initiation in the sense of initiating people into a sect; it was a baptism of initiation only in the much wider sense in which those people baptized became members of the community of those who, by repentance, baptism and righteous living were prepared to face the Coming One and his twofold eschatological baptism.

This interpretation is denied by some who point to the account of Josephus in which we read that 'John . . . was bidding the Jews who practised virtue and exercised righteousness towards each other and piety toward God, to come together for baptism'.[1] This last phrase, 'to come together for baptism' (*baptismō sunienai*), it is held, indicates that those baptized by John were initiated into a sect. The argument is a weak one,

---

[1] *Antiquities*, XVIII, 5, 2. Goguel renders *baptismō sunienai* as 's'unir par un baptême'; for his view see *Jean-Baptiste*, p. 16 n., p. 19. See also H. G. Marsh, *The Origin and Significance of the New Testament Baptism*, p. 64.

however, and most likely the phrase means simply 'that the people were invited to come as a people must, in numbers rather than each one separately'.[1] The great mass of people were not enrolled in a sect or made members of a religious community; having received baptism, they returned to their daily tasks.

The indications are that 'the disciples of John' were few in number, and they must have been a very small percentage of those who were baptized by John. John 4.1 tells us how, quite near the beginning of his ministry, Jesus was 'winning and baptizing more disciples than John'. Josephus does not speak of John's disciples, and our main source of information is the New Testament in which they are mentioned on a number of occasions. In the Clementine literature there are references to the disciples of John, according to which they were thirty in number and included Simon Magus, Dositheus, and 'one woman who was called Luna'. These accounts preserve for us the fact that John did have a group of disciples, but are entirely unreliable with regard to details.[2]

What was the nature of this group, and what exactly was a disciple? In Greek, a disciple (*mathētēs*) is a pupil or a learner; the word is frequently used, for example in Plato, of the pupil of a philosopher. In the New Testament the word is used for John's disciples, for 'the disciples of the Pharisees', and very frequently for the disciples of Jesus.

Various analogies have been cited in the attempt to shed some light on the true nature of the disciples of John. The scribes or Rabbis had their pupils, *Tolmide Hakamim*,[3] 'disciples of the learned', who surrounded their teachers 'with an atmosphere of reverent devotion'.[4] The 'disciples of the Pharisees' were probably such pupils of Rabbis. John, however, does not appear in the role of a scribe, teaching pupils the subtleties of scriptural exegesis. The mention by Thomas of the followers of Judas the Galilean is even less helpful, although Banos, whose

---

[1] C. H. Kraeling, *John the Baptist*, p. 119.
[2] On the evidence of the Clementine literature, see further pp. 190-5.
[3] See G. F. Moore, *Judaism*, I, p. 43.
[4] C. Guignebert, *The Jewish World in the Time of Jesus*, p. 68.

disciple (*zēlōtēs*) Josephus was, may provide a closer analogy.[1] Obviously, however, the closest and most useful analogy is to be found in the disciples of Jesus, who learned from him and were the recipients of his teaching, but who in addition entered into a close personal relationship with him, seeking to obey and serve him as well as listen to him. To some extent the *mathētēs* of the Greek philosopher, and certainly the pupil of a Rabbi, was not merely a learner but an adherent of his teacher. But it is in the New Testament that this aspect of discipleship is especially stressed, as can be seen from a text such as John 15.8—'This is my Father's glory, that you bear fruit in plenty and so be my disciples'. Jesus' disciples share his ministry of preaching and even of exorcism (Luke 10.17-19), and also help to attend to his personal needs (e.g. John 4.8).

In all probability we should therefore see in the disciples of John a small group of men, having been baptized by him, who chose to remain close to him in order to hear his preaching and teaching, and to aid him in his ministry. That there was any formal organization of this group is unlikely; certainly nothing as complicated as the Qumran sect, and probably not even an inner circle as in the case of Jesus.

Two pieces of information regarding the practices of this group during John's lifetime have been preserved for us.

Firstly, we gather that they had special prayers. In Luke 5.33 we read that 'John's disciples are much given . . . to the practice of prayer, and so are the disciples of the Pharisees'; while in Luke 11.1, Jesus' disciples say to him, 'Lord, teach us to pray as John taught his disciples'. The latter text especially must certainly be historical as no Christian writer would ever invent the idea that the Lord's Prayer was given in imitation of the practice of John. Clearly what is referred to here is not the normal prayers which a Jew would use, such as the Shema, a form of the Shemonah Esreh, grace at meals, and so on. We are dealing here with special prayers composed by John for use by his disciples. A fairly close analogy to this is to be seen in the practice of the Rabbis who composed prayers which were pre-

[1] See J. Thomas, *Le Mouvement Baptiste*, p. 89.

served by their disciples; a considerable number of such prayers are to be found in the Talmud.[1]

The word used in Luke 5.33 is *deēsis*, which means a request or petition, and probably John's prayers would be petitionary in character. The closest analogy we can hope to get to John's prayers is probably the Lord's Prayer itself for, as Kraeling points out, 'there is little in it that could not have been made the subject of petition in Baptist circles quite as appropriately as in Christian circles'.[2] It has been suggested that the phrase, 'Thy holy spirit come upon us and cleanse us', which appears as part of the Lord's Prayer (Luke 11.2) in a few manuscripts, was originally part of a prayer of John's; but this is extremely far-fetched.[3] The furthest we can go is to suggest that John's prayers, like his preaching, would be predominantly eschatological in outlook; they would probably include petitions for the forgiveness of sins, and for God to be merciful at the coming day of judgement.

The second piece of information that we have about the disciples of John is that they practised fasting. It was frequently commented on that John's disciples and the disciples of the Pharisees fasted, while the disciples of Jesus did not (Luke 5.33; Mark 2.18; Matt. 9.14). In this, John's disciples were following the example of their master, whose asceticism contrasted with the example of Jesus, as we learn from Matt. 11.18—'John came neither eating nor drinking. . . .' The parallel passage in Luke has—'John the Baptist came neither eating bread nor drinking wine' (Luke 7.33).

While it is true that ascetic ideas and practices have never dominated Judaism, nevertheless an 'ascetic strain' can very definitely be discerned, and more and more attention has been called to it in recent years.[4] Israel's faith was born in the desert and the Israelites did not forget the desert's discipline, even

---

[1] G. F. Moore, *Judaism*, II, pp. 214f.

[2] C. H. Kraeling, *John the Baptist*, p. 79.

[3] See J. Thomas, *Le Mouvement Baptiste*, p. 93, n. 4; J. Steinmann, *Saint John the Baptist and the Desert Tradition*, p. 75.

[4] See J. A. Montgomery, 'Ascetic Strains in Early Judaism', *JBL*, 51 (1932), pp. 183-213, especially p. 185. Cf. also M. Black, *The Scrolls and Christian Origins*, p. 15.

when settlement in Palestine brought to them the pleasures of civilization. In the Old Testament fasting is associated with individuals such as Moses (Ex. 34.28) and Daniel (Dan. 10) and we also hear of an ascetic order of Rechabites,[1] possibly connected with the later order of Nazirites, though the Nazirite vow usually seems to have implied only a temporary asceticism.[2] In John's day many people seem to have made a practice of fasting twice a week (Luke 18.12), on Mondays and Thursdays. Ascetic influences are especially strong in the nonconformist, baptist sects, as we have already noted. In Judaism prayer and fasting were often linked, as they are in Luke 5.33— 'John's disciples are much given to fasting and the practice of prayer'.[3]

Concerning John's asceticism we have two pieces of information; he neither ate bread nor drank wine (Luke 7.33), but he did eat locusts and wild honey (*akrides kai meli agrion*, Mark 1.6; Matt. 3.4). The locusts and honey represent the food of the desert, and it is curious how much difficulty they seem to have occasioned. The apocryphal *Gospel of the Ebionites* substitutes for *akris* (locust) the word *egkris*, denoting a cake made with oil and honey. To this day travellers in Palestine are shown carob-pods or 'locust-beans', known as 'St John's Bread'.[4] Yet strange as it may seem to some, locusts were eaten and indeed still are eaten in parts of the East. Two points about John's diet of locusts deserve mention. Firstly, the locust was a clean animal and its consumption is specifically permitted by the Law (Lev. 11.22), a clear proof, of course, that locusts were eaten. Secondly, if John ate locusts he was not a vegetarian. Almost certainly it was the vegetarianism of the Ebionites which made them remove the reference to locusts, and

---

[1] II Kings 10.15f; Jer. 35. See C. Guignebert, *The Jewish World in the Time of Jesus*, p. 192.

[2] Num. 6.1-21. See D. Eaton, 'Nazirite', *HDB*, III, pp. 497-501.

[3] J. A. Montgomery, 'Ascetic Strains in Early Judaism', *JBL*, 51 (1932), p. 188; G. F. Moore, *Judaism*, II, pp. 259, 260.

[4] See W. H. Brownlee, in K. Stendahl, *The Scrolls and the New Testament*, p. 33. For another modern attempt to explain away the locusts see A. E. J. Rawlinson, *The Gospel According to St Mark*, Westminster Commentary, Methuen (1925), p. 9.

several of the baptist sects were strongly vegetarian. With this aspect of the baptist movement, therefore, John was not in sympathy.[1]

When we ask why John confined himself to such a diet, and refrained from bread and wine, we are confronted with a number of possible answers.

1. It might be that John fasted of necessity, that a meagre diet was imposed on him by the wilderness where he lived. This is unlikely, since John would have been able to obtain food if he desired at a nearby town such as Jericho. To suggest that the wilderness was the cause of John's asceticism is to put the cart before the horse; much more probably it was because of his ascetic principles that John chose to live in the wilderness.

2. It has been held that John was a Nazirite.[2] Regulations for a temporary Nazirite vow are given in Num. 6.1-21, during the period of which no wine or strong drink is to be taken, the head is not to be shaved, and all contact with the dead is to be avoided. The vow was terminated by offering certain sacrifices and although the whole custom dates back to fairly early times, it seems still to have been common in the New Testament period (see Acts 21.23f). In addition to the usual temporary vow there seems also to have been such a thing as a Nazirite vow for life, where a person was dedicated to the Lord by his parents before his birth; examples of this are Samson, and probably also Samuel.

---

[1] According to the Slavonic version of Josephus, John ate no flesh or bread and drank no wine; 'wood-shavings served him for his meals'. Eisler notes that this ascription of a vegetarian diet 'flatly contradicts the Gospel tradition of his feeding on locusts', but he prefers to follow the Slavonic version and some later traditions which state that John confined himself to a vegetable diet (*The Messiah Jesus and John the Baptist*, p. 236). Eisler believes that what John ate was *akrodrua*, 'tree-fruits', but that this was 'maliciously distorted into *akridas* by the hand of an enemy of the Baptist's sect, desirous of making the Baptist appear as one feeding on vermin, naturally loathsome to Gentile Christians of the educated classes'. The 'wood-shavings' of the Slavonic Josephus, a strange diet indeed, do not worry Eisler; he supposes that the words *karpōn xulinōn*, 'wood fruits', i.e. wild fruits, were altered to *karphōn xulinōn*, 'chips of wood', probably by Josephus himself as a 'caustic punning witticism'. Such 'reconstructions' are unlikely to convince anyone, and all attempts, ancient and modern, to make John into a vegetarian, are doomed to failure.

[2] See D. Eaton, 'Nazirite', *HDB*, III, pp. 497-501.

It is to this latter, permanent type of Naziriteship that John, it is suggested, may have adhered. The only real piece of evidence in support of this is found in Luke 1.15 where the angel says to Zechariah that John 'will be great in the eyes of the Lord. He shall never touch wine or strong drink. From his very birth he will be filled with the Holy Spirit.' Here the writer of the Infancy Narrative does seem to picture John being consecrated as a Nazirite before his birth just as Samson was (Judg. 13.3ff). But, as we have seen, this narrative is probably legendary to a great extent, and it is likely that the writer reads back John's later asceticism into the story of his birth in order to bring out the resemblance to heroes of the Old Testament.[1]

Apart from this reference, there is no mention of the fact that John was a Nazirite, and no indication that he was fulfilling a vow. There is no mention of John letting his hair grow, which was the characteristic mark of the Nazirite. There is no evidence that John observed the laws of purity very strictly as the Nazirite had to do. Indeed, by conducting a public ministry instead of living in a strict monastic community John demonstrated that this was just where he differed from a sect such as that of Qumran with their tremendous stress on ritual purity. John's asceticism in one respect actually went beyond that of the Nazirite for there were no restrictions as to what a Nazirite might eat. But it was John's meagre diet and his abstention from bread which attracted public attention. While, therefore, John may have been influenced by the ascetic tradition of the Nazirite vow, it does not seem likely that he was a life-long Nazirite.

3. John's asceticism has been connected with the Essenes, who were well known for their shunning of all luxuries. Philo implies that honey was part of the frugal diet of the Essenes since he mentions that among their tasks 'some superintend the swarms of bees'.[2] Further, the Damascus Document has a short passage on food laws which says:

[1] Cf. C. H. Kraeling, *John the Baptist*, p. 13. 'There is in the earliest tradition, no tangible basis for the later view that John was observing the sanctifying dietary regimen of the Nazirite.' See also M. Goguel, *Jean-Baptiste*, p. 286.
[2] *Hypothetica*, IX, 9, 8.

Let no man defile his soul with any living being or creeping thing by eating of them, from the larvae of bees (in honey) to all the living things that creep in water. And as for fish, let them not eat them unless they have been split while alive and their blood has been poured away. And as for all locusts in their various kinds, they shall be put into fire or water while they are alive, for this is what their nature requires.[1]

This passage allows locusts to be eaten provided they are roasted or boiled alive, and also, as Rabin explains, apparently allows honey to be eaten provided that it is filtered.[2] Here then is evidence that John's diet was also characteristic of the Essene movement.

Such a presentation of the case is, however, rather one-sided, for the Qumran sect at least was not so ascetic as some writers imagine. One characteristic of their life was their common meals, and at some of them at least, meat was consumed.[3] If a member could be punished by having his food ration cut by a quarter (1 QS 6.24), the normal diet can hardly have been the bare minimum. Furthermore, whatever may have been the case in the rest of the baptist movement, the Qumran sect at least did partake of bread and wine at their sacred meal, while it is definitely stated that John refused to partake of either bread or wine. It would seem therefore that John was more rigorous in his asceticism than was the Qumran sect.

Allegro has suggested that John's diet of locusts and honey 'may indicate that the food he was able to eat was strictly limited owing to his purity vows taken in the Qumran community'.[4] Probably Allegro has in mind here what Josephus says of the Essenes:

Those who are convicted of serious crimes they expel from the order; and the ejected individual often comes to a most miserable end. For, being bound by their oaths and usages, he is not at

---

[1] C. Rabin, *The Zadokite Documents*, Oxford, 1954, pp. 60–63.
[2] C. Rabin, op. cit., p. 61.
[3] J. Allegro, *The Dead Sea Scrolls*, p. 116. An agricultural settlement linked with the Qumran monastery has been discovered at 'Ain Feshka; see R. De Vaux, 'Fouilles de Feshka, Rapport Préliminaire', *RB*, 66 (1959), pp. 225–55.
[4] *The Dead Sea Scrolls*, p. 164.

liberty to partake of other men's food, and so falls to eating grass and wastes away and dies of starvation. This has led them in compassion to receive many back in the last stages of exhaustion, deeming that torments which have brought them to the verge of death are sufficient penalty for their misdoings.[1]

If John had at one time been a member of the Qumran sect but had then been expelled, he might likewise not have been 'at liberty to partake of other men's food', and so might have been reduced to locusts and wild honey.

It cannot be said, however, that this variant form of the Essene theory is very convincing either. In the Gospels John is not pictured as a miserable outcast unable to touch any other men's food; his fasting is rather a matter of principle. Moreover, John enjoined the practice on his disciples; and surely we are not to assume that all his disciples had likewise been expelled from Qumran.

4. In the light of the foregoing we can take it that John was not compelled to fast by circumstances, but did so of his own free will and as a matter of principle. The key to his asceticism is therefore to be sought in his view of life.

The fact that John's food 'grows by itself in nature, without cultivation or breeding', Brownlee thinks, 'may represent a repudiation of civilization as corrupting'.[2] Some such idea probably lay behind the asceticism of Josephus' teacher Banos, who 'dwelt in the wilderness, wearing only such things as trees provided, feeding on such things as grew of themselves'.[3] In view of the fact that both Moses and Daniel fasted as a preparation for revelation it has also been suggested that John may have thought that his asceticism would better fit him to understand God's will.

While we do not rule out these possibilities, much the likeliest explanation is that John's motives must principally be understood in the light of the prevailing Jewish conception of fasting, namely that it expressed humiliation before God and

---

[1] *The Jewish War*, II, 8, 8.
[2] In K. Stendahl, *The Scrolls and the New Testament*, p. 33.
[3] Josephus, *Vita*, 2.

symbolized repentance for sin. This was the significance of fasting as a liturgical practice in Judaism, especially in the case of the Day of Atonement. In the classic instance of repentance in the Old Testament, that of Nineveh, in the Book of Jonah, the people proclaim a fast as a symbol of repentance (Jonah 3.5). A text such as Ecclus. 34.26 is also revealing—'If a man fasts for his sins, and goes again and does the same things, who will listen to his prayer? And what has he gained by humbling himself?' The idea of fasting as a penance for sin is prominent in the inter-testamental literature.[1] Remembering how the call to repentance lay at the very heart of John's message, we can see how in their fasting John and his disciples were demonstrating in their lives, for all to see, the repentance and humility before God which they demanded in their preaching.

Could it be that John and his disciples conceived of their task as including something more than this? J. A. T. Robinson, in a thought-provoking article, puts forward the hypothesis that they may have thought of themselves as in some way a redemptive group, making atonement for the sin of Israel.[2] This conception, Robinson suggests, may have been taken over by John from the Qumran community, the final object of whose 'discipline, repentance and purification' was that they might 'become the embodiment of the Servant ideal, the Elect of God for his atoning work'.[3] Robinson suggests that this would help us to understand why Jesus was attracted to John and why he spoke of him so highly, facts which are not easy to understand if John was merely a stern prophet of doom.[4]

In support of Robinson's ideas it may be noted that fasting was sometimes thought of as having some atoning significance. Those who practised the semi-weekly fasts may have thought that they were thus showing 'a vicarious piety which might incline God to overlook the deficiency of others and be gracious to the whole nation'.[5]

---

[1] G. F. Moore, *Judaism*, II, pp. 257-9.
[2] 'The Baptism of John and the Qumran Community', *HTR*, 50 (1957), pp. 175-91.
[3] Op. cit., p. 187.   [4] Op. cit., p. 186.
[5] G. F. Moore, *Judaism*, II, p. 262.

Plausible though it may seem at first sight there are, however, too many objections to Robinson's theory to allow us to
accept it. For one thing, the idea of redemptive suffering is not
nearly so prominent in the Dead Sea Scrolls as he suggests.
It is present in a few texts, but can hardly be claimed as a
leading idea. More seriously, there is no support for this theory
whatsoever, in our main sources, Josephus and the Synoptic
Gospels. On the contrary, John stressed each man's responsibility for his own sin; the merits of the fathers would not atone
for a man's misdeeds, so it is most unlikely that he thought of
himself and his group as atoning for sin. Robinson finds that his
hypothesis fits in well with the Fourth Gospel's view of John,[1]
but the passages he cites all clearly reflect, as we shall see, not
what John actually said, but rather the theology of the later
Christian Church. In view of these objections, Robinson's
theory cannot be accepted.

Thus we can gain at least a sketchy picture of the group of
disciples who gathered round John, aiding him in his ministry,
and sharing in his life of prayer and asceticism. There is no
evidence that they thought of themselves as making atonement
for the sin of Israel, nor is there any evidence that they performed the rite of baptism, but no doubt they would play
their part in warning the people of the approaching end, and
calling them to repentance.

[1] Op. cit., pp. 189-91. See further pp. 149f.

IX

John and Jesus

So far we have been concerned solely with John the Baptist, his message and ministry, and his group of disciples. Now we turn to a question which has always been of great interest, but which is nevertheless extremely difficult to answer; namely, what exactly was the relationship between John and Jesus?

Josephus has nothing to contribute here, and we are left with the Gospels as our only source of information. The Gospels do testify to a connection between John and Jesus. Indeed two of the best attested facts of the New Testament are that Jesus was baptized by John, and that Jesus later spoke very highly of John. These facts would never have been invented by the early Church, for they caused it some embarrassment, and for the sake of the Church's ideas on the uniqueness, the sinlessness and the pre-existence of Christ it would have been much more convenient to forget about John's dealings with Jesus. The fact that they are recounted in the New Testament is due principally to the way in which they were so firmly embedded in the earliest accounts of Christian origins.

We noted in Chapter II,[1] however, that while the New Testament evidence is reasonably reliable with regard to factual details of John's life and the broad outlines of his message, yet there are points at which the evidence is inconsistent and contradictory, and at which there are clear signs of the material

[1] See pp. 15, 16.

having been adapted to serve the interests of the early Church. It is with regard to the relations between John and Jesus that these trends are the most noticeable, and we must therefore consider the evidence with great caution.

There are some striking differences between the Synoptic Gospels and the Fourth Gospel in their treatment of John and Jesus and it will be helpful to indicate these differences before attempting an assessment of the evidence as a whole.

In all three Synoptic Gospels, following their accounts of John, Jesus appears abruptly on the scene, out of the blue. 'It happened at this time that Jesus came from Nazareth in Galilee and was baptized in the Jordan by John,' says Mark (1.9; cf. Matt. 3.13). In Luke, the entry is even more abrupt, for Jesus appears in the middle of a sentence—'During a general baptism of the people, and when Jesus too had been baptized...' (Luke 3.21).

The accounts of the baptism of Jesus are short and similar (Mark 1.10, 11; Luke 3.21, 22; Matt. 3.16, 17), and all three Synoptics affirm that immediately after his baptism Jesus went into the wilderness. Thereafter Jesus and John never again came into personal contact. Matthew and Mark, immediately after their Temptation narratives, tell of how Jesus, hearing that John had been arrested, went to Galilee and began his ministry there (Mark 1.14; Matt. 4.12); Luke tells of Jesus' return to Galilee (Luke 4.14), having already mentioned John's arrest (Luke 3.19, 20). Apart from the undeniable fact that Jesus was baptized by John, personal contact between the two is reduced to a bare minimum; Jesus only comes to John to be baptized, and as soon as he is baptized the two part never to meet again.

It is the Q source which records the one other, indirect encounter between John and Jesus, namely John's question from prison, 'Are you the Coming One?' (Matt. 11.2-6; Luke 7.18-23). This passage is an important one, and it raises the difficult question as to why John, if he recognized and hailed Jesus as The Coming One at the time of his baptism, should almost at the end of his life appear to be in doubt about the matter and send to Jesus asking whether or not he was the Coming One.

We cannot solve the problem by denying the historicity of the question from prison. The fact that it is a Q passage favours its authenticity; the terms of the question agree with John's Messianic expectation; Jesus' refusal to give a direct answer, and the way he leaves John to make the leap of faith bears all the marks of authenticity; and the very fact that the passage appears to contradict the general New Testament view suggests that it is not an invention.

Turning now to the Fourth Gospel, we find a rather different picture. Jesus' baptism by John is not even specifically mentioned; we are left to infer it from the words of John, 'I saw the Spirit coming down from heaven like a dove and resting upon him (Jesus). I did not know him, but he who sent me to baptize in water had told me, "When you see the Spirit coming down upon someone and resting upon him you will know that this is he who is to baptize in Holy Spirit" ' (John 1.32, 33). The Fourth Gospel seems here to gloss over Jesus' baptism and any idea of subordination which it might be taken to imply, even to the point of not actually narrating the baptism.

Whether the Fourth Gospel thinks of John and Jesus as being in contact prior to the baptism it is not easy to say. The verse in the Prologue, 'Here is John's testimony to him: he cried aloud, "This is the man I meant when I said, He comes after me, but takes rank before me, for before I was born, he already was" ' (John 1.15), and also John's remark to the deputation from Jerusalem, 'Among you, though you do not know him, stands the one who is to come after me . . .' (John 1.26, 27) both come before the allusion to the baptism in John 1.32, 33. If either of these sayings has any historical basis they may have been spoken before the baptism. But the chronology is vague, and we cannot make positive assertions. What we can say, however, is that Jesus does not appear on the scene with the abruptness which characterizes the Synoptic account.

According to the Fourth Gospel, about the time of the baptism, John publicly hailed Jesus by a series of titles, he who 'was before me', the Lamb of God, the Son of God, 'he who is to baptize in Holy Spirit'. Not only are these titles entirely missing from the Synoptic account, but they are quite out of keeping with John's message as we have reconstructed it on the basis of the Synoptics, and indeed they seem to reflect very strongly the theology of the Christian Church.

The Fourth Gospel goes on to recount a period of contact between John and Jesus interrupted, if the present order of the Gospel be correct, by visits by Jesus to Galilee and Jerusalem. During this period of overlap Jesus gathers disciples around him and conducts a ministry in Judaea parallel to John's ministry (John 3.22). This contradicts the Synoptic view that following Jesus' baptism (and temptation) there was no contact at all between John and Jesus, due to the fact that John had been put in prison. As if to block any future attempts at harmonization, there comes the clear statement, 'This was before John's imprisonment' (John 3.24).

There is no indication in the Fourth Gospel as to when the period of overlap came to an end, or of when John was arrested and executed. Jesus' reference to John in John 5.33-35, where he calls John 'a lamp, burning brightly' seems, however, to be a reference back to John after the period of overlap had come to an end.

In addition to these differences between the Synoptics and the Fourth Gospel, there is yet another problem posed by the New Testament evidence. It is clear that there was some connection between John and Jesus, and it is certain that Jesus submitted to John's baptism and also spoke very highly of him. Yet John's message, as we have reconstructed it, differs very considerably from the message which Jesus went on to proclaim. How could Jesus think so highly of John, and yet differ so widely from him?

We must now attempt to assess this confused evidence and to solve these various problems concerning the relations between John and Jesus. It will be convenient to deal with the various points in chronological order.

A. *Prior to Jesus' Baptism*

Although there is no definite account of dealings between

John and Jesus prior to Jesus' baptism, it is hard to believe that this was their very first meeting, or that Jesus went from Galilee to the Jordan in order to be baptized, as the Matthean re-writing of Mark would have us believe (Matt. 3.13). It may well have been that it was on a journey to Jerusalem by means of the longer route through Peraea,[1] that Jesus first heard the fiery preacher by the fords of Jordan; or it may have been reports of John's ministry that brought Jesus south from Galilee. Other Galileans had also come to Judaea, for we know that Andrew and Simon were disciples of John (John 1.35ff). We may assume that Jesus heard for himself the preaching of John, thought deeply about it, relating it to his own ideas, and that in all probability he conversed with John and his disciples before submitting to baptism.

B. *The Baptism of Jesus*

We are not concerned here with a detailed discussion of what the baptism meant for Jesus, and of what it meant for the Christian Church and for later Christian theology. We are trying to look at matters from John's point of view, and to discover what the baptism can tell us about the relations between John and Jesus.

Probably Q had no account of the baptism. The earliest account is therefore that of Mark, which is followed quite closely by Matthew. In the Marcan account it is quite clear that it is Jesus, and he alone, who sees the vision and hears the voice (Mark 1.10, 11; cf. Matt. 3.16, 17).[2] In this original account of the baptism we have, very probably, an account by Jesus himself of an experience which was of tremendous importance to him personally. As only Jesus experienced the vision, it must be to him that we owe the description of the heavens opening, the Spirit descending, and of the heavenly voice; in the same way, Jesus himself is the only possible source

---

[1] For the dangers of the more direct route cf. Luke 9.51ff, and Josephus, *Antiquities*, XX, 6, 1.

[2] The contention of some older scholars (cf. H. R. Reynolds, *John the Baptist*, Hodder and Stoughton, 1874, p. 132) that the subject of *eiden* in Matt. 3.16 is *ho Iōannēs* is quite unacceptable, as comparison with Mark clearly shows.

of the temptation narrative, since the temptation was also a personal experience peculiar to Jesus himself.

When we move on to Luke's account, we find that he alters the wording to make the vision and voice more objective— 'heaven opened and the Holy Spirit descended on him in bodily form (sōmatikō eidei) like a dove; and there came a voice from heaven . . .'. This, however, still does not state that John, or anyone other than Jesus, saw the vision or heard the voice.

It is only when we turn to the latest account, in the Fourth Gospel, that we find the narrative altered so that John says, 'I saw the Spirit coming down from heaven like a dove and resting upon him' (John 1.32). This is to ascribe to John a knowledge and awareness of Jesus' inner consciousness which he could not possibly, at the time, have possessed.

We can now see therefore that in the Synoptics there is no contradiction at all in John's attitude to Jesus. Q probably had no account of the baptism, and in it the question from prison is the first suggestion that John had any idea that Jesus might be the Coming One. Mark does not of course contain the question from prison so that in Mark there is no suggestion at all that John thought of Jesus as the Coming One. It is only when Luke, who has the question from prison, begins to make Jesus' baptismal experience into something more objective that any suggestion of a contradiction begins to arise. Even then the only real contradiction occurs when we place the question from prison alongside the Fourth Gospel's account which makes John see the descent of the Spirit and makes him hail Jesus as Son of God, Lamb of God and so on. The conclusion is inescapable that at this point the Fourth Gospel is not strictly historical but has altered the facts from theological motives. The earliest and most reliable sources indicate that at the time of the baptism John never hailed Jesus as the Coming One; it was only when he was in prison that this possibility dawned on him.

The Gospel accounts of Jesus' baptism are brief and lacking in detail, the one exception being Matthew's account of John's objection to baptizing Jesus (Matt. 3.14, 15); this is clearly a later addition reflecting the Church's embarrassment that Jesus, who was sinless, should have submitted to a baptism of repentance for the forgiveness of sins. This concern of the Church was carried a step further in the *Gospel According to the Hebrews* which contained this passage:

> Behold the mother of the Lord, and his brethren said unto him, John the Baptist baptizeth unto the remission of sins; let us go and be baptized of him. But he said unto them: Wherein have I sinned that I should be baptized of him, unless peradventure this very thing that I have said is a sin of ignorance?[1]

This trend is continued in the *Gospel of the Ebionites* which makes John, after he has baptized Jesus and seen 'a great light', fall down before him and say, 'I beg you, Lord, baptize me'.[2]

Having regard to what we have been able to reconstruct of the meaning and purpose of John's baptism, we can appreciate that when Jesus was baptized, along with the crowds who had heard John preach he was aligning himself with those who believed that they were living in the last days and that God was about to break into human history. He was demonstrating his approval of John's movement and his sympathy with John's view that orthodox Judaism was lacking in something and that men must make a decision and, by repentance and righteous living, prepare to enter the Kingdom. Repentance was certainly demanded by John, but we will remember how repentance signified a positive turning towards righteousness, just as much as a turning from sin.

Jesus' baptism has posed a problem for Christian theology, the solution to which has been sought along various lines. Jesus has been thought of as undergoing baptism in order to consecrate the sacrament and provide the example for Christians to follow; or his repentance has been thought of as not being on his own behalf, but on behalf of others; or his submission has been thought of as part of his complete self-identification with sinners.[3]

---

[1] Quoted in Jerome, *Contra Pelagium*, III, 2.
[2] Quoted in Epiphanius, *Against Heresies*, XXX.
[3] See O. Cullmann, *Baptism in the New Testament*, pp. 18, 19; A. Richard-

c. *John's References to Jesus*

As we have already seen, the Synoptics give us no sayings of John which are directly applied to Jesus, and it is only in the Fourth Gospel that we find a series of sayings in which John publicly hails Jesus by a series of titles. Comparison of the Synoptic and of the Fourth Gospel's accounts has shown how the latter cannot be accepted as strictly historical. Of course, if one sets out on the assumption that the Fourth Gospel is literally true down to the last word, then it is necessary to argue that John must have anticipated, by divine inspiration, the later Christian doctrines which are placed on his lips. By studying various Old Testament passages, it may be said, he was guided to apply the ideas of Son of God and Lamb of God to Jesus years before the Christian Church did so. This position, however, would seem to be extremely difficult if not impossible to maintain by anyone making a critical and unbiassed survey of all the evidence.

The Fourth Gospel makes John hail Jesus as '*Son of God*' (John 1.34). Undoubtedly Jesus was conscious of a unique relation to God, and undoubtedly the baptism played a part in his realization of this, but to make John speak out loud the inner thoughts of Jesus is an anachronism. Later in his ministry Jesus is portrayed as revealing a consciousness of his Sonship (see for example Mark 8.38; Matt. 25.34), but it was only in the early Church and especially the Hellenistic Church that Jesus' special relationship to God came to be denoted by the term 'Son of God'.

Similarly, John hails Jesus as 'the *Lamb of God* who takes away the sin of the world' (John. 1.29; cf. 1.36). This expression, in the New Testament, reflects a mixture of several Old Testament ideas, the Passover Lamb, the lamb to which the suffering servant is likened in Isaiah 53, the ram sacrificed in the place of Isaac, and possibly also the scapegoat of Lev. 16.21f.[1]

son, *An Introduction to the Theology of the New Testament*, SCM, 1958, pp. 180, 181.

[1] See A. Richardson, *An Introduction to the Theology of the New Testament*, pp. 225-9; O. Cullmann, *The Christology of the New Testament*, pp. 71, 72;

Particularly in view of the phrase 'who takes away the sin of the world', there can be little doubt that the expression is used in the Fourth Gospel in the full Christian sense as a symbol of the atoning death of Christ. To place the expression on John's lips is therefore to make him anticipate both the death of Christ and the theological interpretation of it which was worked out in the early Church. The earliest literary evidence for this interpretation is found in I Corinthians, written some twenty-five years after John's ministry, in which Paul declares that 'Christ, our paschal lamb, has been sacrificed' (I Cor. 5.7, RSV). Once again, the writer of the Fourth Gospel is guilty of an anachronism.

This conclusion has been disputed not only by those who claim that by divine guidance John could have foreseen the redemptive efficacy of Christ's death through the study of the Old Testament, but also more recently by some who believe that the ideas of Messiah and Suffering Servant were already combined in the Dead Sea Scrolls.[1] If this were the case, since John may well have had some connection with the Qumran sect, it would be quite understandable that he should predict a suffering Messiah. In answer to this, it must be said that there is no clear evidence whatsoever of the identification of Messiah and Suffering Servant at Qumran; the only suffering referred to is that of the whole community.[2] It is very doubtful indeed if there was any pre-Christian identification of the two concepts, and certainly the Synoptic Gospels depict the disciples as being unable to grasp the idea, and only understanding it after the death and resurrection of Jesus. We have noted already the suggestion that John's disciples may have thought of themselves as making atonement for the sin of Israel.[3] If this were so, it might have been the reason why Jesus was so attracted to John; Jesus may have seen his own baptism, not as a confession of sin, but as a 'setting foot on the path of redemptive

C. K. Barrett, *The Gospel According to St John*, SPCK, 1955, pp. 145, 147.

[1] See W. H. Brownlee, in K. Stendahl, *The Scrolls and the New Testament*, pp. 50, 51. Cf. J. A. T. Robinson, *HTR*, 50 (1957), p. 189.

[2] See M. Burrows, *More Light on the Dead Sea Scrolls*, p. 66.

[3] See pp. 140, 141.

suffering'.[1] Attractive as this suggestion may appear at first sight, we have seen that it is most unlikely that John's group did entertain such ideas about themselves. And in any case there is still a wide gap between the idea that the group had some atoning function and the hailing by John of an individual as the Lamb of God who takes away the sin of the world. A suffering Messiah is quite incompatible with the stern Messianic judge whom John expected, and who was not to give his life for sinners, but rather to burn them up in a river of fire. It should also be noted that the phrase 'who takes away the sin of the world', expressing as it does a thought 'grandly universalistic', could hardly have been spoken by John.[2] When all is said and done, the evidence we have at present indicates that the idea of a suffering and dying Messiah originated either in the mind of Jesus or in the early Church; to attribute the idea to John is not historically accurate.

The Fourth Gospel further makes John declare of Jesus, 'This was he of whom I said, "He comes after me, but takes rank before me", for before I was born, he already was' (John 1.15, 30). This is to make John anticipate the doctrine of the pre-existence of Christ, a doctrine which arose fairly early in the Church as the pre-Pauline Christ-hymn of Phil. 2.1-11 shows, but which clearly could only have arisen after the resurrection and the first Christian preaching.

Similarly, John hails Jesus as the bestower of the Holy Spirit (John 1.33). It is true that John expected the Coming One to baptize with holy spirit, but to make John speak these words at the time of the baptism is to make him anticipate the day of Pentecost and the thought of the early Church.

Another type of defence has been made of the historicity of John's hailing of Jesus as Son of God and Lamb of God. It has been argued that John did use these actual terms, but that he did not read into them the ideas which the early Church did; instead he used them simply as Messianic titles. There is some evidence that 'Son of God' was used in this sense in John's day,

---

[1] J. A. T. Robinson, *HTR*, 50 (1957), p. 186.
[2] See G. H. C. Macgregor, *The Gospel of John*, p. 28.

though the references are few in number.[1] Similarly, in the apocalyptic literature the lamb, or the horned ram, sometimes stands for the conquering Messiah as, for example, in *Testament of Joseph* 19.8, where the Messiah is pictured in these terms—'There came forth a lamb, and on its left all the beasts and all the reptiles attacked, and the lamb overcame them and destroyed them'.[2]

This view is, however, open to serious objections. The main one is that, as we have already argued, the earliest and most reliable evidence shows that John did not hail Jesus as Messiah at all, whether as Son of God or under any other title. Lamb of God, in the Messianic sense, signified a military and conquering Messiah, but this is quite at variance with John's conception of the Coming One. Again, the phrase 'who takes away the sin of the world' suggests that the Fourth Gospel uses the term Lamb of God not in the earlier Messianic sense, but instead in the full Christian sense of an atoning sacrifice for the sins of the world.

There is a further testimony by John to Jesus in John 3.27-30, where John again emphasizes that he is not the Christ, 'It is the bridegroom', he says, 'to whom the bride belongs. The bridegroom's friend, who stands by and listens to him, is overjoyed at hearing the bridegroom's voice. This joy, this perfect joy, is now mine. As he grows greater, I must grow less.' The 'friend of the bridegroom', according to Jewish custom,[3] played an important role in arranging the marriage contract, taking part in the ceremony and presiding at the wedding feast; but his was a purely subordinate role, and he joyfully gave chief

[1] See II Sam. 7.14; Ps. 2.7; 89.27; Matt. 16.16; 26.63. Cf. W. Manson, *Jesus the Messiah*, p. 105; O. Cullmann, *The Christology of the New Testament*, pp. 273-5.

[2] See A. Richardson, *An Introduction to the Theology of the New Testament*, pp. 225-9. C. H. Dodd (*The Interpretation of the Fourth Gospel*, pp. 230-8), quoting Test. Levi 18.9, Ps. Sol. 17.29, Apoc. Baruch 73.1-4, argues that the Messiah could 'remove sin' without this being thought of in terms of atoning sacrifice, and he suggests that John 1.29 refers to 'God's Messiah who makes an end of sin'. But it is very difficult to accept that this is the sense in which the term 'Lamb of God' is used in the Fourth Gospel.

[3] I. Abrahams, *Studies in Pharisaism and the Gospel*, II, p. 213; C. K. Barrett, *St John*, pp. 185, 186.

place to the bridegroom. The metaphor aptly describes, for the author of the Fourth Gospel, John's important though subordinate relation to Jesus. It is impossible to accept that John ever actually said this of Jesus, for it reflects the later Christian view of the relation between the two. Almost certainly it is based on Mark 2.18ff (and parallels), where Jesus is compared with the bridegroom at a wedding feast. Similarly, the concluding saying, 'As he grows greater, I must grow less', represents what happened later, rather than anything John actually said.

D. *The period of overlapping ministries*

We turn now to the other major contradiction in the sources which deal with the relation of John and Jesus: was the contact between the two men the brief encounter of the Synoptics or was there an overlap of ministries as the Fourth Gospel indicates? It has been argued that here we have another example of the Fourth Gospel altering the historical facts for theological reasons; the period of overlap brings John and Jesus together so that John may witness to Jesus as the Christ and the superiority of Jesus may be convincingly demonstrated.[1]

But this argument cannot carry much weight. It is quite true that the period of overlap does allow John to witness to Jesus, but there has already been ample opportunity for that at the time of the baptism. If the author of the Fourth Gospel wanted to provide a further opportunity for John to witness to Jesus, why did he go to the length of inventing not only an overlap, but a period of joint ministries during which Jesus baptized as well as John? (John 3.22, 26; 4.1). This is an idea which has proved troublesome, and indeed we have only to look at John 4.2 to see a scribal gloss inserted in an effort to correct the impression that Jesus baptized alongside John.

---

[1] See G. H. C. Macgregor, *The Gospel of John*, p. 90; see also pp. 46, 47. It should be noted that it is only Mark and Matthew who conflict with the Fourth Gospel. Luke omits the Marcan phrase 'after John was arrested' (Luke 4.14; Mark 1.14), and therefore Luke's account can be harmonized with the Fourth Gospel. G. C. Darton suggests that e.g. Luke 5.33 can be placed at a time when Jesus and John were still both preaching; cf. *St John the Baptist and the Kingdom of Heaven*, pp. 47-49.

Furthermore, this section of the Fourth Gospel contains factual details, such as the information that John went to Aenon near Salim while Jesus ministered in Judaea, which suggest an early source, not an invention. While the Fourth Gospel is the latest one and the least concerned with strict historical accuracy the paradoxical fact is that it also draws upon early and accurate sources unknown to the Synoptic writers. Here there seem to be definite traces of such an early source which knew of a Judaean ministry exercised by Jesus parallel to the ministry of John.

What exactly the relations were between John and Jesus during this period of overlap it is difficult to say. If Jesus merely baptized, then it would be possible to regard him as one of John's disciples, sharing in John's ministry. This may well have been the case initially, but we are told that Jesus himself called disciples (John 1.35ff), and that they were associated with him during the joint ministry (John 3.22). This seems to imply a certain degree of separation, and this is borne out by the fact that John and Jesus baptized at different locations (John 3.22, 23), and that Jesus began to have greater success than John (John 4.1). Was this a friendly separation, and a division of spheres of work between equals? Or does it signify a period of friendship followed by a break?

Immediately following the account of the simultaneous ministries, we read that 'a discussion arose between John's disciples and a Jew (*meta Ioudaiou*) over purifying (*peri katharismou*)' (John 3.25, RSV). This passage seems to break the sense, and it is difficult to understand; who was this Jew? Some manuscripts read *Ioudaiōn*, 'Jews', but the plural form does not improve matters much. A very probable emendation is therefore that John's disciples were disputing either with Jesus or with Jesus' disciples (reading *meta Iēsou* or *tōn Iesou*). The change is a small one and it makes sense of the passage, particularly in its context. If the emendation is accepted, we can see how tension must have arisen between John and Jesus, so that some of John's disciples came to Jesus and disputed with him. A sudden break between John and Jesus is not necessarily implied, but only a gradual parting of the ways. The context suggests that the discussion may have been about baptism, but we have seen that 'purification' suggests rather a reference to the various Jewish rites of ritual purity.[1] In this case, we may conjecture that Jesus and his disciples were not strict enough for John's liking (cf. Mark 7.1-23).

The idea of a period of co-operation and then a definite break has been worked out in detail by Maurice Goguel.[2] He rejects the Synoptic separation of the ministries of John and Jesus holding that their view is quite inadequate to explain, among other things, the very high opinion of John which Jesus undoubtedly held. The early chapters of the Fourth Gospel are a much more reliable witness to the facts and behind them Goguel detects a special source, independent from the Synoptics, as is shown by the facts that it makes Jesus' disciples come over from John instead of being called in Galilee, and makes Peter a native of Bethsaida (John 1.44) instead of Capernaum as the Synoptics indicate (Mark 1.29).

Goguel goes on to reconstruct an early period when Jesus preached a message similar to that of John and, like him, baptized. Traces of Jesus' preaching at this time are to be seen for example in the Sermon on the Mount with its demands for perfection. But after a while Jesus' thought developed; he broke with John and stopped baptizing. John believed that if men repented and were baptized they would be rewarded by the Messiah; they were to be the wheat gathered into the granary. But Jesus, his thought dominated by the absolute transcendence of God, came to see how nothing which men do can make them deserve entry into the Kingdom. All are debtors; all are 'unprofitable servants' (Luke 17.7-10). Hence Jesus was led to the preaching of the 'Gospel', stressing the love and forgiveness of God. God is not the stern Judge of John's preaching; he *wants* men to be saved. Jesus gave up baptism because of the danger that people would think that it guaranteed entry into the Kingdom. He gave up asceticism and left the wilderness in order to take the message of salvation to

---

[1] See p. 95.   [2] M. Goguel, *Jean-Baptiste*, pp. 235-74.

sinners, thus demonstrating God's initiative in salvation, as opposed to John who expected people to come to him.

Goguel develops his 'interprétation psychologique' in a very interesting fashion, though his theory does go far beyond the evidence. Its chief defect is the way Jesus' teaching is chopped up, in arbitrary fashion, and assigned either to before or after the break with John. The teaching of Jesus is far more of a consistent whole than Goguel is willing to recognize. God's free offer of salvation does not presuppose the kind of character delineated in the Sermon on the Mount, but can it not work towards the production of such a character in the forgiven sinner? On the other hand, much of what Goguel has to say about the development of Jesus' conception of the Gospel in contrast to the outlook of John, is highly probable.

There can be little doubt that John and Jesus, after a period during which they were closely associated, did move apart, but not necessarily with either ill-feeling or a definite break. Jesus' preaching of his own distinctive Gospel probably began when he moved to Galilee about this time. John was arrested, so that the question of direct relations between the two did not arise again. Two small indications show that it is wrong to think of a quarrel or a violent break. One is John's question to Jesus from prison; this may indicate puzzlement on John's part, but hardly open opposition between him and Jesus. More incidental, and therefore more valuable, is the comment which Matthew adds after telling of how John's disciples buried their master, 'and they went and told Jesus' (Matt. 14.12). If the disciples of John went to share their sad news with Jesus, the two groups could hardly have been at loggerheads. Rather, they had been maintaining a friendly though separate existence.

E. *After John's imprisonment*

We have already dealt with the apparent conflict between John's question from prison, 'Are you the Coming One, or are we to expect some other?' and John's hailing of Jesus as the Son of God, and so on. When we realize that John did not, in fact, apply the various titles to Jesus, the conflict is removed.

There are those, however, who try to reconcile the two narratives. It can be supposed that John did recognize Jesus as the Coming One at the time of the baptism, but that his faith failed, as he lay in prison, and as reports of the ministry of Jesus came to him which did not square with his idea of the Messiah. Alternatively, it has been suggested 'that the question was asked for the sake of John's disciples, who needed strengthening or correcting in their beliefs'.[1] In view of what has been said above, however, neither of these explanations are very convincing, and we can take it that it was only when he was in prison that the possibility dawned on John that Jesus might be the Coming One for whom he had sought to prepare.

Although there was no other contact between John and Jesus, we must not fail to note the sayings of Jesus about John which are preserved, particularly in the Q source.

Following the episode of John's question from prison, Jesus ironically asked the crowds what spectacle drew them to the wilderness, 'A reed-bed swept by the wind? No? Then what did you go out to see? A man dressed in silks and satins? Surely you must look in palaces for that. But why did you go out? To see a prophet? Yes indeed, and far more than a prophet...' (Matt. 11.7-9; Luke 7.24-28). Jesus, as we have already seen, is here hailing John as the eschatological prophet, the returning Elijah.

This is followed by the tribute, 'I tell you this: never has there appeared on earth a mother's son greater than John the Baptist, and yet the least in the kingdom of Heaven is greater than he' (Matt. 11.11; Luke 7.28). This saying reflects the idea that the Kingdom is already present, at least partially. John was a supremely great man, but he did belong to the old dispensation. Now that the Kingdom has come, those in it, i.e. Jesus' disciples, are 'greater' than John. 'They are greater, not in their moral character or achievements, but in their privileges.'[2]

Another saying is preserved in different versions by Matthew

---

[1] A. Plummer, The Gospel According to St Luke, ICC, T. and T. Clark, 1896, p. 202.

[2] S. E. Johnson, Interpreter's Bible, 7, p. 382.

and Luke, 'Ever since the coming of John the Baptist the kingdom of Heaven has been subjected to violence (*biazetai*) and
violent men (*biastai*) are seizing it. For all the prophets and the
Law foretold things to come until John appeared' (Matt. 11.12,
13); 'Until John, it was the Law and the prophets: since then,
there is the good news of the kingdom of God, and everyone
forces his way in' (*biazetai*) (Luke 16.16). The saying is a very
difficult one, and we cannot reconstruct the original wording
with any confidence.[1] It is generally held that Matthew's form
is on the whole nearer to the original. *Biazetai* could be either
passive, 'suffers violence', or as Otto suggested, middle, meaning 'exercises force' or 'shows its power'. *Biastai* has been
variously interpreted as men of violence, zealots, or demonic
powers; or alternatively, in a good sense, 'men of spiritual
force'. The basic idea is either that the kingdom is under attack
by enemies, human or demonic; or, that those willing to take
risks and make sacrifices are pressing their way into the kingdom. The point which concerns us here, and which is valid
regardless of the differing interpretations of the rest of the
saying, is that Jesus regards the ministry of John as a turning
point in history. There are two eras; the old era, that of the
Law and the prophets, and the new, that of the kingdom.
Though John marks the dividing line, yet he actually belongs
to the *old* era; 'until John, it was the Law and the prophets'
and the kingdom is 'since then'.

More straightforward is the reference to John in this passage:

How can I describe the people of this generation? What are they
like? They are like children sitting in the market-place and
shouting at each other,

> 'We piped for you and you would not dance.'
> 'We wept and wailed, and you would not mourn.'

For John the Baptist came neither eating bread nor drinking
wine, and you say, 'He is possessed'. The Son of Man came
eating and drinking, and you say, 'Look at him! a glutton and a
drinker, a friend of tax-gatherers and sinners!' And yet God's

---

[1] On the saying see T. W. Manson, *The Sayings of Jesus*, p. 134; C. H.
Kraeling, *John the Baptist*, pp. 156, 157; M. Goguel, *Jean-Baptiste*, pp. 65-69.

wisdom is proved right by all who are her children. (Matt. 11.16-19; Luke 7.31-35.)

The picture is of children playing: one group propose a game of 'Weddings', but their companions object; so a game of 'Funerals' is proposed, and this too is rejected. So the 'people of this generation', in their perversity, criticize John for his asceticism and Jesus for his lack of it.

All three Synoptic Gospels relate the question about authority (Mark 11.27-33; Matt. 21.23-27; Luke 20.1-8), in reply to which Jesus himself asked a question, 'The baptism of John: was it from God, or from men?' This trapped the questioners, for if they replied, 'From God', they would be asked why they had not believed John; while if they answered, 'From men', they would have reason to fear the people, 'for all held that John was in fact a prophet'. Jesus held, therefore, that John's ministry and his baptism were 'from God', that is, divinely authorized.

Matthew alone preserves another word of praise for John, 'For when John came to show you the right way to live, you did not believe him, but the tax-gatherers and prostitutes did; and even when you had seen that, you did not change your minds and believe him' (Matt. 21.32).

These are all the references to John by Jesus which the Synoptics preserve.[1] The Fourth Gospel, significantly, records no such words of praise, the only possible exception being John 5.33-35, words spoken by Jesus to the 'Jews', 'Your messengers have been to John; you have his testimony to the truth. Not that I rely on human testimony, but I remind you of it

---

[1] Some scholars hold that the passage about 'the sign of the prophet Jonah' (Matt. 12. 38-41; Luke 11.29-30) refers to John. See C. H. Kraeling, *John the Baptist*, pp. 136, 137; T. W. Manson, *The Sayings of Jesus*, pp. 89-91; G. R. S. Mead, *The Gnostic John The Baptizer*, pp. 18f. It is held that it is John, the great preacher of repentance, who is the only sign; he preached repentance to Israel just as Jonah did to the Ninevites. Manson points to the similarity between the names 'John' and 'Jonah'; Mead suggests connections with legends about the Great Fish. But, as the original Lucan version shows, it is clearly Jesus himself by *his* preaching of repentance (Mark 1.15), who is the only sign—'just as Jonah was a sign to the Ninevites, so will the *Son of Man* be to this generation' (Luke 11.30).

for your own salvation. John was a lamp, burning brightly, and for a time you were ready to exult in his light.' Apart from the doubtful authenticity of the saying, it has in any case to be read in the context of the Fourth Gospel; John may have been a 'lamp, burning brightly', but in the eyes of the writer his true and only function was to prepare for and to witness to Christ, who is the true Light.

Any attempt to understand the significance of the inter-relationship between John and Jesus must begin with the un-doubtedly high opinion which Jesus held of John. He was the eschatological prophet, the greatest of those born under the old order; his baptism was 'from God'. Here we come up against the problem of how Jesus could think so highly of John and yet differ from him so radically.

The differences between John and Jesus are obvious. John was an ascetic, while Jesus certainly was not; this was one of the most striking differences noted by the people (cf. Luke 7.31-35; Matt. 11.16-19). John remained for the most part in the wilderness, and the people had to go there to hear him; Jesus, on the other hand, travelled freely and sought people out, even entering the houses of notorious sinners. John's message was essentially a stern one, while Jesus' message was essentially the Gospel, 'the good news'. For John, the coming Kingdom is still in the future, albeit the immediate future, whereas for Jesus the Kingdom is partially present, already breaking in. A proof of this is the mighty acts of Jesus; John, on the other hand, 'gave no miraculous sign' (John 10.41, a verdict with which the Synoptics would agree). John, we may assume, gave a central place to the Law, to which his own practices of prayer and fasting were additional burdens. Jesus accepted the Law in a sense, but contrasted what was said to the men of old with his, 'But what I tell you is this . . .'. John's ethical teaching was typically Jewish, whereas Jesus demanded a much more radical ethic. John's teaching implies that by the performance of certain acts man can earn the right of entry into the Kingdom; but Jesus taught that whatever men do, they are still 'unprofitable servants' in the sight of God.

These differences, combined with Jesus' high opinion of John, do pose a problem. A few possible lines of solution may be briefly indicated.

Firstly, allowance must be made for *the development of Jesus' thought*. He had to start from somewhere, from the section of Judaism with which he was the most nearly in sympathy, and then go on to make clear to his followers his own distinctive contribution. Although we have rejected Goguel's dividing up of the Gospel material, yet his general position has much to commend it. Jesus began as a disciple of John, but then went on to exercise an independent ministry.

Secondly, stress must be laid on *the points on which John and Jesus did agree*. These would certainly include dissatisfaction with current trends in Jewish thought and practice, fervent eschatological expectations, conviction of the need for decision, for repentance and for righteous living, and of the need for dedicating oneself wholly in the service of God. We must remember also that there was a stern side to Jesus' teaching, which can be overlooked when he is contrasted with John. Jesus, like John, could address his hearers as, 'You vipers' brood!' (Matt. 12.34; cf. Matt. 3.7; Luke 3.7), and could give warning that 'when a tree does not bear good fruit it is cut down and burnt' (Matt. 7.19; cf. Matt. 3.10; Luke 3.9). Jesus' high opinion of John is the main reason for holding that John must have given a place to the Kingdom of God in his preaching; this argument must be used, however, with great caution.

Finally, Jesus' approval of John must be seen in proper perspective. Jesus did not accept John's preaching and teaching in detail. He did not even accept John's ministry as part of the Kingdom; 'until John, it was the Law and the prophets: since then, there is the good news of the kingdom of God' (Luke 16.16). What Jesus held was that John had a place in God's purposes. God's purposes, however, were developing. John's role was an important one, but it was only a stage in the process which was culminating in the person of Jesus himself. John's ministry was divinely authorized and used by God to call the people to repentance; now, however, the new age was actually breaking in, and the age of the Gospel was succeeding the age of the Law. Jesus' attitude to John has therefore been accurately summed up by the later Church which saw in John the herald and precursor of the Kingdom.

To attribute to John a precise knowledge of the nature of the Kingdom and of the Christ is a historical error; but this does not alter the fact that in his providence, God used John as the forerunner of the Kingdom.

X

The Samaritan Ministry

WE have seen how the ministries of John and Jesus overlapped for a certain period, during which Jesus and his disciples were in Judaea (John 3.22), but John and his disciples went to 'Aenon near Salim' (John 3.23). The latter location has for long proved to be a puzzle to commentators, some of whom have ranged as far afield as the Negeb to locate it. 'Aenon' means 'springs', and 'Salim' means 'peace', and it has been suggested that the name is to be interpreted symbolically. This is a very far-fetched suggestion, however, and the Fourth Gospel gives many exact locations. In fact, only two alternatives are worthy of serious consideration.

Several ancient writers, and many scholars following them, claim that Aenon near Salim lay about eight miles south of Scythopolis, on the west bank of the Jordan. This identification is attested from the fourth century AD onwards, but there is no proof that the tradition is a really early one.[1] Against this view there is the fact that there is no record of there being a town called Salim in this location in the first century AD, whereas the way in which the author of the Fourth Gospel locates Aenon as being 'near Salim' suggests that this Salim was a well-known place. A more serious objection, which really disposes of this site, is the fact that it would be quite pointless to

---

[1] This is the opinion of Eusebius and of Jerome; it tallies with the place marked on the mosaic map of Madeba, and also with the account of the pilgrimage of Silvia of Aquitania. See E. Nestle, 'Salim', HDCG, II, p. 551.

say that 'water was plentiful in that region' (John 3.23), if it was a place on the west bank of the Jordan; that would be too obvious to require saying.

The second alternative is to regard Salim as the well-known town of that name which lay about three miles east of Shechem, in Samaria. Seven miles to the north-east there is still a village called 'Ainun. Between the two lies the great Wady Far'ah where there is 'a succession of springs, yielding a copious perennial stream, with flat meadows on either side, where great crowds might gather'.[1] It has been objected that this place is not 'near Salim', being seven miles away, but Salim is the nearest place of any size by which it could be identified. This identification has the support of Tristram, and also of Conder, who says, 'The site of Wady Far'ah is the only one where all the requisites are met—the two names, the fine water supply, the proximity of the desert, and the open character of the ground'.[2]

A major stumbling-block in the way of accepting this second site has been the fact that it lay in the heart of Samaria. C. W. Wilson, for example, says that 'it has been objected to this site that, as it was in Samaria, the Jews would have not gone to it to be baptized'.[3] Wilson goes on to point out, however, that Scythopolis, a town of the Decapolis, was nearby and it had a large Jewish population. But if John was concerned with preaching to Jews only, then he made himself curiously inaccessible by going to Aenon near Salim. We must seriously ask ourselves whether John did not in fact go to Samaria in order to preach to the Samaritans.

At first sight, such an idea may seem to be extremely un-

---

[1] W. W. Moore, 'Aenon', *HDCG*, I, p. 35.

[2] W. W. Moore, op. cit., p. 35. This identification has been consistently defended by W. F. Albright, see e.g. *HTR*, 17 (1924), pp. 193, 194; 'Recent Discoveries in Palestine and the Gospel of St John', *The Background of the New Testament and its Eschatology*, Cambridge, 1956, p. 159. Although within the Roman province of Judaea, this site could hardly be regarded as being within 'the wilderness of Judaea'. 'The wilderness' in general might, however, be regarded as stretching into Samaria, for much of the terrain there is similar to that which lies immediately to the south in the wilderness of Judaea proper.

[3] C. W. Wilson, 'Salim', *HDB*, IV, p. 354.

likely, for John was certainly a Jew, who preached most of the time to Jews, and 'Jews have no dealings with Samaritans' (John 4.9, RSV). A closer examination of Samaritanism, however, and of Samaritan sectarianism, especially in the light of recent studies and discoveries, sheds quite a different light on the situation.

1. The Samaritans

Until comparatively recent times injustice has been done to the Samaritans, in so far as the sources for their history have been found in the Old Testament, Josephus, and later Jewish writings, all of which are strongly biassed by Jewish hatred and contempt for the Samaritans. The basis for the Jewish account is found in II Kings 17, which tells of how, upon the fall of the Northern Kingdom (in 721 BC), the native Israelite population was deported, and 'people from Babylon, Cuthah, Avva, Hamath, and Sepharvaim' were 'placed in the cities of Samaria instead of the people of Israel' (II Kings 17.24). These foreigners intermarried with the remnants of the native Israelites, and although Jahweh worship survived, these peoples also 'served their own gods'. In origin the Samaritans were therefore of impure race and syncretistic religion. After the Exile there was active hatred between the returned Jews and the Samaritans. The Samaritans set up a rival sanctuary on Mount Gerizim; they accepted only the Pentateuch which they altered so as to justify their own claims. Down to the New Testament period and beyond it, the Jews had no dealings with the Samaritans.

This is the essence of the Jewish account. In comparatively recent times, however, the Samaritans and their literature have been rediscovered, allowing us to see them from a very different point of view, which of course in its own way can be just as biassed as the Jewish.[1]

Modern critical scholarship recognizes that the Jewish-Samaritan split goes much further back than the time of the

---

[1] See J. A. Montgomery, *The Samaritans, The Earliest Jewish Sect*, pp. 3-12.

fall of the Northern Kingdom; north-south rivalry goes back at least to the time of the conquest, and the division may be earlier still if, as some think, only the northern tribes were in bondage in Egypt. During the divided monarchy there was intermittent warfare between north and south, but that did not prevent a great deal of intercourse between the two countries, both regarding themselves as sharing the same racial and religious heritage. After the fall of the Northern Kingdom, some deportations did take place, but they were not large in number.[1] Undoubtedly colonization also took place, but in spite of this the northern Israelites continued to worship Jahweh as did their brothers in the south. There continued to be some contacts on the religious level (cf. II Chron. 30), and the prophets looked for a reunion of Israel and Judah (Isa. 11.11ff; Jer. 31.3-5; Ezek. 37.15ff). Up to the time of the Exile at any rate the rivalry between north and south was a political rather than a religious one. After the Exile, the Samaritans offered to help to rebuild the Temple, an offer which was promptly rejected. The attempts of Sanballat to frustrate the rebuilding of the walls of Jerusalem were again political in inspiration. There is, moreover, no evidence that the racial policies of Nehemiah and especially of Ezra were directed against the Samaritans, or that Samaritans as such were considered racially impure.[2] The religious break between the two sections is probably to be placed roughly between the mid-fifth and mid-fourth centuries BC. Thereafter the rivalry and the hatred intensified. The Samaritans suffered badly during the Maccabaean period, but after 63 BC Samaria was freed from the Jews and became part of the Roman province of Syria.

One of the main characteristics of the Samaritans is that they accept only the Pentateuch, which they have in a version of their own. Another characteristic is their view that the true site of the Temple is on Mount Gerizim; in support of this the Samaritan Pentateuch compresses the Massoretic Text's Ten Commandments into nine and adds a long tenth command-

---

[1] J. A. Montgomery, *The Samaritans*, pp. 49f.
[2] W. O. E. Oesterley, *A History of Israel*, Vol. II, Oxford, 1932, pp. 152-6.

ment which refers to the selection of Gerizim as the Holy Mount.

It is quite wrong to suppose, as has often been done,[1] that the Samaritans had no eschatological or Messianic beliefs; new doctrines were introduced by means of the supplementary oral law.[2] Samaritan Messianic beliefs obviously could not take the same form as Jewish expectations, since they did not accept the prophetic books, and since anything connected with Jerusalem or with the house of David was abhorrent to them. Thus it is that their belief centred in the Taheb (or Shaheb), meaning the 'Restorer'. Authority for this figure had to be sought in the Pentateuch and he was therefore conceived of as the 'prophet like unto Moses' of Deut. 18.15. This figure was never a supernatural Messiah, but rather a mortal man who would be used to restore the Divine Favour to the true people of God.[3] This belief is undoubtedly pre-Christian since the proof text, Deut. 18.15, is embedded in the Samaritans' Tenth Commandment, the text of which cannot be later than the second century BC.

It is interesting to note an account Josephus gives of a rising among the Samaritans which was crushed by Pilate. The Samaritans believe that in the time of Eli (whom they regard as a schismatic) the vessels of the Temple were hidden in a cave in Mount Gerizim. This event marks the beginning of the period of God's disfavour which will only be terminated when the Moses-like prophet comes and recovers the Temple vessels. That this belief existed in pre-Christian times is attested by Josephus' story:

> But the nation of the Samaritans did not escape without tumults. The man who excited them to it was one who thought lying a thing of little consequence, and who contrived everything so, that the multitude might be pleased; so he bade them get together on Mount Gerizim, which is by them looked upon as the most holy of all mountains, and assured them that, when they were come thither, he would show them those sacred vessels which were

[1] See M. Gaster, *Samaritan Oral Law and Ancient Traditions*, Vol. I, *Samaritan Eschatology*, Search Publishing Co., 1932, p. 1.
[2] M. Gaster, *The Samaritans*, Oxford, 1925, pp. 48f.
[3] See M. Gaster, *Samaritan Eschatology*, pp. 221-77.

laid under that place, because Moses put them there. So they came thither armed, and thought the discourse of the man probable, and as they abode at a certain village, which was called Tirathaba, they got the rest together to them and desired to go up the mountain in a great multitude together. But Pilate prevented their going up, by seizing upon the roads with a great band of horsemen and footmen, who fell upon those that were gotten together in the village; and when they came to an action, some of them they slew, and others of them they put to flight, and took a great many alive, the principal of whom, and also the most potent of those that fled away, Pilate ordered to be slain.[1]

Thus we see that the Samaritans, in their Messianic expectations, could be just as fervent and even fanatical as the Jews.[2]

2. Samaritan Sectarianism

In addition to the orthodox Samaritanism of the first century AD there is evidence of the existence of sects on the fringe of Samaritanism, just as there was a non-conformist sectarian movement on the fringe of orthodox Judaism. Unfortunately this evidence, coming as it does from Jewish, Christian, Moslem and Samaritan sources, is very confused and contradictory.[3] One of the fullest sources is the Samaritan historian Abu'l Fath (fourteenth century AD) whose accounts clearly incorporate much earlier material.

We hear of at least four sects of the Samaritans, the *Gorothenians*, the *Masbothaeans*, the *Sabbaeans* and the *Dositheans*. The Gorothenians and the Masbothaeans, mentioned by Hegesippus and Epiphanius, are known to us virtually only by name, although the word 'Masbothaeans' by derivation probably means 'Baptists' and suggests that they practised rites of baptism.[4] The Sabbaeans may also have been 'Baptists'; the accounts of their origin are historically very doubtful, but they do seem to have been in existence prior to the Christian era. From Abu'l

---

[1] *Antiquities*, XVIII, 4, 1.

[2] It may be added that John 4.25 provides further evidence of Samaritan 'Messianic' expectations.

[3] A good summary of the available data will be found in J. A. Montgomery, *The Samaritans*, pp. 252-60.

[4] See M. Black, *The Scrolls and Christian Origins*, p. 56.

Fath we gather that in the fourth century, the Sabbaeans had their own ecclesiastical organization, and refused to co-operate with the great Samaritan High Priest, Baba Raba.

The most important evidence is that associated with the Dositheans, who are said to have been founded by one, Dusis or Dositheus. Here we are confronted with an amazing mass of contradictory evidence, Dositheus being assigned by various sources to periods ranging from the time of Alexander the Great to the fourth century AD! Some scholars think that only one sect existed, others that as many as six are needed to account for all the evidence. In all probability, however, we are dealing with two main groups.

1. There are references which show the existence of an early sect of Dositheans, said by Abu'l Fath to have originated in the time of Alexander the Great. They had their own strict laws of purity, and of the Sabbath, and they separated themselves from the orthodox Samaritans. A number of Patristic references support the early existence of this sect,[1] and testify to the fact that it denied the resurrection. There is evidence that it continued to exist for a very long time. We hear in Photius of a Samaritan sect around AD 600 which followed 'a certain Dosthes or Dositheos'. They claimed that he was the prophet foretold by Moses, that he had taught that the world is incorruptible, and that he denied the resurrection.

2. Separate from this sect there are many references to another group, but unfortunately, while there may originally have been a distinction in the name, this is now lost. This sect originated at the beginning of the Christian era; Patristic references confirm this, speaking of a certain Dositheus who was associated with Simon Magus.[2] The references to this sect agree that, unlike the other one, it affirmed the resurrection. The members practised ritual immersion, and prayed while in the water, with their bodies veiled. They buried their dead girded, and with sandals and staff. Abu'l Fath lists a number of sects which were derived from this one. This second Dosithean sect

[1] J. A. Montgomery, The Samaritans, p. 255.
[2] J. A. Montgomery, op. cit., p. 255.

was an important and influential one, and it seems likely that many of their beliefs and practices passed into orthodox Samaritanism.[1]

From even this brief survey it will be apparent that there are similarities between Samaritanism, and particularly sectarian Samaritanism, and the Jewish baptist movement which, we have suggested, formed the background of John the Baptist's life and ministry. This tentative conclusion has been confirmed in a startling way by the Dead Sea Scrolls which furnish us with many parallels between the Qumran sect and Samaritanism.

On many points of belief the two sectarian movements held very similar views. Samaritans believe in 'Fanuta', the period of Divine disfavour (Deut. 31.18), which will last until one day 'Rahuta', the period of God's favour, will return; similar periods, the 'time of wrath', and the 'time of favour' are mentioned in the Dead Sea Scrolls.[2] The veneration of Moses is a prominent feature of Samaritanism; as they did not accept the prophetic books, for them Moses is the only true prophet. Similarly, the Essenes revered Moses very highly, anyone who blasphemed him being punished with death.[3] The expectation of the Moses-like prophet, noted above as a feature of Samaritan Messianic belief, is characteristic of the Dead Sea Scrolls sect. It is noteworthy that in the Qumran 'Testimonia', a collection of Messianic proof texts, the passages Deut. 5.28, 29 and Deut. 18.18, 19 are combined in exactly the same way as they are in the Samaritan Pentateuch's tenth commandment.[4] Belial, as the power of evil, occurs in Samaritanism, and is frequently mentioned in the Dead Sea Scrolls.[5]

Strict Sabbatarianism is a feature of Samaritanism, being

[1] Cf. J. Bowman, 'Contact Between Samaritan Sects and Qumran?', VT, 7 (1957), p. 187.
[2] See M. Gaster, The Samaritans, pp. 9, 19, 90; CD 1.5; 1 QH 15.15, cf. 9.8; 'The New Covenant' fragment (T. H. Gaster, The Scriptures of the Dead Sea Sect, p. 290).
[3] J. A. Montgomery, The Samaritans, pp. 225-32; Josephus, The Jewish War, II, 8, 9.
[4] See T. H. Gaster, The Scriptures of the Dead Sea Sect, pp. 353-5.
[5] T. H. Gaster, op. cit., p. 311.

specially mentioned in connection with both the Dosithean sects. Ultra-Sabbatarianism was characteristic also of the Essenes, and the Damascus Document contains a very strict Sabbath code.[1] Similarly, strict laws of ritual purity, which are said to have characterized both Dosithean sects, are typical also of the Essene movement.[2] Ritual immersion was practised by the later Dosithean sect and probably by the Masbothaeans and Sabbaeans, as in the sects of the Jewish baptist movement. In their opposition to the Jewish Temple at Jerusalem Samaritans and Jewish sectarians would find common ground. As we have already seen,[3] it is doubtful just how far the Jewish sects did cut themselves off from the Temple, and also just how far this was a matter of principle. Nevertheless, when we learn of how some of the Samaritan sects gave up their devotion to Gerizim, we can see how closely the two sectarian movements could approach each other.

One of the most striking similarities has been revealed by the discovery of texts of the Pentateuch, used by the Qumran sect, and almost identical with the Samaritan version. The first of these to be published was a portion of Exodus, with close affinities to the Samaritan text. Not only do the two texts often agree in their readings, but where the Samaritan version has additions or expansions of the text (e.g. at Ex. 8.19; 11.2; 17.13) so does the Qumran version; and where the Samaritan text has omissions (e.g. Ex. 29.21; 30.1-10) so does the Qumran version.[4] Equally startling has been the discovery that the Qumran sect had their own calendar, this being one of their points of difference from orthodox Judaism. Jaubert has found affinities between this sectarian calendar and the calendar of the Samaritans.[5] To this may be added the fact that differences concerning

[1] J. A. Montgomery, The Samaritans, pp. 33, 170; CD 10.14-11.18; Josephus, The Jewish War, II, 8, 9.
[2] Cf. CD 10.11-13; 12.11-18; Josephus, The Jewish War, II, 8, 10.
[3] See pp. 38, 107.
[4] See J. Allegro, The Dead Sea Scrolls, pp. 67-69; P. W. Skehan, 'Exodus in the Samaritan Recension from Qumran', JBL, 74 (1955), pp. 182-7.
[5] A. Jaubert, 'La Date de la dernière Cène', Revue de l'histoire des religions, 146 (1954), pp. 140-73; 'Le Calendrier des Jubilés et les jours liturgiques de la semaine', VT, 7 (1957), pp. 35-61.

the calendar are noted as features of the Sabbaeans and of the earlier Dosithean sect.

From all this it is clear that there was a Samaritan sectarian movement parallel to the Jewish sectarian movement and having a number of remarkable affinities with it. Noting some of these affinities, Montgomery suggested that the Jewish Essenes had extended their influence northwards and that they were responsible for the coming into being of one of the Dosithean groups.[1] It is noteworthy that Epiphanius actually states that the Essenes were a Samaritan sect; Epiphanius is not the most trustworthy of writers and this statement has often been regarded as completely false and misleading. In the light of the evidence now available, however, this judgement must be revised. If 'Essenes' was a general term, referring to Jewish sectarian groups, it could well have been applied also to the Samaritan sectarians, who have so many similarities with the Essenes. Essenism would then have consisted of two main divisions, a southern and a northern, a Jewish and a Samaritan.

The question must be seriously raised, however, as to which sectarian movement influenced the other. Even with the Dead Sea Scrolls discoveries, some scholars discount the affinities and explain them as being due merely to similar influences being brought to bear on the different groups. Thus Burrows considers that the similarities between the Jewish sectarians and the Samaritans 'do not indicate any direct contacts but are to be explained by the fact that their backgrounds were similar ... they were exposed to the same winds of doctrine that were blowing through the whole region'.[2] While this might account for some of the similarities, it does not explain the possession by the two groups of very similar texts of the Pentateuch and calendars. These features point to a common origin dating far into the past. This is the view argued by M. Black, who attaches great importance to the Samaritan-type Pentateuch found at Qumran, and who holds that 'it is a sign of the very

[1] J. A. Montgomery, *The Samaritans*, p. 263.
[2] M. Burrows, *More Light on the Dead Sea Scrolls*, p. 262. See also J. Bowman, *VT*, 7 (1957), pp. 184-9.

great antiquity of the groups possessing such a book, for any fundamental differences in this connection must antedate the work of Ezra'.[1] While it has been usual to think of the Jewish Essenes influencing the Samaritans, Black suggests that 'we may have to reverse this and look for the formative influences in Judaean sectarianism in the ancient religion of Israel, or rather in its remanent descendants in Samaria'.[2] To explain how this came about, Black puts forward the view that 'while the Second Temple was renewed and reformed at the time of the Restoration, its priesthood must have preserved, with the conservative tenacity of a priestly institution, much of the pre-Ezra type of indigenous Hebrew religion; it would then be this conservatism of the Zadokite exiled priests which constituted the link with the descendants of the Northern Kingdom'.[3]

The evidence we have surveyed does indicate that though the hatred and contempt of orthodox Judaism and orthodox Samaritanism for each other were proverbial in New Testament times, yet on the sectarian level matters were very different. Whatever may have been the facts with regard to the origin of the two sectarian movements, there can be no doubt that they led a parallel existence, and had many similarities in doctrine, practice and general outlook.

3. John the Baptist and the Samaritans

In view of this situation, we can see how any objections to a ministry by John among the Samaritans, on the grounds that they were anti-Jewish and would not be receptive to his message, fall to the ground. We can now see in fact that a ministry by John in Samaria makes extremely good sense.

It may have been that members of Samaritan sectarian groups had already come south to hear John and to be baptized by him, and that they then persuaded John to return with them to Samaria. The separation between John and Jesus necessitated that one or other of them should move away. The decision,

---

[1] M. Black, *The Scrolls and Christian Origins*, pp. 59, 60.
[2] M. Black, op. cit., p. 61.
[3] M. Black, op. cit., p. 61.

however it was arrived at, apparently was that Jesus should remain in Judaea, while John moved north to Samaria. It is difficult to imagine a strict Jew like John ministering among orthodox Samaritans, but remembering the situation which we have just been surveying, we can understand how a Jewish sectarian leader like John would find many points of contact for his message among Samaritan sectarians. Although John was strict in many ways, he must also have had his more tolerant side, and in going to the Samaritans he doubtless had in mind the prophetic passages which hope for a reconciliation between north and south, between Israel and Judah. There is no evidence that John ever took his message to Gentiles; but he did make this advance over orthodox Judaism, that he was willing to include the schismatic Samaritans in his appeal for repentance by God's people.

While in Samaria, John may have modified his preaching and his general approach to suit his hearers' point of view, yet we can see how the Samaritans would be able to grasp two of the chief characteristics of John's ministry, his claim to the prophetic office, and his call to repentance.

John's claim to the prophetic office. Orthodox Samaritanism probably acknowledged Moses as the only prophet, while certain sects did acknowledge other prophets, but all Samaritans as we have seen, were agreed in the expectation of a future prophet. Anyone claiming to be the eschatological prophet would therefore command the interest and respect of the Samaritans. We have seen previously that John did claim to be the coming prophet. We also saw that although in Christian sources John is represented as the second Elijah, probably John himself did not adhere definitely either to the Elijah or the Moses form of the belief.[1] The Samaritans, of course, would interpret his ministry in terms of the Moses-like prophet, this being the form the belief took in Samaritanism. The fact that John was an ordinary man, who 'gave no miraculous sign' (John 10.41) would be no drawback, for the Samaritans did not expect the Taheb to be endowed with any supernatural

[1] See p. 129.

powers. The Samaritans 'expected only a man endowed with human qualities of a higher nature, but nothing divine'.[1]

John's call to repentance was the keynote of his ministry, and such a call to repentance was exactly what the Samaritans would expect from the Taheb. M. Gaster, in discussing the ancient traditions of the Samaritans, says that they 'envisaged the means of turning away the Fanuta (the Divine disfavour) to be repentance, cleansing from sin, outwardly and inwardly'.[2]

Thus we can see that John would find very definite points of contact in Samaria, and it is not surprising that 'people were constantly coming for baptism' (John 3.23).

Just as John prepared the way for the ministry of Jesus and for the early Christian Church in Judaea, so in his ministry in Samaria he was also preparing the way. The close link between Samaria and the earliest Christian Church is in fact another indication that John did exercise a ministry in Samaria. For although the Jewish-Christian Gospel of Matthew records Jesus at one point as saying, 'Do not enter any Samaritan town' (Matt. 10.5), elsewhere Jesus is shown as betraying a very sympathetic attitude towards them (cf. Luke 9.51ff; 10.31ff; 17.11ff). Jesus' visit to Samaria, as a consequence of which 'many came to believe in him', is related in John 4. The first Christians were to be witnesses 'in Jerusalem, and all over Judaea and Samaria, and away to the ends of the earth' (Acts 1.8). The very first Christian mission, led by Philip, took place in Samaria (Acts 8). The early Christians, therefore, so far from having no dealings with the Samaritans, came into very close contact with them. We can understand this much more easily if the ground had already been prepared to some extent, and if there were already certain points of contact.

In this connection, the account of Jesus' Samaritan ministry in John 4 is worth further study, in particular the passage, John 4.31-38, in which Jesus tells his disciples that 'others toiled and you have come in for the harvest of their toil'. Who were these 'others' who prepared the way for this ministry in

[1] M. Gaster, *Samaritan Eschatology*, p. 223.
[2] M. Gaster, op. cit., pp. 251, 252.

Samaria? Various suggestions have been made and Cullmann has argued very ingeniously that they were the Hellenists, led by Philip, the author of the Fourth Gospel reading back later events into the narrative.[1] In the light of what we have been discussing, however, a more straightforward explanation commends itself. Verses 36 and 37 seem to point opposite morals. Verse 36 obviously refers to the immediate situation and the quick results which Jesus' contact with the Samaritan woman has brought about. No sooner has he planted the word in her heart than a whole crowd of Samaritans come flocking to hear him (John 4.28-30), so that sowing and reaping can be said to take place together (v. 36). But that is only one side of the picture; it is also true that 'One sows, and another reaps' (v. 37). In this case, Jesus tells his disciples, 'others toiled' first. Since the word is plural, it cannot refer to Jesus himself. But this narrative follows almost immediately after the account of the overlapping ministries when John baptized at Aenon near Salim (John. 3.23). There is a very strong case, therefore, for regarding the 'others' who prepared the ground for Jesus' mission to Samaria as being John and his disciples.

Two further pieces of evidence linking John with Samaria deserve mention. One is the references in the Clementine literature which link John with Simon Magus and Dositheus.[2] The historical value of these accounts is extremely doubtful, yet they may just preserve an accurate memory of the fact that John did have a connection with Samaria.

The other evidence concerns the tradition that John was buried in Samaria. From the time of Theodoret (AD 393-457) there has been a firm belief that the disciples of John brought him to Samaria for burial. Two churches dedicated to John and purporting to be built on or near the site of his burial date from the fourth to fifth century AD and the seventh century AD,

---

[1] See O. Cullmann, *The Early Church*, SCM, 1956, IX, 'Samaria and the Origins of the Christian Mission', pp. 185-92; also O. Cullmann, 'The Significance of the Qumran Texts for Research into the Beginnings of Christianity', in K. Stendahl, *The Scrolls and the New Testament*, pp. 18-32. For the interpretation offered here cf. J. A. T. Robinson, 'The "Others" of John 4.38', *Twelve New Testament Studies*, SCM, 1962, pp. 61-66.

[2] On this see further pp. 192, 193.

respectively.[1] These traditions are not nearly early enough to be reliable, yet there seems little reason why anyone should invent Samaria as the place of burial, unless there was some early tradition to that effect. Parrot suggests that John's disciples might have buried him nearer Machaerus, where he was executed, 'but they chose to go further afield to Samaria, thus avoiding Herod's jurisdiction'.[2]

John was probably arrested soon after his return from Samaria and we can easily imagine either a group of his Samaritan disciples requesting his body for burial, or else, his Jewish disciples thinking it best that their master's mortal remains should rest somewhere outwith the domains of Antipas, and therefore handing them over to some of John's Samaritan followers.

[1] See A. Parrot, *Samaria, the Capital of the Kingdom of Israel*, SCM, 1958, pp. 122, 124.
[2] A. Parrot, op. cit., p. 126.

XI

Arrest and Martyrdom

JOHN met his death at the hands of Herod Antipas, one of the sons of Herod the Great, and the ruler of Galilee and Peraea. In so far as John's ministry was exercised in 'the wilderness of Judaea' he would be within the Roman province of Judaea, and the same would be true of the period spent in Samaria. John's ministry extended further than this, however, for John 1.28 tells of how he baptized in 'Bethany beyond Jordan'.[1] Wherever exactly this was, the fact that it was 'beyond Jordan' places it clearly in Peraea, the domain of Herod Antipas. When the period of overlapping ministries came to an end, Jesus and his disciples left Judaea and went north to Galilee (John 4.3). This would leave John free to return to the scene of his former ministry, and we may conjecture that he did so almost immediately. If our interpretation of John 4.38 as referring to John and his disciples is correct, then it would appear that John had already left Samaria when Jesus passed through on his way to Galilee. We do not know, however, just how accurate the narrative of the Fourth Gospel is here and it would be unwise to try and draw up a strict timetable of the exact movements of John and Jesus. We can take it, nevertheless, that John, after his Samaritan ministry, did return to Peraea; it was there that he was arrested, and it was there that he met his death.

John's arrest, imprisonment and death are narrated both in the Gospels and in Josephus.

[1] On the location of this see p. 90.

Mark's account is the fullest (Mark 6.17-29) and tells of how Herod Antipas imprisoned John because of his denunciation of Antipas' marriage to Herodias, the wife of his brother Philip. Antipas really respected John, according to the Marcan account, but Herodias plotted against him and with the help of her daughter, tricked Herod into executing John. Matthew gives a shorter summary of the Marcan story (Matt. 14.3-12) and Luke is content with only a brief mention (Luke 3.19, 20).

Alongside the Gospels must be laid the narrative of Josephus in *Antiquities*, XVIII, 5, 1 and 2. This tells of how Antipas married the daughter of Aretas, King of Arabia. When Antipas was on a visit to Rome, however, he lodged with a half-brother of his named Herod, with whose wife, Herodias, he fell in love. Herodias agreed to elope with Antipas on condition that he divorced his wife. His wife, however, got word of what was happening and, pretending to be ignorant, asked to be allowed to go to Machaerus. Antipas, suspecting nothing, granted this request, but his wife promptly fled and made her way to Arabia to her father. Aretas thereupon raised an army and made war on Antipas whom he soundly defeated.

Some of the Jews, Josephus goes on to tell us, thought that the defeat of Antipas was a well-deserved punishment sent from God because of what Antipas had done to John the Baptist. Here follows Josephus' account of John, which includes the statement that Antipas, fearing that John's great hold over the people might tempt him to raise a rebellion, took him prisoner, sent him to Machaerus, and there put him to death.

The accounts of the Gospels and of Josephus have been assailed as being inconsistent and contradictory. There are certain difficulties, it is true, but both accounts seem to be basically reliable, and to be complementary rather than contradictory.

The Gospel account cannot, of course, be taken entirely at its face value for it is obviously a story which has grown in the telling. To object to the promise of Antipas that he would give to the dancing girl 'up to half my kingdom' (Mark 6.23) is to misunderstand the nature of the story in which exaggeration certainly plays a part.[1] It has also been objected that 'a princess of the proud Herodian house' would not 'demean herself by dancing like a slave girl in the presence of a half-intoxicated crowd of men'.[2] By ordinary moral standards it certainly would be outrageous for a princess to perform an Oriental solo dance in this fashion, but when we remember the moral standards of the Herodian family, we can believe anything. Rawlinson sums up well by calling the Marcan story 'an account, written with a certain amount of literary freedom, of what was being darkly whispered in the bazaars or market places of Palestine at the time'.[3] It is possible, however, that in the early Christian community there were better sources of information than mere rumours. Luke 8.3 lists among the women who ministered to Jesus and his disciples, 'Joanna, the wife of Chuza a steward of Herod's'; as steward (*epitropos*) Chuza would be the manager of Herod's household and estates. Acts 13.1 mentions among the 'prophets and teachers' in the Church at Antioch one, Manaen a *suntrophos* of Herod the Tetrarch. *Suntrophos* means literally 'foster-brother', but may mean merely, 'a member of the court'; at any rate, a position of some influence and authority is certainly implied. Some account of John's death as seen from within the court of Herod might therefore have found its way into early Christian circles, via either Chuza or Manaen.[4]

The account of Josephus, taken by itself, presents only one minor, chronological difficulty. On the basis of Luke 3.1, the death of John must have taken place about AD 29-30. The

[1] It has also been held that the story was composed on the basis of Elijah's dealings with Ahab and Jezebel, John being the new Elijah; and also under the influence of the story of Esther's appearance before King Ahasuerus (Esth. 5.1f), who promised to grant any request of Esther 'even to the half of my kingdom'. This phrase had probably become proverbial, however, and the Old Testament parallels are not close enough to warrant the conclusion that the New Testament story is a pure fiction.

[2] A. E. J. Rawlinson, *The Gospel According to St Mark*, p. 82.

[3] A. E. J. Rawlinson, op. cit., p. 82.

[4] On Chuza, see A. Plummer, *St Luke*, *ICC*, p. 216; on Manaen, see H. Cowan, 'Manaen', *HDB*, III, pp. 228, 229, which mentions the possibility of a connection with Manaen the Essene, who won the favour of Herod the Great.

defeat of Antipas at the hands of Aretas occurred in AD 36. This indicates a longer lapse of time between the two events than is suggested by the narrative of Josephus. The punishment does not necessarily need to follow so closely upon the crime, however, and the death of John may well have made such an impression that it was easily brought forward as the explanation of events which took place five or six years later.

More serious difficulties arise when the two accounts are compared, for there are some apparent contradictions between them.

1. The Gospels say that Herodias was the wife of Antipas' brother Philip (Mark 6.17; Matt. 14.3), whereas according to Josephus, Herodias was married to a man called Herod, a half-brother of Antipas. It is possible to argue that the man had a double name, Herod Philip, and thus harmonize the two accounts. In fact there was a Herod Philip, a half-brother of Antipas, but he was someone quite distinct from Herodias' husband; he was tetrarch of Ituraea and Trachonitis and died in AD 34. He, moreover, married Salome, the daughter of Herodias. It seems therefore that the Marcan account has made a mistake and confused Herodias' husband with her son-in-law. Considering the fantastically complicated Herodian family tree, with its marriages lawful and unlawful, such confusion can be both understood and excused. That it is the Marcan account which is at fault is further confirmed by the fact that though Matthew (14.3) follows Mark, Luke (3.19) drops the name Philip, thus avoiding the historical error.[1]

2. A second apparent contradiction concerns the place of John's execution. Taken by itself, the Marcan story might be thought to have taken place at Tiberias. This is suggested by the fact that the banquet was attended by Herod's chief officials and commanders and the leading men of Galilee (Mark 6.21).[2] Josephus, on the other hand, definitely says that John was

---

[1] The reading of the AV 'his brother Philip's wife' is an inferior reading (ACKX and some versions) which harmonizes Luke with Mark and Matthew, and is clearly to be rejected.

[2] For this argument see C. H. Kraeling, *John the Baptist*, pp. 92, 201, 202.

imprisoned and executed at Machaerus, the castle by the Dead Sea.

Actually the indications of place in the Gospel story are very slight, and there is no real difficulty in accepting Josephus' version. Machaerus was a palace as well as a prison, and the court could well have been in residence there.

3. The most noteworthy divergence between the two accounts lies in the motive assigned to Antipas. According to the Gospels, John was imprisoned because of his denunciation of the marriage of Antipas and Herodias. This was a clear breach of Jewish law. It is true that under the law of Levirite marriage, where two brothers are living together and one dies, leaving no son, the surviving brother has the duty of taking the widow to wife; the eldest child of this union then succeeds to the name and inheritance of the deceased brother.[1] This law, however, had no relevance in this case, for Herodias' husband was still living. The marriage therefore violated the law of Lev. 20.21, 'If a man takes his brother's wife, it is impurity' (cf. Lev. 18.16). Thus John had no hesitation in declaring boldly, 'You have no right to your brother's wife'(Mark. 6.18).

The Gospel account gives the impression that the whole matter was a domestic affair and that John's death was due to the personal anger of Antipas, and especially of his wife, Herodias. Josephus, on the other hand, presents the incident wholly from a political point of view. We have here, however, to make allowance for the viewpoint of the different writers: Josephus was interested in political events; the Gospel writers were not.

Kraeling has shown very clearly how, for a person like Antipas, such a 'personal' matter was at the same time inevitably political. Antipas' first wife was the daughter of Aretas II, ruler of the Nabataean Kingdom. Modern exploration and discoveries have shown how this extensive kingdom, with its capital at Petra, was a power to be reckoned with. Control of caravan routes made it economically strong, and its desert warriors

[1] The law is found in Deut. 25.5-10. On Levirite marriage, see S. R. Driver, *Deuteronomy*, *ICC*, T. and T. Clark, 1902, pp. 280-5.

could give it an extremely effective fighting force. Antipas ruled Peraea, a narrow strip of territory east of the Jordan, which was very much open to Nabataean influence and infiltration. Antipas' marriage to Aretas' daughter can only be viewed as an attempt to consolidate and secure his hold east of Jordan.

Similarly, Antipas' treatment of his wife would also be viewed in a political light. When she heard of Antipas' intentions and fled to her father, he naturally viewed this not only as a personal insult, but as a breach of a political alliance. Possibly he saw it also as a good excuse for extending his kingdom, and so he fitted out his expedition against Antipas. He was just too successful, however, for his victory over the forces of Antipas prompted the intervention of a Roman army under Vitellius.[1]

Bearing in mind this background, it can be readily appreciated that when John came forward and denounced Antipas' marriage to Herodias, this was a move fraught with political consequences. John preached by the Jordan, some of the time on the east side, actually in Peraea. To condemn Antipas' split with the Nabataeans could easily be interpreted as subversive activity, an attempt to rouse the Jews of Peraea against their king. This, from the political side, was the reason for John's arrest.

It will be noted that Josephus nowhere states that John preached rebellion; it was as a precaution against this that he was arrested. Antipas 'feared that John's so extensive influence over the people might lead to an uprising (for the people seemed likely to do anything he might counsel). He thought it much better, under the circumstances, to get John out of the way in advance, before any insurrection might develop, than for himself to get into trouble and be sorry not to have acted, once an insurrection had begun.'[2]

When this is taken along with the Gospel account, we can see now how the two fit perfectly together. John's condemna-

---

[1] Josephus, *Antiquities*, XVIII, 5, 1 and 3.
[2] Josephus, op. cit., XVIII, 5, 2.

tion of the unlawful marriage, and Antipas' political fears were in fact different aspects of the same series of events. Nothing shows more clearly that John's Messianic preaching must have been completely *non*-political. If he had foretold the advent of an earthly leader and a warrior king, Antipas would have acted right away, and the attitude of Josephus to John would have been far less favourable. John denounced Antipas on moral grounds, however, and it was only because of the political consequences of this that Antipas was forced to arrest him as a potential revolutionary, even though John had no intention of being a revolutionary in this sense.

In regard to the main essentials of the story, therefore, the accounts of Josephus and of the Gospels complement rather than contradict each other. The arrest and death of John seem to have made a great impression at the time, and this impression is reflected by Josephus and the Gospels, from their own particular viewpoints.

The characters in the story are vividly portrayed for us, although Antipas appears in the Marcan account in a curiously favourable light. He arrested John, yet nevertheless 'he liked to listen to him', knowing that he was 'a good and holy man' (Mark 6.20). The impression Mark gives is that John was taken into a sort of 'protective custody', and the blame for his death is laid entirely on Herodias. This hardly squares with the picture Josephus gives us, and it is interesting to see how Matthew has altered the narrative, asserting that it was Antipas himself who wanted to put John to death from the very first, the only reason preventing him being his fear of the reaction of the general public (Matt. 14.5). This account is nearer to the view of Josephus, and is more likely to be correct.

The characterization of Herodias in the Gospels, on the other hand, is exactly in line with what we know about her. She was an ambitious and an unscrupulous schemer who egged on her husband unmercifully until she brought disaster upon both of them. Jealous of Agrippa's kingly rank, she prevailed upon the reluctant Antipas to go to Rome and seek the favour of the Emperor Caius. Agrippa informed the Emperor against them, however, and Antipas was shorn of his possessions and money, and banished, along with Herodias, to Lyons, in Gaul. Thus, we might add, Herodias was also punished for her part in the death of John.

Above all, this episode gives us a wonderful insight into the character of John himself. It shows us a true prophet, meeting the fate of a prophet with high courage and a firm faith in God. The story of his dealing with Antipas shows how John was prepared to condemn sin wherever it was found, and whatever the consequences. How far John understood the political implications of his action is not easy to say, but certainly he can have had no illusions about the danger in which he was placing himself by attacking Antipas.

The ruins of Machaerus remain to this day on the spur of a hill overlooking the eastern shore of the Dead Sea. Alexander Jannaeus was the first to build a fortress on the site, but Antipas inherited it from his father Herod the Great. Josephus tells us that

> when Herod came to the throne, he decided that no place would better repay attention and the strongest fortification, especially in view of the proximity of Arabia; for its situation was most opportune, commanding as it did a view of Arab territory. So he surrounded a large area with walls and towers, and founded a city there, from which an ascent led up to the ridge itself. Not content with that he built a wall round the very summit and erected towers at the corners, each ninety feet high. In the middle of this enclosure he built a palace, breathtaking in the size and beauty of the various rooms; and at carefully chosen spots he constructed a number of tanks to receive rain-water and maintain a constant supply. He might well have been competing with nature in the hope that the impregnability the place had received from her might be outdone by his own artificial defences. He further provided an ample store of weapons and engines, and managed to think of everything that could enable the occupants to snap their fingers at the longest siege.[1]

Modern explorers have surveyed the site,[2] although it still

---

[1] *The Jewish War*, VII, 6, 2. Translation by G. A. Williamson, in *The Jewish War*, Penguin Classics, 1959, p. 397.

[2] See H. R. Reynolds, *John the Baptist*, pp. 411, 412; H. V. Morton, *In the Steps of the Master*, pp. 282–91.

awaits a thorough and competent archaeological investigation. As well as the fortress, there is also a town on a nearby hill, with a causeway connecting the two. The dungeons of the fortress are still to be seen.

The view from the hill-top of Machaerus is an exceptionally fine one, and if John was allowed any freedom at all, he could see below him the blue waters of the Dead Sea; northwards, the river Jordan and the wilderness of Judaea, where he had lived and worked; and in the far distance, the hills of Samaria. On a clear day he could see almost to Jerusalem itself, and on the opposite shore of the Dead Sea he would certainly see the monastery of Qumran. The scene of a whole lifetime's activities would be spread out before his eyes.

The Gospels indicate that John was imprisoned for a period of time before being put to death, and that during this period he had a certain amount of freedom in so far as his disciples could visit him and relay messages. Josephus mentions no interval, but his account is not inconsistent with the Gospels; he simply tells of how, 'because of Herod's suspicion, John was sent as a prisoner to Machaerus, the fortress already mentioned, and there put to death'.[1]

We have already dealt with John's question to Jesus. What John's response was, when his disciples brought back Jesus' reply, we shall never know. Certainly he must have thought hard and long about the reports of the ministry of Jesus, reports which described a rather different kind of Coming One from the figure whom he had been led to proclaim. Did John end his life defeated and disillusioned, or aflame with new faith and hope? The question cannot be answered. We can only say that if he died as he had lived, then John must have faced his executioner bravely, knowing that he was now to be numbered among the prophets, saints and martyrs who had given their all in the service of God.

[1] *Antiquities*, XVIII, 5, 2.

XII

The Baptist Sect

WE have already noted how some of John's disciples transferred their loyalty to Jesus (John 1.35f), and it is very likely that after the death of John, many more would follow suit. At the time of John's death, however, the group of John's disciples was still in being, for they 'came and took his body away and laid it in a tomb' (Mark 6.29; Matt. 14.12). There is moreover a considerable body of evidence that the group of disciples of John was not wholly swallowed up in the growing Christian Church, but rather continued its separate existence for a considerable period of time. This evidence must now be considered.

1. *The evidence of Acts.* In Acts 18.24-28 we are introduced to Apollos, a Jew from Alexandria, who came to Ephesus, 'an eloquent man, powerful in his use of the scriptures. He had been instructed in the way of the Lord and was full of spiritual fervour; and in his discourses he taught accurately the facts about Jesus, though he knew only John's baptism.' Then in Acts 19.1-7, we hear of how, when Paul came to Ephesus, he found there about a dozen disciples, who had not received the Holy Spirit.[1] 'Then what baptism were you given?' he asked.

---

[1] On the meaning of Acts 19.1-7, see Chapter V, p. 73, note 1. G. C. Darton, arguing that Luke's method 'is always to convey the large momentous lesson by the small particular story about real people', holds that Acts 19.1-7 is presented as a typical incident from which we are to understand that 'in many of the towns which Paul visited, he found disciples of John, even as far away as Ephesus'. See *St John the Baptist and the Kingdom of Heaven*, pp. 39, 40.

'John's baptism', they answered. Paul then told them how the Coming One, foretold by John, was in fact Jesus; he baptized them, laid hands on them, and they received the Holy Spirit.

Although Apollos and these disciples are mentioned close together in the book of Acts, and although they are both located at Ephesus, they do not necessarily fall into the same category.[1] The dozen disciples of Acts 19.1-7 cannot possibly be regarded as Christians; they did not know about Jesus, or at any rate did not know that he was the Coming One, and they did not possess the Holy Spirit. Confession of Jesus as the Christ, and possession of the Holy Spirit were the two most important and absolutely essential distinguishing marks of the Christian from the earliest days. On the other hand, these people had been baptized into John's baptism, and therefore the inescapable conclusion is that they were members of the group of John's disciples.

In opposition to this, it is common to point out that the author of Luke-Acts calls them 'disciples' (mathētai). This term, it is argued, is confined solely to members of the Christian Church, and therefore the disciples at Ephesus must have been Christians.[2] But there is no doubt, whatever interpretation we accept, that in this passage we have a very special case, and it is dangerous to apply a general rule to an exceptional case. In any case, although the term 'disciple' can generally be assumed to be the equivalent of 'Christian believer' in the New Testament, the author of Luke-Acts himself uses it of the disciples of the Pharisees and of the disciples of John, during their master's lifetime (Luke 5.33; 7.18, 19). The determining factor in the interpretation of 'disciples' in Acts 19.1 must therefore be the context, and the rest of the passage. This indicates clearly that these people were not Christians at all, and that they can only be classed among the disciples of John.

[1] Cf. J. Thomas, Le Mouvement Baptiste, p. 96; M. Goguel, Jean-Baptiste, p. 100. On these passages see also, J. B. Lightfoot, Colossians and Philemon, p. 402.

[2] See e.g. J. L. Teicher, 'Has a Johannine sect ever existed?', JJS, 4 (1953), pp. 143f. It has to be admitted that many scholars have too easily assumed the existence of the baptist sect; for a word of caution see J. A. T. Robinson, NTS, 4 (1958), p. 279, n. 2.

The case of Apollos is rather different. Unlike the dozen disciples, he 'taught accurately the facts about Jesus' (Acts 18.25).[1] Whereas Paul re-baptized the disciples, there is no word of Apollos being re-baptized; he merely receives some additional teaching. The disciples did not receive the Spirit until after their Christian baptism, whereas Apollos was already 'fervent in the spirit' before Priscilla and Aquila took him in hand.[2] We cannot therefore be certain into which category Apollos is to be assigned; he may well represent a very primitive type of Christianity, before baptism was re-introduced.[3] On the whole, it is best not to regard him as a 'disciple of John', in the same class as the dozen disciples.

2. *The evidence of the Lucan infancy narrative.* We have already seen how behind the narrative of Luke 1, there lay an early source, probably written in Hebrew, and which not only displayed a detailed interest in the birth and infancy of John, but which also thought of him much more highly than any Christian would. This is further borne out by the highly distinctive character of the sections which deal with John; we noted especially (in Chapter IV) the use of *kurios* to mean God and not Christ, the exalted conception of John not as precursor of the Messiah but as forerunner of God himself, and also the priestly emphasis in the narrative. It was also shown how the *Magnificat*, and the whole of the *Benedictus* originally belonged to the narrative of John, which thus regards him very highly indeed. The only conclusion which can be drawn from this evidence is that the account was produced, not in the Christian

[1] The phrase is *ta peri tou Iēsou*. Comparison with Mark 5.27 and Luke 24.19 suggests that this phrase means the facts of the earthly ministry of Jesus, and not Christian belief or doctrine.

[2] Acts 18.25, 26. It is open to question, of course, whether *zeōn tō pneumati* means the Holy Spirit in the full Christian sense.

[3] There is no evidence that Jesus or his disciples baptized, from the time of the Galilean ministry onwards. The absence of any command by Jesus to baptize, apart from Matt. 28.19 is most striking. The authenticity of Matt. 28.19 has often been questioned; it is in any case a command of the risen Christ, given only some time after his death and resurrection. The early chapters of Acts do speak of baptism from the day of Pentecost onwards, but is Luke here not reading back the practice of a later day? There certainly is a strong probability that for a period, albeit a short one, the earliest Christians did not practise a baptism of their own.

Church, but among a group which continued to revere John. The narrative may not have very great historical value as far as the infancy of John is concerned, but it is of considerable value as a testimony to the existence of a continuing baptist sect in which John was given an exalted, almost Messianic position, and in which there was a decidedly priestly emphasis. Indeed, we may agree with Kraeling when he says that the main value of the narrative derives from the fact that it is 'a record of the piety of the Baptist circles that created it'.[1]

3. *The evidence of the Fourth Gospel.* W. Baldensperger was by no means the first to show how the Fourth Gospel contains a powerful polemic against John and his followers, but he set out the idea and carried it to its extreme limits.[2] Pointing to Acts 18 and 19, he suggested the existence of the baptist sect at Ephesus, the place of origin of the Fourth Gospel. Not only the first chapters, but the whole Gospel, so Baldensperger believed, has as its main aim, anti-Johannine polemic.

It certainly is true that the Fourth Gospel seizes upon every opportunity to emphasize the inferiority of John to Jesus.[3] E. F. Scott sums up the Fourth Gospel's references to the Baptist, 'Indeed it is not too much to say that John is introduced into the narrative for no other purpose than to bring out this fact of his inferiority'.[4] Baldensperger carries his argument much too far; for him the point of the whole Gospel is to show that Jesus is the Christ, and not John, as the baptist sect held. Setting aside such an extreme position, the evidence is nevertheless strong enough to permit us to say that one of the aims of the Evangelist was to counter excessive claims which were being made for John the Baptist. Such claims could only have been put forward by a continuing sect of John's disciples.

4. *The evidence of the Clementines.* Further valuable evidence is preserved for us in the Clementine *Recognitions* and *Homilies*, both of which have a fictitious narrative in which are embedded

[1] C. H. Kraeling, *John the Baptist*, pp. 20f.
[2] In his book, *Der Prolog des vierten Evangeliums*, J. C. B. Mohr, 1898.
[3] See especially, John 1.6-8, 15, 19ff; 3.30; 10.41.
[4] E. F. Scott, *The Fourth Gospel: Its Purpose and Theology*, T. and T. Clark, 1906, p. 78.

considerable doctrinal sections represented as discussions between Clement and Peter. Modern studies have shown that
'most probably both are recensions of a common source, produced in Syria in the early third century AD, itself being a
compilation of earlier works. They represent a type of Jewish
Christianity though there are differences and inconsistencies
in doctrine'.[1]

Direct references to the 'disciples of John' are found in the
Recognitions. In *Recognitions* 1.53, Peter relates how he went up
to the Temple, after the death of Christ, 'to bear witness concerning him, and at the same time to charge the Jews with
many foolish things which they were doing. For the people
was now divided into many parties, ever since the days of John
the Baptist.' Chapter 54 lists these various sects, mentioning
the Sadducees, the Samaritans, and the scribes and Pharisees,
and continues:

> Yea, some even of the disciples of John, who seemed to be great
> ones, have separated themselves from the people, and proclaimed
> their own master as the Christ.

Peter and the other apostles then proceed to answer the arguments of the various parties in a kind of public disputation on
the steps of the Temple (*Rec.* 1.55f), in the course of which,

> One of the disciples of John asserted that John was the Christ,
> and not Jesus, inasmuch as Jesus himself declared that John was
> greater than all men and all prophets. 'If then,' said he, 'he be
> greater than all prophets, he must be held to be greater than
> Moses, and than Jesus himself. But if he be the greatest of all, then
> he must be the Christ.' To this Simon the Canaanite answering,
> asserted that John was indeed greater than all the prophets, and
> all who are born of women, yet that he is not greater than the
> Son of Man. Accordingly Jesus is also the Christ, whereas John
> is only a prophet: and there is as much difference between him

---

[1] M. R. P. McGuire, 'Clementine Literature', *Encyclopaedia Britannica*,
London, 1959, 5, pp. 797-9. See further, G. Uhlhorn, 'Clementina', *The New
Schaff-Herzog Religious Encyclopedia*, New York, 1909, 3, pp. 141-3; E. J.
Goodspeed, *A History of Early Christian Literature*, Chicago, 1942, pp. 127, 128.
The quotations from the *Homilies* are taken from the *Ante-Nicene Christian
Library*, Vol. XVII, T. and T. Clark, 1870, and those from the *Recognitions*
from the *Ante-Nicene Christian Library*, Vol. III, T. and T. Clark, 1867.

and Jesus, as between the forerunner and Him whose forerunner he is; or as between Him who gives the law, and him who keeps the law. (*Rec.* 1.60)

Recognitions 1.63 sums up the different arguments, reminding the reader how the apostles taught 'the disciples of John, that they should not suffer John to be a stumbling block to them'.

While the narrative framework is completely fictitious, there is nevertheless preserved for us here the fact that a sect did exist, which exalted John to the rank of the Messiah. The *Recognitions* give a detailed reply to arguments which were evidently being put forward, claiming that John was greater than Jesus.

The *Clementines* link John with Simon Magus and Dositheus. Relating the story of Simon, *Homilies* 2.23, 24 says,

> There was one John, a hemerobaptist, who was also, according to the method of combination, the forerunner of our Lord Jesus; and as the Lord had twelve apostles, bearing the number of the twelve months of the sun, so also he (John) had thirty chief men, fulfilling the monthly reckoning of the moon. . . . Of these thirty, the first and the most esteemed by John was Simon; and the reason of his not being chief after the death of John was as follows: He being absent in Egypt for the practice of magic, and John being killed, Dositheus desiring the leadership, falsely gave out that Simon was dead, and succeeded to the seat.

A similar account appears in the *Recognitions* (2.8):

> For after that John the Baptist was killed . . . when Dositheus had broached his heresy, with thirty other chief disciples, and one woman, who was called Luna . . . this Simon, ambitious of evil glory, as we have said, goes to Dositheus, and pretending friendship, entreats him that if any one of those thirty should die, he should straightway substitute him in the room of the dead. . . .

These apparently parallel passages have in fact, significant differences.[1] The reference to John in the *Recognitions* is a purely chronological one, and he is not linked at all with the heretical sect which is mentioned. The *Homilies*, on the other hand,

---

[1] For a discussion of these passages, see J. Thomas, *Le Mouvement Baptiste*, pp. 127-9.

make two startling assertions—that John was a hemerobaptist, and that he was the founder of a sect of thirty disciples, which included Simon Magus and Dositheus. The *Recognitions* only mention John in the passing, whereas the *Homilies* show a highly hostile attitude towards him. The link with Simon and Dositheus was in fact one of the biggest insults which could be directed against John; Simon, to early Christian writers, was 'the source and spring of all later heresy',[1] and to present him as the disciple and successor of John is to make John the arch-heretic. Probably the naming of John as a hemerobaptist is meant to be an insult too. Evidently then, the *Homilies* were in bitter opposition to John, regarding him as the father of all heresy; whereas the *Recognitions* have omitted the assertion that John was a hemerobaptist, and so altered the rest of the narrative as to remove the connection between John and the heretics, Simon and Dositheus. Comparison of the two accounts suggests that the *Recognitions* are a later form and are an orthodox revision much more favourable to John.

It is worth noting that the passage from *Recognitions* 1.54 cited above may also contain an echo of the argument that John and his disciples were linked with the heretic Simon. The account says that 'some even of the disciples of John, who seemed to be great ones, have separated themselves from the people . . .'. The phrase, 'who seemed to be great ones' recalls Acts 8.9, 10, where Simon is introduced as 'claiming to be someone great', and where the people said of him, 'This man is that power of God which is called "The Great Power" .'

No historical value can be attached to the claim that John was associated with Simon; the *Clementines* contain the only assertion to this effect, an assertion obviously inspired by malice. Yet, as we have already suggested, there may be a grain of truth in the story if John did sojourn for a period in Samaria.

In addition to these references, there is further, indirect evidence in the *Clementines* of a continuing sect. This is to be found in the theory of 'pairs' (*suzugiai*) which is set forth in

[1] A. C. Headlam, 'Simon Magus', *HDB*, IV, pp. 520-7; quotation from p. 520.

the *Homilies*. God, 'teaching men with respect to the truth of existing things, being himself one, has distinguished all principles into pairs and opposites . . .' (*Hom.* 2.15). Of these pairs, the first part is always inferior to the second; God placing before man 'small things first, and great ones afterwards, such as the world and eternity' (*Hom.* 2.15). Examples of such pairs are given, such as Cain and Abel, Esau and Jacob, and *Homilies* 2.17 then continues, 'In like manner, the combination with respect to Elias, which behoved to have come, has been willingly put off to another time, having determined to enjoy it conveniently hereafter. Wherefore, also, he who was among the sons of men came second.' The text here is corrupt, but the general meaning is clear. 'Elias' is John the Baptist, 'he who was among those born of woman' (cf. Luke 7.28; Matt. 11.11). He is paired with 'he who was among the sons of men', that is, Jesus. By the law of pairs, Jesus is therefore superior to John.

A similar reference is to be found in *Homilies* 3.22:

> But a companion was created along with him (i.e. with man), a female nature, much differing from him, as quality from substance, as the moon from the sun, as fire from light. She, as a female ruling the present world as her like, was entrusted to be the first prophetess, announcing prophecy with all those born of woman. But the other, as the son of man, being a male, prophesies better things to the world to come as a male.

Here again, John 'born of woman', is contrasted with Jesus, 'the son of man', who is superior and who 'prophesies better things'.[1]

The *Recognitions* also deal with the theory of pairs (*Rec.* 3.59, 61), but in their list all mention of John has been dropped, and it is 'the tempter' who is paired with the 'son of man'. Undoubtedly the passage has again been revised by a more orthodox editor, who wished to delete the ideas which were so unfavourable to John.[2]

---

[1] See J. Thomas, *Le Mouvement Baptiste*, pp. 126, 127. For male and female pairs, cf. *Homilies* 2.15.

[2] Cf. J. Thomas, op. cit., pp. 125, 126.

Though Gnostic in origin, and though applied to Peter and Simon Magus, this theory of pairs is principally directed against the view that John must be superior to Jesus because he preceded him in point of time. The length to which the writer goes to work out such an elaborate theory shows how concerned he is to combat excessive claims being made for John. Some scholars, such as Goguel who quotes only *Recognitions* 1.60, suggest that the *Clementines* may only reflect an *argumentum ad hominem*, put forward by persons who had no connection with a baptist group.[1] The above survey shows, however, what an inadequate explanation this is. Not only do the *Clementines* definitely state that 'some of the disciples of John ... separated themselves from the people, and proclaimed their own master as the Christ', but they display bitter opposition to John, depicting him as the father of all heresies and as a false prophet, in the succession of Eve, Cain, Ishmael, Esau, Aaron and Anti-Christ. Such feeling against John can only have been generated by conflict with the continuing baptist sect.

5. *The evidence of Ephraem.* The fourth century Syrian father Ephraem, giving a list of the various Jewish heresies, mentions 'the disciples of John', who glorify him and claim that he is greater than Christ, as he himself testified when he said that among those born of woman there is none greater than John. Ephraem may have drawn on the same source as the *Clementines*, in which case his reference cannot be reckoned as an independent piece of evidence; in any case it does not add anything to the evidence of the *Clementines*.[2]

Though we could wish for fuller information concerning John's disciples, the evidence we have surveyed gives convincing proof of their continued existence, and allows us to reconstruct at least a partial picture of the sect.

One of the sect's main features was its claim that John was the Christ. The Lucan infancy narrative, as we have seen, has almost reached this position. Behind the insistence of the

---

[1] M. Goguel, *Jean-Baptiste*, p. 107.

[2] There are certain similarities between this passage in Ephraem and the passage in *Recognitions* 1.54f. See J. Thomas, *Le Mouvement Baptiste*, pp. 116-18.

Fourth Gospel that John was not the Light, and not the Messiah, very probably lies a desire to counter a group who were making just such claims. The *Clementines* state specifically that some of the disciples of John 'proclaimed their own master as the Christ'.

Another clearly recognizable feature of the Johannine sect is their claim that John must be greater than Jesus since he preceded him in point of time. As Cullmann has reminded us,[1] the chronological argument was of great weight in antiquity; Jewish apologists, for example, were concerned to show that Moses preceded the Greek philosophers in point of time. John certainly preceded Jesus, and spoke of him as 'he that comes after me'. Here then was a strong argument for the disciples of John.

The history of this dispute can be traced through several stages. Cullmann thinks traces of it can be found even in the Synoptics. Mal. 3.1 and Isa. 40.3 are quoted in Mark 1.2, 3 to show that it was the divine intention that John should precede Christ; Matt. 11.11b was 'preserved to serve as a reply to the chronological argument utilized by champions of the baptist sect'; Matt. 3.11 stresses that 'the one who comes after me is mightier than I'.[2] Whatever may be thought of this, there is no room for doubt when we turn to the Fourth Gospel. It accepts the validity of the argument that precedence in time implies superiority, but counters the baptist sect with the doctrine of Christ's pre-existence, so that John says 'He comes after me, but takes rank before me, for before I was born, he already was' (John 1.15, 30).

We can now see in clearer perspective the fantastic lengths to which the source underlying the *Clementines* went in order to combat the disciples of John. They either neglected or rejected the Fourth Gospel's approach, and instead set about to refute the whole accepted idea that priority in time implies superiority. Hence the elaborate theory, with proofs from the Old Testa-

---

[1] On this section see O. Cullmann, 'Ὁ ὀπίσω μου ἐρχόμενος', *The Early Church*, 177–82.

[2] O. Cullmann, op. cit., p. 180.

ment, that in each pair it is the evil principle which comes first
and the good second.

The baptist sect apparently found this chronological argument a most powerful one, and used it with effect in disputes
with the Church.

Another feature of the sect was their continuance of the rite
of baptism. The disciples of John at Ephesus were baptized
with 'John's baptism' (Acts 19.3) and we may assume that the
rite continued to be a distinguishing feature of the sect. The
designation of John as a 'Hemerobaptist' by the *Clementine
Homilies* is, as we have seen, quite unreliable, and is no proof
that a repeated baptism was practised by the sect. Presumably
it was a once-for-all baptism which was continued, and probably as time went on the idea of baptism as the token of
initiation into a sect would become more prominent, while the
idea of baptism as a preparation for the imminent judgement
would fade a little, due to the obvious delay in the arrival of
the last day.

The priestly character of the Lucan infancy narrative has
been noted, and although this feature does not appear in any
of the other sources, it may well have been typical of the
continuing sect. The priesthood was certainly important in
other sects of the baptist movement.[1] Since John himself was
of priestly descent, we can well imagine that priests were
specially honoured by his disciples. The infancy narrative suggests that the sect looked back to a time when the Temple
worship was something to be honoured, and they may well,
like the Qumran sect, have looked forward to a time when the
true priesthood would be restored.

Apart from these features, we can only assume that the life
and doctrine of the sect were essentially Jewish. If any other
features were introduced, for example of a Gnostic character,
they did not come from John. It may well be, as some have

[1] For the Essenes, cf. Josephus, *Antiquities*, XVIII, 1, 5, and *The Jewish War*,
II, 8, 5. The Dead Sea Scrolls show us just what an exalted position the priests
had in the Qumran sect; as M. Burrows says, 'the ultimate power, both legis-
lative and judicial, seems to have been reserved to the priests' (*More Light on
the Dead Sea Scrolls*, p. 358).

claimed, that the sect was drawn into the syncretistic process, but there is really no definite evidence of this.[1]

The origins of the sect are largely obscure. To those of John's disciples who did not become Christians, but continued a separate existence, the first and greatest problem must have been posed by the death of John itself. Did this not invalidate his message? The first Christians faced a problem which was superficially similar, but which was in fact made radically different by the resurrection appearances of Christ. John did not rise from the dead, and his followers had to seek a different type of explanation.

When we remember that John was thought of, and also thought of himself as the eschatological prophet, the probability is that his disciples would think in terms of a martyr prophet. The Old Testament prophets constantly faced opposition, persecution and even death. In the inter-testamental literature the idea of martyrdom becomes especially prominent, and the Maccabaean martyrs were particularly revered.[2] We know that lists of martyrs were kept,[3] and Jesus seems to be quoting from a lost wisdom martyrology in Luke 11.49. There is evidence that there existed in New Testament times a cult of the martyred prophets; Jesus refers to those who 'build up the tombs of the prophets and embellish the monuments of the saints' (Matt. 23.29; Luke 11.47).

Thus, even allowing for their belief that John was *the* pro-

---

[1] B. W. Bacon, 'New and Old in Jesus' Relation to John', *JBL*, 48 (1929), pp. 40-81, seems to think that various sects, such as the Dositheans, the followers of Simon Magus, the Masbothaeans, Sabaeans and Hemerobaptists can all be traced back to John the Baptist via Simon and Dositheus. Apart, however, from the doubtful references in the *Clementines*, the only evidence he can find to support his contention is that such sects continued the rite of John's baptism. John may have been part of the baptist movement, but it is quite wrong to make him its originator; baptist sects, as we have seen, existed long before John's time, and quite independently of him. It is equally wrong to accept uncritically the assertions that Simon Magus and Dositheus were disciples of John, and that they were the originators of all Gnostic heresy.

[2] On this subject see especially the many interesting references collected by E. Stauffer in *New Testament Theology*, pp. 331-4, Appendix 1, 'The Principal Elements of the Old Biblical Theology of Martyrdom'; see also Chapter 21, 'The Passion of Christ's Forerunners', pp. 98-100.

[3] Cf. IV Macc. 16.20-22; 18.11f.

phet, the last and greatest of the prophets, John's disciples could nevertheless have seen that he stood in a noble succession and that by his death he merely suffered the traditional fate of the prophet. Undoubtedly God would speedily act and avenge his death.

In this connection, we note Mark 9.13 where Jesus, in an obvious reference to John, says, 'However, I tell you, Elijah has already come and they have worked their will upon him, as the scriptures say of him'. This last phrase, 'as the scriptures say of him' seems to refer to some writing which foretold a martyr's death for the returning Elijah. This may have been an uncanonical book, part of an Elijah literature traces of which are known to us,[1] and if this is the case such a book would be of cardinal importance to the disciples of John and would assure them that John's death did not invalidate his claim to be the eschatological prophet, but rather supported it.

Of special interest here is the early Christian *Ascension of Isaiah* which incorporates a non-Christian, Jewish *Martyrdom of Isaiah*, the original of which must have been written in Hebrew.[2] This Jewish *Martyrdom* pictures the apostasy of Israel under Manasseh; this results in a withdrawal to the wilderness by Isaiah and many of the faithful prophets, where they live an ascetic life clothed in garments of hair. Isaiah, however, is accused by the false prophet Belchira, is seized and then martyred by being sawn asunder. The *Martyrdom* was known by Justin Martyr, and almost certainly also by the author of Hebrews (11.37), and most probably dates from the first half of the first century AD. It is therefore an important witness to the concept of the martyr prophet. It may even be more than this. With what group did such a work originate? One possible answer is the Qumran community to whom the pattern of

[1] See E. Stauffer, *New Testament Theology*, p. 98, and Note 267. Some commentators hold that Jesus is here referring to an Old Testament text; but no text fits this reference. Another way out of the difficulty is to rearrange the text of Mark 9.11-13; cf. A. W. F. Blunt, *The Gospel According to St Mark*, The Clarendon Bible, 1939, p. 208; A. E. J. Rawlinson, *St Mark*, p. 121.

[2] See R. H. Charles, *The Ascension of Isaiah*, A. and C. Black, 1900; R. H. Charles, *Apocrypha and Pseudepigrapha*, II, pp. 155-62; J. Armitage Robinson, 'Ascension of Isaiah', *HDB*, II, pp. 499-501.

apostasy—withdrawal to the wilderness—martyrdom of a prophetic leader would be familiar. On the other hand, it might even be that the *Martyrdom of Isaiah* originated with the continuing sect of John's followers themselves, to whom Isaiah, sawn asunder by the wicked king, would be the prototype of John, beheaded by Herod. In the *Martyrdom*, Isaiah preaches against Judah and Jerusalem, calling them Sodom and Gomorrah, and this would be very much in keeping with the fiery preacher of repentance who prepared the way in the wilderness. If the baptist sect did produce this work, it could easily have passed into the Christian Church where it would receive the later Christian additions. This must remain an interesting hypothesis, incapable of proof, but at any rate it does help us to see how a martyred prophet could be held in great honour.

The next stage or stages in the development of the sect would see an ever-increasing regard for their martyred founder. The Lucan infancy narrative would seem to represent an intermediate stage; John is not yet regarded as the Messiah, but he is well on the way to it. The particular group of disciples who produced the infancy narrative was located in all probability in Judaea. Though it must have been small, yet their thoughts and beliefs as reflected in the narrative give us glimpses of a sincere, pious and vital group.[1]

When we recall the part played in John's ministry by his sojourn in Samaria, we can perhaps detect one influence which would hasten the acknowledgement of John as the Messiah. We saw that Samaritan eschatology knew only one 'Messianic' figure, the Moses-like prophet. While John was preaching to Jews his prophetic ministry would undoubtedly be interpreted in terms of the forerunner of the Coming One. When he moved to Samaria he would doubtless stress the subordinate status which he believed himself to hold. But after his death, possibilities of misunderstanding would arise, especially among his Samaritan followers. John had been a prophet; was he not

---

[1] MacNeill suggests that the narrative was the work of a group rather than of an individual; he calls it 'the precipitate of the life and feeling of a probably rather isolated religious community'. See 'The Sitz im Leben of Luke 1.5-2.20', *JBL*, 65 (1946), p. 126.

therefore the Taheb of Samaritan expectation? To the Samaritans, the Taheb was no mere forerunner; he was *the* eschatological figure. It is easy to see how, in this situation, John could be elevated into the position of a Messiah.

It appears, however, that this development was a gradual one for, to begin with, the baptist sect seems to have maintained reasonably friendly relations with the early Christian movement; it was only at a later stage that real opposition developed. We have already seen that the separation of John and Jesus, during the period of their overlapping ministries, was a friendly one. When John was put to death, his disciples went and told Jesus. John was held in high regard by Jesus and by the first Christians. The Q source reflects this early period of friendship, devoting much space to John, and portraying him in a favourable light. The combining of the infancy narratives of John and Jesus, however exactly this took place, also presupposes some kind of friendly contact between the two groups, in spite of the differences that were developing. This phase probably lasted until about AD 50-60 (taking this as a likely date for the compilation of Q), but it can hardly have lasted much longer.[1] The differences would become too marked, and the groups would diverge from each other, each making stronger and more exclusive claims for John and Jesus respectively. In the Synoptics, the portrait of John is not so favourable as that of Q; by the time we come to the Fourth Gospel there is clearly a background of enmity with the baptist sect and a need to combat the claims it made for John.

As far as geographical extent is concerned, the sect of John's followers was not confined to Judaea. Acts and the Fourth Gospel show how it had spread to Asia Minor and was active in Ephesus, while the *Clementines* attest its presence in Syria.

As regards time, the New Testament testifies to the existence

[1] Cf. H. L. MacNeill, op. cit., pp. 123, 130, who thinks that the narratives represent 'the earliest, very primitive and very imperfect, linking or blending of what later were again regarded as two quite distinct and separate movements'; they were 'the product of a community somewhere in Judaea, outside Jerusalem, in the period between AD 50 and 60, probably not long before AD 60.'

of the sect in the first century AD: the *Clementines* to its existence in the second and probably also the third century AD.

It is evident, however that the disciples of John were at their strongest in the mid-first century AD, but thereafter declined rapidly. It is sometimes asked why, if there was a continuing sect, it is not mentioned by more early Christian writers. The answer may be partly that it does not appear in the lists of Christian heresies, because it was not considered Christian at all.[1] But basically the answer is that by the second century it was too small and unimportant to deserve attention. The *Clementines* do not come from the mainstream of Christian tradition, and probably by the second century the disciples of John were to be found only in some Syrian backwater.

It has been held by scholars that the disciples of John did not fade out altogether, but have in fact survived to the present day in the shape of the Mandaeans. We have, however, already examined the evidence,[2] and concluded that this is not the case. The Mandaean literature contains no reliable early traditions concerning the life or teaching of John, and cannot be regarded as having originated in the continuing sect of John's disciples.

[1] See J. Thomas, *Le Mouvement Baptiste*, p. 137.
[2] See pp. 23-31.

XIII

What Manner of Man?

W<small>E</small> stressed at the outset that the picture we gain of John the Baptist depends upon our sources and upon the use we make of them. Stauffer comments very truly that 'the portrait of John the Baptist has undergone a good deal of change in the course of time. Of our oldest sources, the Gospels paint an apocalyptic figure, the Greek Josephus a moralist, the Slavonic Josephus a political, Byzantine art an ascetic, and Mandaean speculation a mythological figure.'[1]

We have seen, however, that the only sources having any claim to historical authenticity are Josephus, whose evidence amounts to one paragraph in the *Antiquities*, and the New Testament, which is thus our chief source of information. Neither of these sources are first hand accounts. They were not committed to writing until some considerable time after the events occurred, and they undoubtedly reveal the interests and the prejudices of their authors.

The larger part of the reliable source material consists of sayings of John, and we are also given a few essential details of his life. The narratives of his birth and infancy are legendary to a great extent, and certainly cannot be relied upon in detail. The genuine source material for the life of John is thus very limited and meagre. We could wish for far greater detail, and this has doubtless been the motive for the compilation of the

[1] E. Stauffer, *New Testament Theology*, p. 21.

different apocryphal accounts which at various dates have sought to expand and supplement the New Testament record.

We can be certain, then, only of a rather sketchy outline of the life of John. He was born of priestly descent, his parents being Zechariah and Elizabeth, in a town of the Judaean hill country, some time before the birth of Jesus. He appeared as a preacher and an ascetic, in the wilderness of Judaea, attracting large crowds of hearers, many of whom submitted to his baptism. A small group of men attached themselves to John as his disciples, aiding him in his ministry. Among these was Jesus, who at first allied himself to John, but who then embarked on an independent ministry. During this period of overlap, John went north into Samaria and ministered there. When Jesus left Judaea, John returned south and entered Peraea where he was arrested by Herod Antipas. After a period of imprisonment at Machaerus, John was put to death.

By reason of the meagreness of our sources, it is an impossible task for us to seek to understand the inner workings of John's mind and heart. What manner of man was John? Much as modern writers would like to answer that question by a detailed analysis of his personality and a romantic reconstruction of his life and character, our sources do not permit this. If we could accept the records of Josephus and of the New Testament as being literally true in their entirety there might be some basis for such an investigation, but the historical unreliability of much of the material, especially the infancy narratives, compels us to draw back from such a task.

The attempt has been made in at least one book, *John the Baptist: A Modern Interpretation*, to 'interpret John's character from the point of view of twentieth-century psychology, and to understand him as a struggling human being'.[1] The author, Margaret Goldsmith, true to her self-imposed task, first analyses John's parents and finds them to have been 'repressed puritans'; 'there was no laughter in their home, and neither of them was

---

[1] Margaret Goldsmith, *John the Baptist: A Modern Interpretation*, Arthur Baker, Ltd., 1935. The quotations in these two paragraphs are taken from this book.

gifted with a sense of humour'. Because of their childlessness, they 'were never free from a feeling of guilt'. The experience of Zechariah in the Temple lends itself well to a psychological analysis; he goes to fulfil his duties 'in a state of abnormal excitement', and the appearance of the angel is a hallucination which lays bare his subconscious mind. His temporary dumbness is a proof that his hallucination was a severe nervous shock. Returning home, Zechariah is now vigorous and full of purpose, for 'his renewed psychological assurance had given him a fresh vitality'. His new mood is communicated to Elizabeth, and when the fear of barrenness thus leaves her, she conceives.

Because of the strange events at the time of his birth, John was from the start 'set apart from his contemporaries', and pointed out as someone special. He was not allowed by his parents to play with other children, or to go to school, since his life was to be wholly dedicated to God. Goldsmith believes that Zechariah brought up John with the idea that 'he was to carry out the ultimate salvation of his people'. The result was that 'his childhood was repressed and unnatural'. So the various aspects of John's character and of his message are given a psychological explanation. His parents were 'obsessed by their faith and by the oppression of their people. They knew a great deal about blind obedience and about retribution, but tolerance and human kindness had little place in their harsh religion.' Because of this, John's conception of God was one of a stern and unmerciful tyrant. Similarly, John's parents imposed on him the Nazirite vow, forbidding him ever to cut his hair or to drink wine; and John grew up in terror of breaking the rules which governed his life, and of offending God. His parents having died when he was in his teens, John withdrew into the wilderness. Desperately afraid of the temptation to sexual sin, John drove himself to a fanatical asceticism.

Goldsmith's analysis is much more extensive, but enough has been said to indicate the main lines of her thought. Her viewpoint is open to various objections such as a rather uncritical use of apocryphal sources, and an overdrawn contrast between a stern Jewish Jehovah and a Christian God of love, but the principal criticism is that the author accepts every detail of the New Testament record as being literally true. Unfortunately, a psychologist does require a certain amount of reliable data to attempt a convincing analysis, and is interested in particular in details of parents, childhood and upbringing. It is just here, however, that our sources are at their weakest, and we just do not possess reliable details of John's upbringing and of his personal life which could make this type of investigation possible. Except in a very general way, no psychological reconstruction can be made, certainly not on the scale attempted by Goldsmith, interesting though her analysis may be.

Nevertheless, while our source material does set limits to our study, particularly of John's inner consciousness, our understanding of John can be broadened by setting what information we have against the background in which John lived and worked. We have seen how a knowledge of the historical and eschatological associations of the area in which John ministered can add considerably to our appreciation of his work.

Noting how John cannot be classed along with either Sadducees, Pharisees or Zealots, we suggested at the outset of our study that John's true background appears to have been 'the baptist movement', consisting of the various non-conformist, sectarian groups which appeared on the fringe of Judaism, concentrated especially in the Jordan valley, from before the first century BC and which continued into the first centuries of our era. Our survey of John's message and ministry have tended to confirm this tentative conclusion that in so far as he can be classified in terms of first century Judaism, and in so far as he was the product of the background from which he emerged, that background was the baptist, sectarian movement.

In the past it has frequently been suggested that John was an Essene, or at least had some connection with the Essenes.[1] So

---

[1] Goguel dismisses this theory on the grounds that John's baptism was not repeated as was that of the Essenes; nothing is said of the cult of angels in connection with John; John's dress is quite unlike that of the white robes of the Essenes; John's ideas of the imminent approach of the Messiah have no parallels in Essene thought. See *Jean-Baptiste*, p. 285.

long as the only accounts available were those of Josephus, Philo and Pliny, no hard and fast conclusions could be reached on this question. The discovery of the Dead Sea Scrolls, however, has considerably altered the picture, and it is significant that the closest parallels to John's thought which we have noted from within the baptist movement come from the Dead Sea Scrolls, such as punishment by the river of fire, eschatological baptism conditional on repentance, the expectation of the Moses-like prophet, and so on.

In addition to the close analogies and similarities to the baptist movement we have also, however, frequently pointed to the fact that John was an original and independent figure.

His differences from the sectarian movement are obvious. As we meet him in our sources, he is clearly not a member of the Qumran sect or of any other group. He did not retire into a monastery and live the sheltered life of a pious, religious community. He was an individual figure, subject to no man. He did, it is true, attract a group of disciples, but there is no evidence that he imposed any kind of monastic discipline upon them. His rejection of monasticism appears to have been due to a desire to make contact with the people. While he did not withdraw from the wilderness, nevertheless he positioned himself near the fords of Jordan where the presence of a main travel route to Jerusalem would ensure him many hearers.

If, as we suggested, the term 'Essene' was a general one describing all, or at least a large part of the sectarian movement, then John may be regarded as an Essene in this broad sense. But we must qualify this by saying that he was an evangelistic Essene, though such a phrase might have been regarded by many in John's day as a contradiction in terms.

It seems certain that John must have known and must have been influenced by one or more of the sects of the baptist movement. But a person such as G. L. Harding goes much too far when he says that 'John the Baptist was almost certainly an Essene, and must have studied and worked in this building (the Qumran monastery); he undoubtedly derived the idea of ritual immersion, or baptism from them'.[1] There is no direct evidence that John was a member of the Qumran sect, and if he was at one time, then certainly he must later have broken away from them. Steinmann suggests that John may have been 'a postulant or novice who left the community before taking the final oath of the Covenant'.[2] We noted the suggestion that John may have been adopted by the sect as a boy; though an attractive hypothesis, it too is incapable of proof.

We must remember in this connection that the Qumran sect was not the only one of its type; it was merely part of the larger baptist movement. It is the only sect of which we have detailed, inside knowledge, since the others are known to us only by means of descriptions from outside sources. The Qumran literature is therefore best regarded as representative of a type of thought within Judaism. It is with this type of thought that John has the closest connections; it is from this type of background that John broke away to exercise an independent ministry.

We must now, therefore, note the most original and outstanding features of John's ministry, features which make clearer his differences from the rest of the sectarian movement.

1. The most fitting way to describe John's ministry is to say that it was prophetic. His proclamation of imminent judgement, including his metaphors of the tree being cut down, and of winnowing, are grounded in the preaching of the prophets, as is the idea of the future outpouring of the spirit. His demand for repentance in the face of the coming judgement, the keynote of his preaching, is likewise a rediscovery of the heart of the prophetic message, and, as in the case of the prophets, John demanded that repentance be expressed in terms of righteous living and social justice. Similarly, in his conception of baptism, John must have owed much to those passages in the prophets which interpret cleansing in a moral and spiritual sense.

---

[1] G. L. Harding, 'Where Christ Himself may have Studied; An Essene Monastery at Khirbet Qumran', *London Illustrated News*, 3rd Sept., 1955, pp. 379-81.

[2] J. Steinmann, *Saint John the Baptist and the Desert Tradition*, p. 60.

The category of 'prophet' is the one ascribed to him by Jesus and by the early Church, and it is the one, so we have contended, which John chose for himself.

This feature of his ministry distinguishes John from his contemporaries; for many long years prophecy had been considered dead, a thing of the past. In orthodox Judaism especially, the red-hot molten metal of prophecy had long since hardened into Pharisaic legalism. Even in the sectarian movement, while the prophetic books were highly valued and intensively studied, the true spirit of prophecy was lacking especially where, as in the case of the Qumran group, the community had become a rigidly organized and strictly governed sect. In John, however, the flame of true prophecy was rekindled.

2. It follows from this that John's ministry was essentially a preaching one. He was a man with a message, and he conceived it as his urgent duty to put that message across to all who would listen. His nickname 'the Baptist' might suggest that his rite of baptism was the most important feature of his ministry, but that was hardly the case, for it was subordinate to his preaching. It was essentially a piece of prophetic symbolism, an acting out of his demand for repentance in face of the coming judgement. Israel needed to be cleansed from sin, and this need was dramatized by those who submitted to John's baptism. Hence we have the significant phrase, 'John came . . . proclaiming a baptism . . .'. Similarly, John's asceticism, which has been the source of so much speculation and dispute is best regarded as being principally a symbol of humiliation before God and of repentance for sin. Neither John's rite of baptism, nor his practice of asceticism could be properly understood of themselves; they only made sense when they were related to his message.

Here again, John stands out in contrast not only with the sectarian movement, but with almost all branches of contemporary Judaism. Pharisees and Essenes for example, were both concerned in their own way with the study and correct observance of the Torah; their leaders were thus teachers, not preachers. There was no room, however, in John's proclamation for study or discussion of Scriptural exegesis. Although grounded in the written Word of the Old Testament, his spoken word had an authority of its own. His word challenged individuals to a decision; there was no room allowed for dispute—the message had to be either accepted or rejected.

Men were challenged by John's preaching to set aside their preconceived notions of who were righteous and who were sinners, and of what membership of the Chosen People implied. In face of the coming Kingdom everyone must be changed at the very core of their being; they must execute a complete 'about turn', for this is the meaning of repentance. Only then can they be accepted into membership of the eschatological community, the new Israel, the righteous and repentant remnant.

The primacy of preaching was thus one of the most marked features of John's ministry.

3. Another notable feature was the simplicity of his message. His metaphors were bold and easily understood. For John there were but two classes of men, the righteous and the wicked. On the righteous would be poured out the blessing of God's spirit; the wicked would perish in the river of fire. John might have been accused of oversimplification, but not of any lack of clarity in his thought. His appeal for repentance and righteousness would be readily understood, and if Luke 3.10-14 is authentic, he was clearly able to expound a practical, down-to-earth, ethical application of his message.

This concentration on essentials is matched by an apparent refusal to go into details, a refusal which marks John off from a considerable part of Jewish apocalyptic expectation. His view of the reward of the righteous, and of the coming Kingdom is barely hinted at. We do know that he spoke of an outpouring of God's spirit, and we have suggested that he did speak of the coming Kingdom. But the emphasis of his preaching was on the coming crisis rather than on the nature of the Kingdom. Similarly, in his view of the coming Messiah, John, we have suggested, appears to have been deliberately vague. He did not commit himself to any particular branch of expectation, but used only the most general title available, 'The Coming One'. In casting himself in the role of the eschatological prophet, he does not appear to have claimed to be either Moses or Elijah come again, but to have contented himself with claiming to be 'the prophet'.

John's message was thus essentially a simple one, and in its simplicity lay its strength.

John's ministry, therefore, was prophetic to the core; it was essentially a ministry of preaching, marked by great simplicity. These factors would all aid greatly John's determination to take his message to the people. John's originality and independence presuppose some sort of call to the prophetic office. Apart from Luke's use of the conventional phrase, 'the word of God came to John' (Luke 3.2), we have no information concerning the experience which led John to appear preaching his baptism of repentance. It may well be that he was partly influenced by a strict upbringing; we have also suggested the influences the wilderness may have had on his thought. But where our sources are so reticent, it would be unwise to speculate further.

It has not been the purpose of this study to attempt a full assessment of John's influence on Jesus, but only to see John as he was in himself. Nevertheless the results of this study obviously have an important bearing on the origins of the Christian faith. Jesus was an adherent of John, before breaking away to form his own movement. Some of John's disciples went over to Jesus, and on John's death more probably would follow suit. Inevitably they must have brought into the early Church many features of the baptist movement. Most notably, the rite of baptism itself must have entered the early Church in this way.

In attempting a final assessment of John as a religious figure, we find it difficult to achieve a balanced judgement. For the greater part of our material we are dependent on Christian sources, and for an independent assessment we have to try and discount the particular prejudices and biasses, not only of the New Testament, but also of centuries of Christian tradition.

In attempting such an assessment, we have to reckon with two contradictory trends.

The first is the tendency in Christian tradition to belittle John. Almost from the start, Christians were very concerned to emphasize the subordinate and inferior status of John. We saw how this tendency is clearly to be traced in the New Testament, especially in the Fourth Gospel. To begin with, this tendency would be aggravated by the existence of the continuing baptist sect. But all down the centuries, John has been pictured as taking very much a second place to Christ. He appeared for the sole purpose of preparing the way for, and witnessing to Christ; with the baptism of Jesus, his work was done, and God's spirit was even thought of as having been withdrawn from him.[1]

But against this tendency to belittle John in Christian tradition, there has also been an opposite tendency at work. The name and fame of John have been preserved and spread abroad throughout the whole earth, in a way which would never have happened were it not for John's connection with Christianity. The continuing baptist sect was never a strong movement, and lacked the power to survive. It may therefore be truly said that his place in the Christian tradition has also tended to give John a greater status than he would otherwise have deserved.

As a leader of one of the several baptist groups operative in the Jordan valley during the first century AD, John certainly made quite an impression on his contemporaries, but hardly did anything to warrant our classing him on the same place as such great figures in the history of the faith of Israel as Moses or Samuel, Elijah or Jeremiah.

He did show originality and imagination and courage, yet it remains true that the greatness he achieved was largely due to the circumstances and situation in which he was placed. He was not born great—his parents were of humble priestly stock; he did not achieve greatness—for his own efforts do not merit

[1] Tertullian in his *Treatise on Prayer*, I, states that 'all John's doings were laid as groundwork for Christ', and expresses the opinion that 'the whole work of the forerunner passed over, together with his spirit itself, unto the Lord'.

such a word; but he did have greatness thrust upon him. Because of his revival of the true spirit of prophecy, because of the simplicity and urgency of his appeal for repentance and cleansing, John's movement provided the starting point for the mission and message of Jesus. Jesus had to start somewhere, to use existing ideas and then go on to show how he differed from them.

John's greatness is thus due primarily to his position in the history of religion. He is the bridge between the Old Covenant and the New; he is 'the clasp of the two Testaments'.[1] He is a bridge between Judaism and Christianity. Dissatisfied with the orthodox religion of his day, rejecting any idea of political or military action, he put all his faith in a dramatic intervention into human history with the advent of the Coming One. He reached forward for something that would shatter the present order of things and introduce a completely new order. His mission was to prepare the people so that they might be fit to take their part in that new order.

Up to a point, of course, John was wrong. There was no dramatic intervention into human history, no dramatic separation of the wicked and the righteous. How John died we do not know, whether crushed with disappointment, or ablaze with hope. But for the Christian, John's hopes and dreams were fulfilled, though in a way which far transcended his limited conception of God and of his workings.

All this does not detract from John's record. He was used by God in a way which went beyond his understanding, yet he was true to the light he saw. Mistaken though he was in thinking that man can ever satisfy God through his own efforts, whether by observance of the Law, or by baptism, or by prayer or fasting, he is nevertheless to be highly commended for his zeal in conducting his ministry, and for his courage in the face of danger.

His message was a stern one, and we have found no evidence to support the view that he and his disciples thought of themselves as making atonement for Israel, or that he expected a

[1] H. R. Reynolds, *John the Baptist*, p. 12.

Messiah who would make atonement for sin. His message was one of hope for those who lived in humble and pious expectation of the end of days; but for few could his preaching have been called 'gospel', 'good news', and for many his preaching must have been a source of terror and dismay. As G. C. Darton says, 'John is of the Old Testament, God seen from behind his back. He denounces, abuses, whips the people towards their salvation; he would force them, frighten them into being godly.'[1] John's faith was strong, faith in the God whom he served; his hope was strong, hope of a swift righting of the wrongs of this puzzling life, but to faith and hope must be added the greatest of the trinity of the virtues, love. It was this quality which was lacking in John's message; and it was this very quality which became incarnate in Jesus Christ.

By and large, therefore, John has not been unjustly treated over the centuries. Modern research uncovers a picture of him which differs in details from that found either in Josephus or in the New Testament. In some respects he was a more original and more independent figure than our sources allow; but at the same time, on his own merits, he hardly deserved the fame that has been his lot because of the part he played in the purposes of God.

[1] G. C. Darton, *St John the Baptist and the Kingdom of Heaven*, p. 17.

INDEX OF SUBJECTS

Abraham, 83f
Abu'l Fath, 168, 169
Aenon near Salim, 90, 116, 154, 163, 164, 176
Agrippa, 20, 184
Andrew, 146
Apollos, 187-9
Apostolic Constitutions, 35, 36
Archelaus, 20, 87, 89n
Aretas, 17, 179, 181f
Asceticism, 38, 39, 47, 56, 134ff, 155, 159, 160, 209
Athrongas, 87

Baba Raba, 169
Banos, 36, 111, 132, 139
Baptism
    Jewish lustrations, 94, 95, 154, 155
    proselyte, 93, 95-102
    sectarian, 36f, 102-10
    of John, 63f, 90-116, 187, 188, 209
    with fire, 67ff
    with holy spirit, 70ff, 144
    of Jesus, 143ff, 146-8
    Christian, 91, 148, 189
Baptist movement, 33-40, 58, 102ff, 170f, 206ff
Baptist sect, 16, 131-41, 187-202
Belial, 109
Benedictus, 51, 52, 55, 189
Bethany beyond Jordan, 90, 178

Caius, 184
'Christianizing', 16, 62, 70, 73n
Chuza, 180
Clementine Homilies and Recognitions, 23, 35, 40, 92n, 190-5, 198n, 201
Coming One, the, 15, 62ff, 74ff, 86, 115, 131, 143, 147, 151, 156f, 196, 200, 202, 211, 213

De Doctrina Apostolorum, 47
Dead Sea Scrolls, 28ff, 35f, 46, 58, 74, 111, 122, 150, 170ff, 207. See also Index of References

Didache, 47
Disciples of John, 131-41, 154, 187-202, 204, 212
Dositheus, 132, 169, 192f, 198n
Dositheans, 168ff, 176, 198n
Dualism, 28

Ebionites, Gospel of the, 23, 135, 148
Egyptian false prophet, 46, 124
Elijah, 15, 45, 53, 74f, 119-30, 174, 180n, 194, 199, 211, 212
Elizabeth, 30, 50f, 204f
Ephraem, 36, 195
Epictetus, 99
Epiphanius, 23, 35, 148n, 172
Epistle of Barnabas, 47, 98
Essenes, 19, 34, 37ff, 58, 59, 103ff, 137ff, 170ff, 206f
Eusebius, 18, 163

Fadus, 124
Form-criticism, 15

Gorothenians, 168

Hasidim, 39
Heavenly Man, 24f
Hebrews, Gospel according to the, 22, 148
Hegesippus, 22, 35, 36
Hemerobaptists, 35, 36, 40, 92n, 103, 192, 193, 197, 198n
Herod, the Great, 57, 178
Herod, Antipas, 17, 18, 20, 21, 85, 88, 127, 129, 177, 178-86, 200, 204
Herod, half-brother of Antipas, 179, 181
Herodias, 20, 179, 181ff
Herodotus, 49
Hippolytus, 22, 92n

James, Book of, 23, 57
Jerome, 148n, 163
Jesus, 11, 19, 41, 47, 49f, 63ff, 85, 86, 88, 121, 126, 127, 132ff, 142-62, 174ff, 204, 211ff

John, the Baptist
  birth, 49-57, 203, 204
  infancy, 58, 59, 203f
  preaching, 60-89, 208ff
  baptism, 90-116
  eschatological prophet, 117-30
  disciples, 131-41, 154, 187-202, 204, 212
  relations with Jesus, 142-63
  Samaritan ministry, 163-77
  arrest and martyrdom, 178-86
  in Christian tradition, 11, 212
John Hyrcanus, 35
Jonathan, 34
Jordan, 20, 27, 37, 41ff, 60, 102, 106, 116, 124, 163, 206, 212
Josephus, 17-22, 34, 37, 38, 40, 45, 58, 79n, 85, 91, 93, 95, 98, 103, 107n, 109ff, 117, 124, 131ff, 138, 139n, 141, 142, 146n, 165, 167, 168, 171n, 178ff, 203, 204, 207
Josippon, 22, 88
Judas of Galilee, 87, 132
Justin Martyr, 22, 98, 125, 199

Kingdom of God, 62, 64, 74, 86, 148, 155, 157, 158, 160ff, 210

Lamb of God, 144, 147, 149-52
Luna, 132, 192

Maccabees, 39, 45, 96, 166
Machaerus, 18, 179, 182, 185, 186, 204
Magnificat, 51, 54, 55, 189
Manaen, 180
Mandaean literature, 23-31, 202, 203
Manichaeism, 29, 31
Marcionism, 31
Martyrs, 198f
Mary, 50f
Masbothaeans, 36, 168, 171, 198n
Messiah, 29, 53, 64f, 74ff, 117, 122ff, 150ff, 157, 167, 168, 192, 196, 200, 210
Morning Bathers, 36
Moses, 44, 121-30, 135, 139, 167, 169, 170, 174, 196, 200, 207, 211, 212

Naaman, 45, 92, 116
Nasarenes, 35, 38
Nazirite vow, 135ff, 205
Nazorenes, 35
Nicodemus, Gospel of, 23

Origen, 18, 22, 57

Pairs, theory of, 193ff
Paul, 98, 101, 150, 187, 189
Pharisees, 19, 33, 39, 79n, 38, 132ff, 191, 206, 209
Philip, the Evangelist, 175, 176
Philip, the Tetrarch, 20, 21, 179, 181
Philo, 34, 37, 38, 96n, 97, 107n, 137, 207
Photius, 169
Pilate, 88, 167
Plato, 132
Pliny the Elder, 34, 37, 207
Polybius, 49
Primal Man, 24f
Prophet, the eschatological, 119ff, 157, 160, 198, 211
Prophetic Symbolism, 113
Psalms of Solomon, 51

Quirinius, 87

Rabbi Eleazar ben Jacob, 98
Rabbi Eliezer ben Hyrcanus, 82, 99
Rabbi Hezekiah ben Hiyya, 84
Rabbi Jose the Galilean, 82
Rabbi Jose ben Halafta, 100
Rabbi Joshua ben Hananiah, 82, 99
Rabbi Joshua ben Levi, 67n
Rabbi Judah the Patriarch, 100
Rabbi Simeon ben Yochai, 82
Rechabites, 135
Redemption myth, 24f
Repentance, 79ff, 108, 111ff, 129, 148, 175, 210

Sabbaeans, 168, 172, 198n
Sacrifice, 38, 96f, 107
Sadducees, 19, 32, 79n, 191, 206
Salome, 181
Samaritanism, 123, 163-77, 191
Samaritan sects, 168-73

Samson, 50, 136
Samuel, 50, 136, 212
Sanballat, 166
Satan, 47, 64, 65, 80
Sectarian movement, *see* Baptist movement
Seleucids, 39
Septuagint, 50, 52, 92f
Shema, 133
Shemonah Esreh, 133
Sibylline Oracles, 36
Silvia of Aquitania, 163
Simon, the Canaanite, 191
Simon, the Essene, 20
Simon, Magus, 132, 169, 176, 192ff, 198n
Simon, of Peraea, 87
Simon, Peter, 146, 155, 191, 195
Slavonic Josephus, 19-22, 87ff, 136n, 203
Sodom and Gomorrah, 45, 200
Son of David, 65, 75f, 79
Son of God, 65, 79, 144, 147, 149-52, 156
Son of Man, 66f, 77f, 79, 159n, 191

Suffering Servant, 64, 140, 149f
Syriac Christianity, 31, 191

Tacitus, 73n
Taheb, 167, 174, 175, 201
Teacher of Righteousness, 29, 35
Temple, 38, 50, 56, 57, 59, 66, 98, 100, 107, 119, 120, 173
Tertullian, 22, 92n, 98, 212n
Thanksgiving Psalms, 51, 52
Theodoret, 176
Theodotion, 66n
Theudas, 46, 124
Thucydides, 49
Toledoth Jeshu, 88
Tosefta, 36

Vegetarianism, 38, 135, 136
Vita Adae et Evae, 36, 116
Vitellius, 183

Way, the, 47
Wilderness, 15, 41-48, 136, 155, 160, 164, 200, 204

Zealots, 33, 89, 206
Zechariah, 30, 54, 127, 137, 204f

INDEX OF AUTHORS

Abrahams, I., 40, 71, 72, 83, 93, 98, 111, 152
Albright, W. F., 164
Allegro, J., 38, 46, 52, 104, 106, 138, 171
Arndt and Gingrich, 92
Aytoun, R. A., 51

Bacon, B. W., 198
Baldensperger, W., 190
Barrett, C. K., 150, 152
Bates, H. N., 36
Bauer, W., 25
Baumgarten, J. M., 38
Beasley-Murray, G. R., 72, 98, 100, 102, 104
Benoit, P., 51
Berendts, A., 19
Beveridge, W., 36
Black, M., 17, 34, 35, 38, 39, 52, 92, 104, 123, 134, 168, 172, 173
Blunt, A. W. F., 199
Bowman, J., 170
Brande, W. G., 96
Brandon, S. G. F., 21
Brandt, W., 24, 34, 36
Brownlee, W. H., 37, 58, 72, 106, 135, 139, 150
Bultmann, R., 15, 25, 28, 50, 55
Burkitt, F. C., 31
Burney, C. F., 17
Burrows, M., 29, 35, 37, 38, 46, 72, 76, 150, 172, 197

Charles, R. H., 36, 76, 78, 116, 199
Conder, C. R., 164
Conybeare, F. C., 34
Cowan, H., 180
Creed, J. M., 21, 22, 24, 50, 55
Cross, F. M., 106
Cullmann, O., 78, 104, 118, 119, 123, 126, 148, 149, 152, 176, 196

Dalman, G., 16, 50
Daniélou, J., 52
Darton, G. C., 85, 153, 187, 214

Dentan, R. C., 120
De Vaux, R., 138
Dodd, C. H., 24, 28, 152
Driver, S. R., 47, 182
Drower, E. S., 23
Duncan, G. S., 75
Dunkerley, R., 21
Dupont-Sommer, A., 38, 52, 104

Easton, B. S., 85
Eaton, D., 135, 136
Eisler, R., 19, 21, 22, 72, 86f, 101, 136

Fitzmyer, J. A., 36, 106
Funk, R. W., 41

Gaster, T. H., 29, 35, 68, 69, 104, 122, 125, 170
Gaster, M., 167, 170, 175
Gavin, F., 96, 99, 100
Geyser, A. S., 58, 59
Ginzberg, L., 36, 121
Goguel, M., 55, 66, 68, 72, 77, 131, 137, 155, 156, 158, 161, 188, 195, 206
Goldsmith, M., 204f
Goodspeed, E. J., 191
Gould, E. P., 128
Grant, F. C., 70
Grass, K., 19
Grintz, J. M., 52
Grobel, K., 64
Grollenberg, L. H., 43
Grundmann, W., 64
Guignebert, C., 18, 32, 35, 47, 96, 132, 135

Harding, G. L., 207, 208
Harnack, A., 50, 51, 55
Headlam, A. C., 193
Hirsch, E. G., 96

Jack, J. W., 21, 22, 88, 89
James, M. R., 23, 58
Jaubert, A., 171
Johnson, S. E., 157

Kraeling, C. H., 50, 54, 56, 61, 66, 68, 72, 77, 80, 115, 132, 134, 137, 158, 159, 181, 182, 190
Kuhn, K. G., 76, 104, 108, 122

Leipoldt, J., 101
Liddell and Scott, 92
Lidzbarski, M., 24
Lightfoot, J. B., 34, 36, 38, 188
Lohmeyer, E., 112
Loisy, A. F., 55

Macgregor, G. H. C., 32, 63, 151, 153
MacNeill, H. L., 52, 53, 200, 201
Manson, T. W., 13, 70, 73, 75ff, 158, 159
Manson, W., 24, 28, 78, 152
Marsh, H. G., 99, 131
Matheson, P. E., 99
Mauser, U. W., 41, 46, 123
McCasland, S. V., 47
McGuire, M. R. P., 191
Mead, G. R. S., 26, 80, 159
Moffatt, J., 51
Montgomery, J. A., 134, 135, 165, 166, 168ff
Moore, G. F., 18, 32, 66, 80, 82, 84, 86, 96, 100, 125, 132, 134, 135, 140
Moore, W. W., 164
Morgan, W., 80
Morton, H. V., 43, 44, 185
Moulton, J. H., 50
Moulton and Milligan, 92, 93
Mowinckel, S., 76, 78, 79

Nestle, E., 163
Niese, B., 18
Niven, W. D., 34
Nöldeke, T., 24

Oepke, A., 90, 92, 94
Oesterley, W. O. E., 166
Otto, R., 78, 158

Parker, P., 90
Parrot, A., 177
Peake, A. S., 94
Pfeiffer, R. H., 36, 37
Plummer, A., 86, 157, 180
Popov, A. N., 19

Purdy, A. C., 32

Rabin, C., 138
Rawlinson, A. E. J., 135, 180, 199
Reitzenstein, R., 24, 28, 29, 30
Reynolds, H. R., 146, 185, 213
Richardson, A., 148, 149, 152
Robinson, J. A., 199
Robinson, J. A. T., 75, 106, 125, 140, 141, 150, 151, 176, 188
Rogers, C. F., 102
Rowley, H. H., 98, 99, 102, 104, 125

Schmidt, K. L., 15
Schürer, E., 95, 97
Schweitzer, A., 74, 75
Scott, E. F., 190
Skehan, P. W., 171
Smith, G. A., 42, 43, 44, 45
Stauffer, E., 76, 102, 116, 125, 198, 199, 203
Steinmann, J., 43, 48, 134, 208
Stendahl, K., 36, 76, 104, 106, 108, 122, 139, 150, 176
Strack and Billerbeck, 82
Streeter, B. H., 13, 49, 50

Taylor, T. M., 97, 98
Taylor, V., 13, 25
Teicher, J. L., 188
Thackeray, H., St. J., 18
Thomas, J., 27, 34ff, 38, 39, 94, 95, 98, 99, 107, 133, 134, 188, 192, 194, 195, 202
Torrance, T. F., 97
Torrey, C. C., 16
Tristram, H. B., 164
Turner, N., 51

Uhlhorn, G., 191

Wells, L. S. A., 36
Williamson, G. A., 21, 185
Wilson, C. W., 164
Winter, P., 53
Wright, G. E., 108

Yadin, Y., 72
Young, F. W., 118, 121, 123

Zeitlin, S., 22, 118

INDEX OF REFERENCES

Genesis

17.15-21	50
19	45
25.25	128
26.3, 5	84

Exodus

3	44
6.23	54
8.19	171
11.2	171
17.13	171
29.4	94
29.21	171
30.1-10	171
30.17-21	94
32.11ff	84
34.28	135
40.12	94

Leviticus

8.6	94
11-15	94
11.22	135
16	47
16.4, 24, 26, 28	94
16.21f	149
18.16	85, 182
19.10	100
20.21	85, 182
24.3-8	100

Numbers

6.1-21	135, 136
8.6, 7, 21	94
19.3	103
19.11-13	92
24.15-17	122

Deuteronomy

1-26	122n
5.28, 29	122, 170
17.14, 15	101
18.15f	121, 122n, 123, 167

Deuteronomy

18.18, 19	122, 170
25.5-10	182
31.18	170
33.8-11	122
34.1-6	127

Joshua

3	45
5.2f	100
15.61, 62	41

Judges

3.28	42
13.2-24	50
13.3ff	137

I Samuel

1.1-23	50
2.1-10	54

II Samuel

7.4	152n
15.28	43
23-26	45

I Kings

18.43	75
19	45
19.3	75
19.19	128
21.17ff	129

II Kings

1.8	128
2.1-12	127
2.8	124
2.11	121
2.13, 14	128
5	45
5.14	92
6.1-4	60
10.15f	135n
13.14ff	113
13.22, 23	84
17.24	165

II Chronicles

30	166

Esther

5.1f	180

Job

21.18	61
38.26	41

Psalms

1.4	61, 72
2.7	152n
22.1	121
35.5	61
51.6-11	113
51.11	70
63.1	45
74.9	118
89.27	152n
118.26	66

Proverbs

14.31	86
28.13	81

Isaiah

1.16, 17	113, 114
9.6	65
10.33, 34	60
11.4	72
11.11ff	166
17.13	61
21.4	93
29.5	61
31.9	67
32.15	71
40.3	15, 41, 46, 47, 126, 127, 196
41.15, 16	61
44.3	71, 73
51.1, 2	84
53.12	64
58.6, 7	86
63.10, 11	70

Jeremiah

19.10f	113
23.10	41
31.3-5	166
31.31-34	109
35	135

Ezekiel

18.21	80
18.30, 31	81
36.25-27	71, 113, 114
37.15ff	166
38.22	67
39.29	71, 72
47.1-12	45, 46

Daniel

7.9, 10	68
7.13	66, 77
10	135

Hosea

2.14, 15	45, 46
13.3	61

Joel

2.22	41
2.28, 29	71, 72, 119

Amos

7.4	67

Jonah

3.5	140

Micah

7.17	80n

Zechariah

13.3-6	118
13.4	128

Malachi

3.1	126, 196
3.1-4	120
3.2	67, 69
4.1	67
4.5, 6	119, 120, 126

Matthew

3.1	41, 42
3.2	62, 79
3.3	127
3.4	128, 135
3.5	79n, 83
3.6	91
3.7	60, 161
3.7-10	13
3.7-12	79n
3.8	79, 81
3.9	83
3.10	60, 70, 161
3.11	63, 67, 79, 112, 196
3.11, 12	13, 16
3.12	62, 63, 66, 70
3.13	143, 146
3.14, 15	147
3.16	91
3.16, 17	143, 146
4.12	15n, 143
4.19	63
5.22	68
5.40	85
7.12	13
7.19	161
9.14	134
10.2	90
10.5	175
10.41	123
11.1f	16n
11.2-6	13, 143
11.3	77
11.7f	41, 157
11.7-11	13, 16, 126
11.11	157, 194, 196
11.12, 13	158
11.13, 14	126
11.16-18	16
11.16-19	13, 159, 160
11.18	47, 56, 134
12.29	65
12.34	161
12.38-41	159n

Matthew

12.43	47
13.40, 42, 50	
	68
14.3	181
14.3-12	127, 179
14.4	85
14.5	184
14.12	156, 187
16.14	121
16.16	152n
17.10-13	126
17.11	121
21.9	65
21.23-27	127, 159
21.32	14, 47, 85, 159
23.15	96
23.29	198
25.34	149
25.41	68
26.63	152n
27.46-49	121
28.19	189

Mark

1.1-8	14
1.2	126
1.2, 3	196
1.3	127
1.4	15, 41, 79, 90, 91
1.5	42, 79n, 83, 91
1.6	128, 135
1.7	63
1.8	67
1.9	143
1.9-11	14
1.10	91
1.10, 11	143, 146
1.14	15n, 143, 153n
1.15	159n
1.17	63
1.29	155
2.18	14, 134
2.18ff	153

Mark

3.18	90
5.27	189
6.14	90
6.15	121
6.17	181
6.17-29	14, 179f
6.18	85, 182
6.20	184
6.21	181
6.24, 25	90
6.29	187
7.1-23	155
7.4	93
8.27, 28	14
8.28	90, 121
8.34	63
8.38	149
9.11	125
9.11-13	14, 126, 199
9.12	120, 121
10.38, 39	93
11.9	65
11.27-33	33, 127, 159
11.28-30	16
11.30-33	14
14.3	90
15.34-36	121

Luke

1.1	54
1.1-4	49
1.5	50, 54
1.5-2. 52	49, 50, 189 200
1.6	56
1.8f	50
1.11f	50, 59
1.14-17	51
1.15	53, 56, 137
1.16	53
1.17	53, 126
1.26-38	50
1.28	59
1.30-33	51
1.31	59

Luke

1.35-37	51
1.36, 39	56
1.39f	50
1.42-45	51
1.43	53n
1.46	53, 54
1.46-55	51, 54, 59
1.51, 59	50
1.56	54
1.67ff	59
1.68, 69	53
1.68-79	51, 55
1.69	50, 55
1.76, 77	53
1.80	41, 43, 58, 59
2.41-51	59
3.1	180
3.1f	14, 49
3.2	41, 127, 211
3.3	43, 79, 91
3.4	127
3.7	60, 161
3.7-9	13, 79
3.8	79, 81, 83
3.9	60, 70, 161
3.10-14	85f, 89, 115, 210
3.15	117
3.16	63, 67
3.16, 17	13
3.17	62, 63, 66, 70
3.18	16
3.19	181
3.19, 20	143, 179
3.21, 22	143
3.27	65
4.6	64
4.14	143, 153n
5.33	133f, 153n, 188
7.18, 19	188
7.18-23	13, 16n, 143
7.19	77

Luke

7.24f	13, 41, 126, 157
7.28	157, 194
7.31-35	13, 159, 160
7.33	47, 56, 134, 135
8.3	180
9-18	122n
9.8	121
9.19	121
9.51ff	146n, 175
9.54	75
10.17-19	133
10.31ff	175
11.1	133
11.2	134
11.20-22	64
11.22	65
11.29-30	159n
11.38	93
11.47, 49	198
12.50	93
13.16	64
16.16	13, 158, 161
17.7-10	155
17.11ff	175
17.29	68
18.12	135
19.38	65
20.1-8	127, 159
24.19	189

John

1.6-8	14, 190n
1.15	14, 63, 144, 151, 190n, 196
1.19-23	117, 190n
1.19-42	14, 75
1.21	15n, 121, 122
1.23	127
1.24	33
1.26, 27	144
1.27	63
1.28	90, 178